CRITICAL INSIGHTS

Ralph Waldo Emerson

CRITICAL INSIGHTS

Ralph Waldo Emerson

Editor
Jericho Williams
Assistant Professor
University of Alaska Fairbanks

SALEM PRESS
A Division of EBSCO Information Services, Inc.
Ipswich, Massachusetts

GREY HOUSE PUBLISHING

Cover photo: By Josiah Johnson Hawes, 1857, via Wikipedia.

Critical Insights: Ralph Waldo Emerson, published by Grey House Publishing, Inc., Amenia, NY, under exclusive license from EBSCO Information Services, Inc.

∞ The paper used in these volumes conforms to the American National Standard for Permanence of Paper for Printed Library Materials, Z39.48 1992 (R2009).

Publisher's Cataloging-in-Publication Data
(Prepared by Parlew Associates, LLC)

Names: Williams, Jericho, editor.
Title: Critical insights : Ralph Waldo Emerson / Jericho Williams, editor.
Description: Ipswich, MA : Salem Press, a division of EBSCO Information Services, Inc. ; Amenia, NY : Grey House Publishing, 2023. | Series: Critical insights. | Includes bibliographic references and index.
Identifiers: ISBN 9781637004401 (hardback)
Subjects: LCSH: Emerson, Ralph Waldo, 1803-1882. | Emerson, Ralph Waldo, 1803-1882 -- Criticism and interpretation. | Emerson, Ralph Waldo, 1803-1882 – Influence. | Transcendentalism. | BISAC: LITERARY CRITICISM / American / General. | LITERARY CRITICISM / Modern / 19th Century. | LITERARY CRITICISM / Subjects & Themes / General.
Classification: LCC PS1638.W55 2023 | DDC 814.E--dc23

First Printing

PRINTED IN THE UNITED STATES OF AMERICA

Contents

Resources

About This Volume

Jericho Williams

The principal goal of *Critical Insights: Ralph Waldo Emerson* is to introduce a perennial figure in studies of American literature, philosophy, and religion to a new generation of readers and to encourage further interest and inquiry. As in the cases of other highly influential nineteenth-century American figures such as Frederick Douglass and Abraham Lincoln, much of Emerson's writing is obscured in the shadow of the persona that precedes it. And like Douglass and Lincoln, Emerson can be a towering and intimidating figure for first-time readers. Yet, as all contributors to this volume might attest, Emerson is still a vibrant force within literary studies.

Emerson has not vanished from the realms of American and global thought. Many of the famous orator and writer's ideas still circulate within intellectual discussions today within a variety of academic disciplines. His ideas comprise what might be described as a common bedrock of American experience, and they remain inextricable from American identity today. This volume aims to celebrate that reality by discussing Emerson's contributions during his lifetime through the present day.

The book originated with the idea of exploring Emerson's writings beyond the essay "Self-Reliance." Chances are that if students encounter Emerson's work in high school or college, they read this essay, which first appeared in *Essays* (1841). A meditation on the self as it relates to American identity, "Self-Reliance" remains thought-provoking today. Some readers proclaim that certain passages are so strongly resonant that they merit excerpting, whereas others decry this approach and insist that the essay must be read in its entirety. This to-excerpt-or-not dilemma also applies to much of Emerson's other work, which also remains eminently quotable. Outside of academic settings, the general public is likely to encounter Emerson via snippets that appear in the public sphere as parts of greeting cards, inspirational speeches, online thoughts of the day, commencements, and eulogies. Cumulatively, they contribute to Emerson's reputation as an American sage. If "Self-Reliance" and Emerson's quotability remain worthy of discussion, the essayists in the volume show that Emerson's other nonfiction essays and poetry also have much to offer. Therefore, a unifying aim of the great diversity of work that follows is a collective goal of inspiring new discussions, debates, inquiries, and analyses regarding Emerson's extensive body of writing beyond "Self-Reliance" and inspirational quotes.

The development of this volume depended upon the work of a dedicated group of researchers, including three pillars of Emerson studies: Sue Dunston, Len Gougeon, and Al von Frank. These scholars, who have contributed to Emerson studies immensely throughout their academic careers, once again offer thoughtful analyses that speak to current conversations in Emerson studies in this volume. Other members of *The Ralph Waldo Emerson Society* have also been generous in terms of their time and support in the development of this book. Readers are encouraged to consult the website of *The Ralph Waldo Emerson Society* (*emersonsociety.org*) for additional information.

Critical Insights: Ralph Waldo Emerson opens with an introductory section consisting of two essays. In the first, "Critique and Celebration: Emerson and Social Reform," Jericho Williams discusses two of Emerson's lesser-known essays: "New England Reformers" and "Farming." Williams argues that these two essays offer differing perspectives on what Emerson offers contemporary readers. "New England Reformers" is cautionary and imparts Emerson's sense that true social reform must begin from within individuals. Calling attention to one of the weaknesses of social movements, Emerson points to the potential consequences of blind acceptance or commitment without the necessary and preliminary change within individuals. Williams suggests that this point resonates today, when social change is also complicated by neoliberalism, those seeking profit and power from fostering social change, the speed in which information is transmitted, and the competition for human attention. While "Farming" does not necessarily offer a viable solution for twenty-first-century problems, the actions of an ideal farmer that Emerson celebrates—looking closely, thinking, acting, assessing, remembering, rebuilding, and regenerating—constitute a blueprint for the active individual mind that can still be empowering despite a more modern set of challenges. LuElla D'Amico's short biography of Emerson focuses on the major changes and developments in Emerson's life that enabled him to become such a profound thinker and inspiration for others. D'Amico details how Emerson participated not just as a writer, but also as an orator and speaker throughout his lifetime, inspiring countless Americans and encouraging independent thinking—perhaps his greatest legacy.

"Critical Contexts," the second section of the book, provides four essays that contextualize Emerson within his time, provide key critical histories, and situate his work in relation to that of one other contemporary figure. Joshua Boyd's "The Paradox of Self-Reliance in an Era of Social Reform" explores two crucial cultural backdrops to understanding Emerson's coming of age and career. First, Boyd explores the historical context in which Emerson lived, from 1803–1882 in the United States. Decades prior to the Civil War, Emerson became a public intellectual associated with Transcendentalism, a philosophical movement that, broadly speaking, energized thought in New England and posed a threat in defiance to social norms associated with the southern states. Boyd discusses how Emerson's belief in the individual and self-culture invited critics from both sides of the social spectrum, some of whom credit him with sparking individual reform that would eventually manifest in societal reform versus others who wished that he would have been more routinely and adamantly outspoken regarding social problems of his time. In the second part of his essay, Boyd describes the religious context that inspired Emerson to develop his own particular beliefs that prompted an exit from the preaching and transition to a lecturing circuit. The next essay is Amy Leshinsky's "The Critical Reception of Ralph Waldo Emerson: A Longstanding Commitment to Individuality and Freedom." Leshinsky's essay contains three parts. First, she details how Emerson's works were received during his lifetime, with an emphasis on content, style, and diction. Next, Leshinsky considers how much of Emerson's career and popularity depended on his oratorical skills and physicality. This portion of her essay reminds readers that the Emerson we encounter today via text differs from the way that many encountered Emerson as a speaker during his lifetime in New England. Finally, Leshinsky discusses Emerson's posthumous legacy. Robert C. Evans's "Emerson's 'Hamatreya': A Critical History" complements Leshinsky's essay by offering a "critical pluralist" overview of the great variety of responses to one of Emerson's more popular poems. Beginning with the 1960s, Evans uncovers the most memorable criticism of "Hamatreya" by decade through to the present day. Lastly, Christopher Black's comparative essay focuses on Ralph Waldo Emerson's influence on Margaret Fuller, especially during the 1840s prior to the publication of Fuller's classic, *Woman in the Nineteenth Century*. Black identifies a similarity in their advocacy of Transcendentalist thought but contrasts their differing views on the principal means for fostering self-improvement in an era given the pressures of societal limitations on women.

The final section of the book, "Critical Readings," consists of nine analytical essays that explore Ralph Waldo Emerson's intellectual development during his time, offer new assessments of his poetry, and discuss the ways he influenced many celebrated artists long after his passing. In "Emerson's Polarity of Loneliness and Friendship," Susan L. Dunston reveals a different side of Emerson as preacher-turned-orator by focusing on the importance of loneliness and isolation in Emerson's lifetime. Citing numerous tragedies including, among others, the abrupt loss of his first wife Ellen and then his first child, Dunston argues that the value Emerson placed on solitude as a means of creative, intellectual, and spiritual growth is connected with his own responses to recurrent personal losses. Friendship, a necessity for Emerson but also sometimes challenging and more valuable in terms of quality rather than quantity, represents another complicated facet of Emerson's life, as Dunston's essay reveals. Trevor B. Williams analyzes Emerson's 1838 "Divinity School Address" in the next essay. Along with Josh Boyd's prior essay in the "Critical Contexts" section, Williams's

"Moral Sentiment and the Salvation of Spirituality in Emerson's 'Divinity School Address' (1838) best addresses Emerson's evolving spiritual beliefs and his relationship to Christianity. Williams argues that "Divinity School Address" is pivotal to understanding Emerson's transcendentalism and his insistence on the relationship between individuals and their own senses of spirituality as separate from tradition or historical doctrine. Next comes two highly relevant essays about Emerson's relationship to one of the pressing cultural issues in his lifetime: slavery. Len Gougeon's "Emerson's Transcendental Antislavery Writings" begins with the compelling premise that of all that Emerson wrote throughout his lifetime, his antislavery writings are among the most routinely neglected works. A significant part of the problem seems to be conceptions of Transcendentalism that emerged after Emerson's death and that emphasized self-reliance and individualism. However, Gougeon contends that Transcendentalists were adamant about a variety of social reforms; that their commitments were inextricable from their beliefs; and that for Emerson, slavery necessitated disapproval and protest because it was antithetical to the development of the individual and a spiritually healthy society. Gougeon focuses on a period in Emerson's life from the 1840s through one of his final lectures in 1878, which proves to be a key difference from Al von Frank's "Emerson and the Central Virtue of Reform: A Subjunctive Investigation into the Early Influence on Him of William Lloyd Garrison," which investigates Emerson's possible intellectual influences during the 1830s. Von Frank's essay presents a deeply human portrait of a younger Emerson coming face-to-face with an increasingly concerning social issue as he developed his own philosophy and beliefs. While acknowledging the speculation of "calling attention to the likelihood of some particular influence bring[ing] publicity to a private mental process," von Frank argues that considering Emerson's likely responses to abolitionist William Lloyd Garrison and his rather different response to young minister Samuel J. May proves to be fruitful in understanding the complexity of Emerson's relationship to antislavery reform, which expanded, at least outwardly, during the subsequent decade.

The three essays that follow offer exciting new readings of Emerson's poetry. Ben Crawford's "'My thunderbolt has eyes to see': The Civil War, Nationalism, and Manifest Destiny in Emerson and Timrod" serves as a bridge from the preceding pair of essays that focuses on Emerson and slavery. Crawford contrasts Emerson's "Boston Hymn" with Henry Timrod's "Ethnogenesis," citing the former as a rebuttal of the latter as both reveal diverging views of nationalism and manifest destiny in relation to the Civil War. Dalicia K. Raymond's "The Multiplicity of Merlin: Emerson's 'Merlin' Poems" looks closely at Emerson's poetic uses of Merlin throughout the course of his career. Raymond argues that Merlin's versatility as a character offered Emerson many possible angles as a poet, in terms of experiments in form and content, and that Emerson continually experimented and developed differing angles of Merlin to engage with universal topics. Finally, in "Ralph Waldo Emerson's Nature Poetry," Charles Rowe focuses on four key poems to illustrate two trends in Emerson's poetic engagements with the natural world. In his analysis of "Each and All" and "The Snow-Storm," he notes Emerson's focus on environments that retain as much agency as the speakers of each poem. Then, more experimentally in poems such as "Threnody" and "Woodnotes II," Rowe describes how Emerson portrays nonhuman perspectives.

The final two essays of the volume showcase Emerson's great impact on two writers from subsequent generations, John Burroughs (1837–1921) and Mary Oliver (1935–2019). In "Master-Enchanter: Emerson's Extraordinary Influence on John Burroughs," Stephen M. Mercier describes Emerson's great impact on Burroughs, who considered him a "spiritual father" from his earliest to latest reading experiences. Mercier's essay focuses more extensively on the impact of Emerson's "Nature" (1836) on Burroughs, and he argues that many of the hallmark qualities of Burrough's insightful naturalist writing emerged from what he learned from reading Emerson. Similarly, in "Writing Dawn and Day in the Work of Mary Oliver and Ralph Waldo Emerson," Jeff Westover notes that Emerson's presentations of "nature, language, the soul, beauty, [and] God" left a profound impression on one of America's most memorable late twentieth-century and early twenty-first century poets. Though Oliver's poetry forges its own path separate from some of the notions of nineteenth-century Transcendentalism, Westover argues that the poet embodies Emerson's notion of living a "spiritually abundant life every day." Collectively, these two essays hint at the great influence that Emerson continues to exert on environmental literature in general, and nonfiction and poetry in particular.

Following the "Critical Readings" section, *Critical Insights: Ralph Waldo Emerson* concludes with additional resources to help facilitate further inquiry into Emerson's life and works. This section includes a chronology of Emerson's life and a list of his more significant writings. A bibliography shares additional resources with readers and information about this volume's contributors and editor appears at the end of the book.

Critique and Celebration: Emerson and Social Reform

Jericho Williams

> "The earth works for him; the earth is a machine which yields almost gratuitous service to every application of intellect. Every plant is a manufacturer of soil." ("Farming" 676)

During the past twenty-five years, Internet use and social media have dramatically changed the ways humans interact with others and their environments. Recent technological advances and their societal effects present an invitation to reconsider the legacy of Ralph Waldo Emerson today. There is no doubt that the rhythms of daily life for Emerson and nineteenth-century Americans—as different as they were depending upon one's race, social class, and geographical location—were far removed from typing, texting, taking and sharing photos, recording and posting videos, and tailoring a desired image of the individual, a second self, online that occupies so much of our society's time today. Public lectures similar to the ones that comprised the bulk of Emerson's career and shaped his thinking and writing still exist. However, they are not central to contemporary culture, although podcasts, perhaps their closest successors, are increasingly popular. As in Emerson's time, face-to-face conversations still occur, but in many cases the use of screens function as mediating devices. With this reality as a beginning point, the question, "What might Emerson think about the quick evolution of screen culture from the early 2000s through the present, as a means of communication and human interaction and as they relate to pressing issues today?," is the underlying concern of this essay, especially in the way that this recent phenomenon relates to possibilities for reform and improvement, education, and fostering the growth of the individual.

The potential for reform via critique and the celebration of a well-lived human life in an Emersonian sense within one's time and place, and in relation to education and human development, are central ideas in two of Emerson's later essays: "New England Reformers" and "Farming." Emerson first presented "New England Reformers" in a lecture hall on Sunday, March 3, 1844, and it later appeared as the ninth and final essay in *Essays: Second Series* (1844). In this work, Emerson addresses the formation of many societal reformation groups in the local Concord area during the preceding twenty-five years, contextualizing what he witnessed and heard within his own Transcendentalist philosophy. Rapidly developing social reform's potential impact on the individual comprises the heart of "New England Reformers," which highlights some of the challenges to fostering meaningful change. A lifelong believer in the notion that the individual's self-development could produce beneficial results for society as a whole, Emerson later turned to a particular subset of Americans, farmers, nearly fifteen years later as a means of highlighting an ideal example of individuals functioning at peak capacity in "Farming," an essay developed from a public address he gave at the Middlesex Cattle Show on September 29, 1858 and that later appeared as the sixth essay of *Society and Solitude* (1870).

Neither "New England Reformers" nor "Farming" has merited as much attention as "Nature," "Divinity School Address," or "Self-Reliance," three of Emerson's hallmark essays and neither would be likely to appear in recommended lists of must-read Emerson essays. However, both remain strikingly relevant today, especially with regard to human behavioral reform and the most pressing environmental issue of our time: global warming. Paired together, "New England Reformers" and "Farming" offer two sides of a hypothetical ideal Emersonian coin: social critique and celebration. In tandem, they convey a compelling message that one reason Emerson still matters today is because of his insistence on these two cornerstones of societal improvement. Emerson suggests that, first, lifelong education must strive to fully develop complex and constantly learning individuals, with the goal of empowering them individually so that they can improve their lives and their environments, to some extent on their own terms. For a portion of Emerson's life, this goal may have been more local in nature. However, it certainly also encompasses a more global, internationalist perspective now, one that Emerson could foresee by the mid-1840s. And second, if the human community is to continue to thrive, we must collectively work to counter the ravages of industrial capitalism that first appeared in Emerson's time and that now manifests as neoliberalism today. Preserving the sanctity of the individual and nurturing the growth of the individual via critique, education, and celebration remain paramount concerns in the face of a deluge of screen-based messaging and advertising that encourages people to align themselves through affinity groups, entangles individualism with consumerism, shapes human identity, and screens the majority of the planet's human population from witnessing the first-hand consequences of environmental disregard and the devaluation of human-environment interaction and collaboration.

Social Critique and "New England Reformers"

At the time he first presented "New England Reformers" in March 1844, Emerson realized that the small town of Concord, where he had lived since 1835, was undergoing significant change. First, a railroad appeared and would begin operation a few months later in June 1844, imparting to Emerson a "sense of linkage to wider publics" for everyone (Buell 249). Less than a month before, in a lecture Emerson delivered to the Mercantile Library Association on February 7, the orator grappled with competing ideas regarding the railroad. On the one hand, it represented marvelous innovation, resembling "a magician's rod, [with] its power to evoke the sleeping energies of land and water" ("The Young American"). In contemporary language, one might conceive Emerson referring to the railroad as a stunning and powerful new technology. The magician's metaphor he employs suggests a great awakening of human potential, one familiar to modern audiences today, and also central to optimistic, pessimistic, and everything-in-between takes on humanity's relationship with evolving machine-based technologies. For Emerson at this time, the railroad represented an engineering feat. He knew it would alter human relationships with landscapes, help transport new ideas at a faster pace, and become central to the future of Concord. However, his lecture also contains what might be described more in terms of deliberation rather than outright resistance. The railroad would operate soon, but its function and use could not be separated from its primary engine: the human mind. Put another way, even the most magnificent human-created tool functioned best in a capacity to nurture and develop individual possibility. To counterbalance inevitable fast-paced change, that is to urge against a blind acceptance of the railroad as a development as normal as, say, the growth of a tree, Emerson imagines a conscientious interrelationship between humans and what the railroad might offer the community. In the same speech, he points to the land surrounding Concord, not as an untapped natural resource waiting for the railroad to devour or exploit, but rather as a means to facilitate "just relations with men and things" ("The Young American").

As in the case of the railroad, Emerson would grapple with another ubiquitous wave of societal change the following month: social reform. However, in contrast with one centralized, quite visible, and indiscriminate new transportation technology, social reform encompassed a variety of different groups and special interests. All were focused on educating the public and, to some extent, either had been or were still competing for citizens' attention. Yet, in contrast to the recent appearance of the railroad, representatives of various causes accounted for a longstanding tradition in New England, which Emerson describes as a period of the prior twenty-five years from roughly 1819–44. They also included Emerson himself, a reformer who repeatedly championed individual growth and personal development over group solidarity in any capacity. Consequently, tension resulting from what Emerson viewed as the health and education of the individual versus the urgency of group-driven reform underpins the heart of "New England Reformers." Certainly neither a stoic nor a hermit, and instead a very public figure, Emerson did not dismiss social reform. He was careful and at times skeptical, though, about what it might entail. Many years before, at the age of twenty, he had written that humans "pay a price for admission to the civilization of society" (*Selected* 95). In the case of "New England Reformers," Emerson considers some situations where the price may be too high. The essay addresses what might be construed as local community members too often given to quickly joining rampant waves of reform movements without much prior thought, thereby undercutting what Emerson believed to be a vital part of the education process.

"New England Reformers" opens with a reference to the "great activity of thought and experimenting" in New England during the prior twenty-five years before transitioning to sharp satire. Emerson mentions a long list of reform groups, ranging from those who criticize various branches of local churches to socialists, temperance society members, agricultural reformers, and others who criticize the institution of marriage or particular professions. In a pointedly critical passage, Emerson adds, "even the insect world was to be defended—that had been too long neglected, and a society for the protection of groundworms, slugs and mosquitoes was to be incorporated without delay" (403). This comment is comical, and it summons attention to what Emerson considers an excessive amount of zeal for reform in the area during his time. Considering it two hundred years later, an average reader is still likely to lack much commitment to the plights of insects, worms, slugs, or mosquitoes, and so Emerson's satire still works. However, our more comprehensive understanding of nonhuman creatures' places within a larger ecosystem complicates matters a bit more, perhaps slightly lessening the effect. Thinking about Emerson's point as it relates to the past versus the way it functions in the present highlights one of the central challenges of social reform. Reformers' good intentions may be impactful in the course of time, or they may not, and it is difficult to know future outcomes in advance.

Partly for this reason, Emerson does not fully decry reform so much as insist on its ideal origin in order for it to become effective. The most compelling example he offers in the early part of the essay is an anecdote of a man who risks censure and excommunication within his church for confronting a proslavery faction with antislavery ideas. The boldness and the risk the man assumes when he stands his ground is honorable from Emerson's perspective. It clearly stems from his identity and convictions. However, when other community members act in a similar fashion without a prior period of internal grappling, (i.e., when they simply hear about and then replicate the prior man's actions), Emerson suggests that the chances of true social reform decrease. He writes that every instance of reform is "good when it is the dictate of man's genius and constitution, but very dull and suspicious when adopted from another" (404). Without all that a deep and pressing personal commitment entails, reform is bound to flounder, and it may also damage the work of others who have experienced a more legitimate and transformative sense of urgency. This represents one of the key facets of Emersonian idealism. Describing what he views as a thrilling, challenging, and sometimes frightening aspect of Emerson's writing, writer John Banville claims, "For him, all is doing, all is risk" (xii). What Banville identifies and champions is the opposite of what troubles Emerson about what might be described as blind commitment. Thoughtful reformers who risk their reputations, safety, and possibly even their lives, no matter the cause, embody all that Emerson celebrates.

Emerson moves from the particular abolitionist example to a more holistic commentary about what causes various reformation movements throughout New England. He writes that "for the last quarter of a century," there has been a "gradual withdrawal of tender consciences from the social organizations" (404). One implied result is the lessening of their ability to achieve convincing results. Motivated by other factors more aligned with succeeding at organizational goals than facilitating conscientious senses of purpose, reform movements risk accusations of becoming more like an indifferent and ineffectual government. In worse cases, fierce criticism and finger-pointing may also appear, collapsing the distance between reform ostensibly motivated by social good and realities of common, everyday customs such as free trade. Emerson identifies a likeness here, questioning the impact of money on people's interactions with others and how they view them. Wealth invites one sort of treatment while poverty another, and according to Emerson, both deprive people of something and become barriers to self-actualization. Class-based categories and biases raise walls that separate people and discourage them from becoming what Emerson sees as the best versions of themselves. Although he does not use the term *labeling*, Emerson's thoughts here call this concept to mind. Societal labels, whether indicative of membership to a reform group, governmental entity, religious institution, or a particular social affiliation or class, work to undo the capacity of what individuals can achieve, if they come to define individuals rather than inform their consciousnesses.

For Emerson, these risks and potential losses, no less than private tragedies that undermine human progress and true reform, relate back to education and individual development. As John Michael Corrigan notes, the orator placed supreme confidence in the concept of the individual soul (11). By the time he was working on "New England Reformers" in 1844, Emerson understood that there was no simple prescription for a lifelong education that would prepare the soul for conflicts brought about by crises of faith or personal tragedies. He had struggled during his twenties with a role he eventually could not continue to fulfill as a pastor. Subsequent conflicts regarding his evolving religious views and the painful losses of two brothers, his first wife Ellen, and a young son also presented difficult challenges. Still, he would maintain that true societal reform—social, scientific, business, or government-related—comes most readily from a deeply engaged person. Cautioning against an opposing scenario, Emerson writes, "The criticism and attack on institutions, which we have witnessed, has made one thing plain, that society gains nothing whilst a man, not himself renovated, attempts to renovate things around him: he has become tediously good in some particular but negligent or narrow in the rest; and hypocrisy and vanity often the disgusting result" (407). In the larger realm of Emersonian criticism, this constitutes one of his strongest statements about the limitations of social reform. Without life experience and enriched, conscientious souls sparking change, social reform is susceptible to becoming a fad and doomed to failure. Emerson believed that the potential and power of individuals, if developed to a maximum evolving capacity, would collectively strengthen "the grand destiny of the American cultural experiment" (Bosco 44).

Emerson is also careful to distinguish between the individual experimenting, learning, and growing versus reformist cultural movements. The foremost examples he cites are the popular communal living experiments of his time, the most famous of which was Brook Farm. This intentional community, roughly twenty miles from Concord and nine miles from Boston, lasted from 1841 through 1847 and temporarily housed co-founder and writer Nathaniel Hawthorne, who later wrote a novel inspired by his experiences and observations entitled *The Blithedale Romance* (1852). If Emerson might have otherwise admired the goal of "unit[ing] liberal culture with an education to labor" at Brook Farm and other similar intentional communities, he ultimately rejected the premise, just as he had previously declined invitations to join (408). He implies that such communities dilute the capacities of distinct and talented individuals, who might become "fractions of men" that they might otherwise become (408). Careful not to imply that he was instead advocating isolationism, Emerson adds, "Friendship and association are very fine things . . . but remember that no society can ever be so large as one man" (409). Instead, he imagines education as nurturing personal development, preparing individuals to organically participate dually as a duo (or more). Emerson conveys this idea via the metaphor of concert, writing, "There can be no concert in two, where there is no concert in one" (409).

The final paragraphs of "New England Reformers" contain generalized tips about how to improve the individual. Emerson identifies a unifying human ideal, the "desire to be made great," as a means of encouraging individuals to seek self-growth and then to share what their hearts and souls have revealed to them (415). "Radical unity" requires "frank and searching conversation" and a selflessness that accepts the fact that people might reject an opinion or point of view solely because they sense that it is not "authentic" (415–16). Though he champions a particular idealistic form of education and insists on its necessity, Emerson does not elaborate extensively about a particular individual or type that might exemplify his thoughts in action. However, to some extent, he would address this concern fourteen years later in an essay entitled "Farming."

Celebration and "Farming"

Originally delivered as a speech to farmers or those with agricultural interests or connections in Concord in 1858, "Farming" first represented an opportunity for Emerson to exalt honorable work within a nation approaching a bitter civil war. Within the coming decade, more than five hundred thousand American lives would be lost and many communities decimated. Immeasurable psychological costs, social and racial unrest, and economic challenges foretold an indefinite future, even as the nation successfully abolished slavery and progressed towards a better and more just future. As an essay published twelve years later as part of *Society and Solitude* (1870), "Farming" appeared in a completely different social and cultural context. Though the bulk of the essay meditates on the best qualities and potential of the independent farmer, addressing its reception is crucial to understanding what was at stake at the time for Emerson and discussing what "Farming" accomplishes.

Couched within the sixth through eighth paragraphs of the essay, Emerson offers a resounding warning about the problematic relationships involving race, slavery, and indentured and industrialized agricultural labor in the United States. Perhaps because he first presented "Farming" to a New England audience, Emerson elected not to place these concerns at the beginning. However, they comprise the heart of an underlying call-to-action aspect of "Farming" that was prescient for both pre- and post-Civil War audiences. A second theory is that he chose to explicitly identify these concerns later in the essay because he hoped to attract a broader readership, even those considered to be his chief critics and skeptics. For example, although southern state economies would still be wedded to agriculture following the Civil War, many writers, journalists, and reviewers in the American South detested Emerson's work. As Matthew Guinn notes, some lampooned him prior to the Civil War, and especially as he attracted more attention as an American orator and philosopher. Generally, southern critics considered Transcendental thought as a "dangerous, alien force" and Emerson's egalitarian vision as a pernicious threat to a "hierarchical, slave-holding society" (Guinn 174). "Farming" does, in fact, validate this second claim. When Emerson writes, "the true abolitionist is the farmer," (675) he explicitly counters an entire region's prevailing ideology and alludes to the necessity of a new conception of a farmer, one that both points to the potential of independent farmers while also conveying farm work in terms of independence rather than dependence upon the labor of enslaved African Americans.

The American South is not Emerson's only target, however, as he also conveys a broader warning about industrialization that extends directly to northern states and England. He realized that slavery was not merely a regional problem limited to one part of the United States. After likening an ideal farmer to an abolitionist, he focuses not on the relationship between farming and abolitionism, but instead upon wealth in the next two sentences:

> We commonly say that the rich man can speak the truth, can afford honesty, can afford independence of opinion and action—and that is the theory of nobility. But it is the rich man in a true sense, that is to say, not the man of large income and large expenditure, but solely the man whose outlay is less than his income and is steadily kept so. (675)

The management and interaction that Emerson refers to here is Earth- rather than capital-centered, and nothing less than a radical attempt at redefining what it means to be wealthy in nineteenth-century America. It is impossible to separate this criticism from factory owners in the northern states who benefited significantly from cotton planted and harvested in the American South. To further develop his criticism, Emerson offers a contrast. He describes a boy in an English factory who works as "a *minder*" who "watches the loom, to tie the thread when the wheel stops to indicate that a thread is broken" (675). A child occupying this position maintains one responsibility that allows industrial production to continue. He is not only a child because this mirrored Victorian realities at one time, but also because Emerson implies that the work the child accomplishes does not in any way nurture his growth as a person. Although not as reprehensible as slavery, this sort of work may be tenable and advantageous from a purely economic standpoint, but comes with a significant social cost. By way of pointed contrast, Emerson redefines "the *minder*" as a more independent farmer, who comes to operate an entire factory himself in the course of time by gaining more and more knowledge of human-environment interaction and agrarian arts and skills (675). Rather than complete one task repeatedly within an industrial work setting, the farmer engages in work that necessitates he read and understand environmental cues in order to become successful. Empowered, his servants are not slaves and "not the Irish, nor the coolies, but [instead] Geology and Chemistry, the quarry of the air, the water of the brook, the lightning of the cloud, the castings of the worm, the plough of the frost" (675–76). Here, Emerson points to the expansion of knowledge and human development rather than control and coercion that he saw as central to industrialization in the United States.

It is difficult to overstate the strength of this contrast today, more than a hundred and fifty years later. One might argue that unfortunately for Emerson and other like-minded critics, industrial expansion would not stop once it began and that it enabled the growth of human populations in the United States and throughout the world. It is also naive to assume that industrial developments did not provide some substantial benefits, particularly in relation to science and medical care that have enabled humans to live longer and healthier lives. Nonetheless, the discovery and ongoing consequences of global warming have complicated more than a century's worth of thinking regarding industrial progress. Human population expansion and pollution today are undeniable factors directly related to environmental degradation that Emerson and others could not clearly foresee during their time, when industrialization appeared more as a threat to the sanctity of the individual. As Wesley T. Mott notes, Emerson held a strong belief in the "centrality of character and the reality of the self" in determining personal and societal outcomes (92). The boy in the English factory performing his task without understanding multiplied by millions of others completing similar work would likely have constituted for Emerson larger global masses of people prevented from understanding the raw materials of a natural world that provide them food and shelter.

The passing of time and changing of environmental conditions begs the questions as to what "Farming"'s celebration of the farmer offers modern readers, given that over four billion people live in urban areas throughout the world now, and by 2050, it is estimated that two of every three humans will as well (Ritchie). The first is optimism. As Todd H. Richardson notes, one of Emerson's important contributions for contemporary readers is his consistent desire to inspire, empower, and help others heal (57). Whereas Emerson alluded to a generalized but also individual-tailored ideal education near the end of "New England Reformers," in "Farming," he explicates what that might look like. The farmer is "the continuous benefactor" of a nation primarily because "he is engaged in small economies, and is taught the power that lurks in petty things" (675; 677). Put another way, the work that the farmer accomplishes is neither easy nor pretty, and it demands careful attention to resource use and "small economies" (677). The farmer looks closely; then thinks; then acts; and later, assesses, remembers, rebuilds, and evolves. In each of these stages, there are inevitably setbacks or struggles, but Emerson focuses on examples of positive energy. Perhaps the modern world would be better off if populations began to shrink to help reduce global carbon footprints, but accompanying that possibility is the need for an optimism that might help generate creative thinking that would help recover damaged environments and work to halt future damage.

The second is Emerson's call for readers to consider how they spend their time and what they pay attention to, and how related decisions impact who they become. "Farming" offers no more emphatic message than that nature shapes one's destiny whether one likes it or not. If, as Emerson asserts, it is true that "cities force growth and make men talkative and entertaining," it also renders them "artificial" (681). Today, we can say with far more certainty than Emerson could imagine during his time that this irregularity poses a risk for our global future. The imbalance between expanding populations living at a distance and screened from the natural world, and increasingly plugged into glossy, manufactured technologies for extended hours each day, versus those working to ensure that they receive food and other natural resource-related products poses a conundrum with no easy answers. The nineteenth-century farmer, in the sense that Emerson celebrates, may be all but gone today. Yet, as John T. Lysaker notes, Emerson extolled the value of individual actions, especially "when we find the world in our way" (3). Instead of insisting that people abandon their new technologies, gather voluntarily and communally, and then reinvent themselves as independent farmers, as one might imagine if one adopted a strategy of the reformers Emerson criticizes in "New England Reformers," Emerson might question the extent to which our daily interactions involve direct engagement with the natural environment. If what we choose to do becomes inevitably integral to the expression of our values, then perhaps a stronger environmental education is necessary in schools, not as a means of forcing students to act a certain way so much as to reconnect with them the natural world and to help them understand the industrial artificiality we inherit as twenty-first century global citizens.

Even if some of its more specific context appears dated, the tandem of Emersonian optimism and the suggestion of the importance of environmental education and engagement are what make "Farming" a valuable essay today. No matter who insists upon it, blind adherence to calls of collective reform, as Emerson identifies in "New England Reformers," is far less likely to achieve productive results in the long-term. It is the "power of the individual mind" that he expresses faith in and celebrates, calling for self-culture and self-development that never loses its sense of connection between humanity and the environment (Maibor 133). Emerson's vision, specific to his time and one that celebrates the wisdom and complexity of the individual farmer in contrast to the social consequences of slavery and labor exploitation, would eventually become much more popular as the United States became more of an industrialized nation, and also find a more vocal champion in writings of Wendell Berry (1934–). Read today, "Farming" is not only an important precursor to Berry's work, but also a plea for more consideration of human relationships with landscapes and how those relationships might become mutually beneficial for individuals and the environment. Neither Emerson nor Berry have stemmed the tide of industrial labor, corporate agriculture, genetically modified crops, factory farming, and the harvesting of human attention, but both call on a new generation who can build upon Emerson's optimism and Berry's faith and become more deeply invested in understanding and engaging with their natural surroundings, hopefully as a means of improving global environments and addressing pressing environmental issues today.

Works Cited

Banville, John. "Foreword." *First We Read, Then We Write: Emerson on the Creative Process,* by Robert D. Richardson. U of Iowa P, pp. ix–xiii.

Bosco, Ronald A. "Ralph Waldo Emerson, 1803–1882: A Brief Biography." *A Historical Guide to Ralph Waldo Emerson*. Edited by Joel Myerson, Oxford UP, 2000, pp. 9–58.

Buell, Lawrence. *Emerson*. The Belknap Press of Harvard UP, 2003.

Corrigan, John Michael. *American Metempsychosis: Emerson, Whitman, and the New Poetry*. Fordham, 2012.

Emerson, Ralph Waldo. "Farming." 1858. *Society and Solitude*. 1870. Reprinted in *The Essential Writings of Ralph Waldo Emerson*. Edited by Brooks Atkinson, The Modern Library, 2000, pp. 671–81.

__________. "New England Reformers." *Essays: Second Series*. Reprinted in *The Essential Writings of Ralph Waldo Emerson*. Edited by Brooks Atkinson, 1844, The Modern Library, 2000, pp. 402–18.

__________. *Selected Journals, 1820–1842*. Library of America, 2010.

__________. "The Young American." 7 Feb. 1844, *American Transcendental Web,* 9 Nov. 2022, archive.vcu.edu/english/engweb/transcendentalism/authors/emerson/essays/youngam.html.

Guinn, Matthew. "Emerson's Southern Critics, 1838–1862." *Resources for American Literary Study*, vol. 25, no. 2, 1999, pp. 174–91.

Lysaker, John T. *After Emerson*. Indiana UP, 2017.

Maibor, Carolyn R. "Teaching the Practical Emerson Through the Sermons and the Early Lectures." *Approaches to Teaching the Works of Ralph Waldo Emerson*. Edited by Mark C. Long and Sean Ross Meehan, The Modern Language Association of America Press, 2018, pp. 131–35.

Mott, Wesley T. "'The Age of the First Person Singular': Emerson and Individualism." *A Historical Guide to Ralph Waldo Emerson*. Edited by Joel Myerson, Oxford UP, 2000, pp. 61–100.

Richardson, Todd H. "Emerson and the Reform Culture of the Second Great Awakening." *Approaches to Teaching the Works of Ralph Waldo Emerson*. Edited by Mark C. Long and Sean Ross Meehan, The Modern Language Association of America Press, 2018, pp. 53–58.

Ritchie, Hanner, and Max Roser. "Urbanization." *Our World in Data*. 2019, ourworldindata.org/urbanization.

Biography of Ralph Waldo Emerson

LuElla D'Amico

Ralph Waldo Emerson (1803–82) was a prominent American philosopher, essayist, and poet who lived and wrote during the nineteenth century. Emerson is best known for his transcendentalist beliefs, which emphasize the importance of individuality, nature, spiritualism, and intuition. His writings have left a profound impact on American literature and philosophical thought. In other words, they are still often referenced today in academic circles and in the wider culture writ large.

In *Democracy Matters: Winning the Fight Against Imperialism*, contemporary philosopher Cornel West writes that Emerson is:

> The indisputable godfather of the deep democratic tradition . . ., a literary artist of dramatic and visionary eloquence and the first full-blown democratic intellectual in the United Sates. Emerson was an intellectual who hungered most of all to communicate to broad publics. He reveled in the burning social issues of his day (the annihilation of Native Americans, slavery), highlighting the need for democratic individuals to be nonconformist, courageous, and true to themselves. (4)

Emerson, therefore, harbors a unique legacy as being both activist and philosopher. Throughout his works, Emerson inspires others to take up his charge of trusting their intuitions to make change. Imminently quotable, he relays in his 1841 treatise "Self-Reliance" that "A foolish consistency is the hobgoblin of little minds, adored by little statesmen and philosophers and divines" (265). For Emerson what matters most is that the public be attentive to their inner selves and conscience—that they rail against thoughtlessly agreeing with the masses, and each other, for the mere satisfaction of approval. Rather, the public must listen to and trust themselves, regardless of social consequences. In this way they can become intellectuals worthy of recognition and esteem. This transcendental focus on radical individualism has become synonymous with an American ethos of self-knowledge and understanding that resonates still today.

Early Life and Education

Ralph Waldo Emerson was born on May 25, 1803, in Boston, Massachusetts, to a lineage of ministers dating back to seventeenth-century Puritan-era United States. His father, William Emerson, was a prominent Unitarian minister, and his mother, Ruth Haskins Emerson, was a devout Anglican. Her well-educated religious background ensured Emerson's influence included British thinkers and writers, such as Samuel Taylor Coleridge, Ralph Cudworth, and Jeremy Taylor. After his father's death in 1811, Emerson was sent to live with various relatives in Boston, Cambridge, and Concord. He attended the Boston Latin School and entered Harvard College at the age of 14, where he studied the Classics, languages, and philosophy.

The death of William Emerson in 1811 left Emerson and his siblings, five of which included brothers, in financial difficulty. To support himself, Emerson began teaching at a school for young women in Boston. Later he became a Unitarian minister, serving as the assistant minister at Boston's Second Church, a post once held by the famous Puritan Increase Mather.

In 1829, Emerson married his first wife, Ellen Tucker. Tragically, she died of tuberculosis only two years after they wed. The grief he felt over her death deeply affected his spiritual beliefs and his writings. Emerson was no longer positive; he held steadfast to the Unitarian views he was preaching. As such, Emerson became increasingly preoccupied with themes of imminent mortality and the spiritual realm.

Despite his grief and changing family situation, Emerson's writing and lecturing career began to takeoff in the 1830s. He eventually resigned from his ministerial post altogether in 1832, citing his growing disagreement with the Unitarian Church's emphasis on tradition and dogma. His focus on individual access to the divine without ministerial intervention became a hallmark of his work following this professional decision.

Early Career and Second Marriage

After leaving the ministry, Emerson focused on honing his writing even further and pursuing that and lecturing as his main career. He published his first major essay, "Nature," in 1836, which established him as the leading voice in what would become known as the Transcendentalist movement.

A year before writing "Nature" in 1835, Emerson met Lydia Jackson at a lecture of his in Plymouth. She envisioned their marriage in a dream and shortly thereafter became his second wife. When they got married, Emerson began calling his wife "Lidian" because he believed the sound of the name had a more romantic, classical quality to it than "Lydia." For Emerson, his image and individual stamp on life remained true even in his romantic and familial relationships. Ralph and Lidian settled in Concord, Massachusetts, where Emerson became part of a literary and intellectual community that included Nathaniel Hawthorne, Henry David Thoreau, and Bronson Alcott. During this period, Emerson continued to write and lecture, traveling throughout the United States to give talks on topics, such as self-reliance, the importance of individualism, and the relationship between nature and the divine. During the course of his lifetime, Emerson gave over 1,500 lectures. Lidian and Emerson had four children together. Although he had suffered financially as a student at Harvard, Emerson's speaking and writing career now easily supported Lidian and their children. Moreover, he inherited an estate from his first wife that was especially helpful during his early married years.

Transcendentalism and Literary Career

In the 1830s and 1840s holistically, Emerson became the world's leading voice for the Transcendentalist movement—the first distinctly American philosophical movement. As aforementioned, Emerson avowed that people should rely on their own experiences and insights rather than conforming to society's expectations. His philosophy can be traced back to his belief in the inherent goodness of human nature and how that can be connected to the divinity of the natural world.

"Nature" is often considered the work that defined Transcendentalism as a movement. Published anonymously in 1836, it is a poetic exploration of the natural world and what Emerson sees as its necessary relationship to human experience. In a praising, 1844 review of the essay—which had just been republished in the United States—fellow transcendentalist thinker Margaret Fuller notes the transatlantic scope of Emerson's ideas, assessing that "Copies of Mr. Emersons first published little volume called 'Nature' have [in England] been sold by thousands in a short time" (par.1). In "Nature," Emerson argues that nature is not simply an external phenomenon or landscape to enjoy: venturing into nature is intimately connected to the human spirit. He suggests that by immersing ourselves in the natural world, humans can awaken our intuition and connect with the divine, or what he calls the "Over-soul." Emerson writes that "Nature is a setting that fits equally well a comic or a mourning piece. In good health, the air is a cordial of incredible virtue. Crossing a bare common, in snow puddles, at twilight, under a clouded sky, without having in my thoughts any occurrence of special good fortune, I have enjoyed a perfect exhilaration. I am glad to the brink of fear" (10). This passage reflects Emerson's notion that nature is a source of both joy and inspiration, as well as a place of deep contemplation and reflection. He suggests that even in difficult or challenging circumstances, the natural world can provide a sense of comfort and renewal, and that by immersing ourselves in it, we can connect with a power larger than ourselves. Emerson felt a sense of wonder and awe in the face of nature, and he believed in its power to transform and uplift the human spirit.

Another of his notable transcendentalist works includes "Self-Reliance." In this 1841 essay, Emerson argued that individuals should seek to connect with their own inner wisdom and intuition, rather than relying on the opinions and beliefs of others. One famous quote from "Self-Reliance" that captures the essence of his view on self-reliance is: "Whoso would be a man, must be a nonconformist.

He who would gather immortal palms must not be hindered by the name of goodness, but must explore if it be goodness. Nothing is at last sacred but the integrity of your own mind" (261). This quote reflects Emerson's belief that true individuality and greatness can only be achieved by breaking free from the constraints of society and tradition. He suggests that conformity and adherence to established norms can stifle creativity and individual expression. Following one's own path and listening to the voice of intuition is the answer to being mundane.

In "Self-Reliance," Emerson also emphasizes the importance of personal integrity and self-trust in whatever current historical moment one lives in. He suggests that individuals must be willing to question and explore their own beliefs and values, and not simply accept what has been handed down to them by tradition or authority. Literary and philosophical tradition ought to be read and understood, but it ought to act as an aid, not a stumbling block, to help generate new, creative ideas in the world. "The American Scholar," and "The Divinity School Address" are two of Emerson's other most famous transcendentalist essays. These two essays likewise emphasize the importance of self-reliance, individualism, and the pursuit of truth.

Although primarily known as an essayist and philosopher, Emerson composed poetry throughout his career, too. Not surprisingly, Emerson's poetry often uses nature as a metaphor for the human experience. Unlike his essays that are rife with theoretical, imagistic, and symbolic language, his language as a poet is characterized by its clarity. He sought to express his more complex transcendental ideas and emotions more simply through the poetic form. Some of Emerson's most famous poems include "The Rhodora," and "Brahma."

In "The Rhodora," Emerson uses the image of a wildflower to explore the beauty and value of individuality. The 1834 poem begins with the phrase: "On being asked, whence is the flower," and Emerson responds:

> "Rhodora! if the sages ask thee why
> This charm is wasted on the earth and sky,

Tell them, dear, that if eyes were made for seeing,
Then beauty is its own excuse for Being." (33)

Emerson attests that nature's simply beauty in this flower provides access to a truer understanding of the world, an understanding that initially stumps "sages" who are lost in ideas rather than intuiting the simple truth found in nature. The poem's message is direct, an homage to nature and how a flower can work to move the soul through its beauty.

In his poem "Brahma"—published in *The Atlantic* in 1857—Emerson uses the Hindu deity Brahma as a symbol for the power of the divine, exploring in a different way the idea of the ultimate unity of all things. Likely having read Hindu works, such as the *Bhagavad-Gita* and *The Upanishads*, Emerson came away with a special interest in this Hindu god Brahma, known as the creator of all things in the universe. In Hinduism, Brahma is characterized as imbuing a universal, connective force and is perhaps most easily likened to Emerson's idea of the "Over-soul." In this poem, Emerson takes on the persona of Brahma. The first lines read as follows:

"If the red slayer think he slays,
Or if the slain think he is slain,
They know not well the subtle ways
I keep, and pass, and turn again." (164)

Emerson asserts that those who kill ("the red slayer") or those who die ("the slain") are never actually dead: there is an afterlife, he asserts. Death is not eternal because Brahma "subtl[y]" is always there, always present, always connecting the universe and all who dwell in it together.

Overall, Emerson's poetry reflects an overriding belief in the power of language to convey complicated spiritual ideas and emotions. His poetry and his essays alike speak to the idea that humans ought to be looking for the eternal and notice the beauty and truth in the natural world that surrounds them.

Later Life and Legacy

In the later years of his career, Emerson's scope as a writer grew once again, this time with an increasing focus on history and politics. He became highly involved in the abolitionist movement, speaking against slavery and supporting the cause of civil rights. Emerson was a frequent contributor to antislavery publications, such as William Lloyd Garrison's *The Liberator* (1831–65). He also delivered a number of antislavery speeches, including a famous address in 1844 entitled "The Young American," in which he called for an end to slavery and urged his fellow citizens to take action to achieve this goal.

Moreover, as West points out at the beginning of this biography, Emerson supported the abolitionist cause through his personal actions. He helped to fundraise for antislavery organizations. And, following the Fugitive Slave Act of 1850—which permitted southerners to go into northern states and take back enslaved peoples who had escaped—Emerson and his Concord neighbors agreed to shelter any escapees who fled to Massachusetts seeking freedom. Emerson was likewise a vocal supporter of abolitionist John Brown and his controversial raid on Harper's Ferry, even giving a speech in Boston in 1859 to aid Brown's family following the raid.

Any critical biography on Emerson ought also to mention that he had a role as a mentor and friend to many of the most important writers and thinkers of his time. Perhaps most famously, he was an extremely close friend and confidant of Henry David Thoreau. Emerson's ideas, and financial help, helped shape Thoreau's famous 1854 work "Walden" as well as his passive resistance ideology, made famous in his 1849 essay, "Civil Disobedience." Emerson was influential in shaping Walt Whitman's career, too, who avowed his debt to Emerson in the preface to the 1855 first edition of "Leaves of Grass." Herman Melville, Frederick Douglass, William James, Emily Dickinson all cited Emerson as influential to their creative careers as well.

Emerson's literary style holistically—a style that combines poetic language with complex philosophical ideas of selfhood and spirituality—has had a lasting impact on American literature and letters. His essays and lectures are characterized by a beauty and depth that continue to inspire, and his work has influenced contemporary writers and thinkers in fields as diverse as literature, philosophy, and political theory.

Emerson died on April 27, 1882, at the age of 78. He was buried at Sleepy Hollow Cemetery in Concord, Massachusetts, a place where he had given a dedication speech years earlier in 1855.

Works Cited

Emerson, Ralph Waldo. *Essays: First and Second Series*. Library of America, 1983.

__________. *The Major Poetry*. Edited by Albert J. von Frank, Harvard UP, 2015.

Fuller, Margaret. "Review of Emerson's Essays [Second Series]," *American Transcendentalism Web*, archive.vcu.edu/english/engweb/transcendentalism/criticism/fulleronemerson.html.

West, Cornel. *Democracy Matters: Winning the Fight Against Imperialism*. Penguin, 2005.

CRITICAL CONTEXTS

The Paradox of Self-Reliance in an Era of Social Reform

Joshua Boyd

Introduction

Ralph Waldo Emerson's famous essay "Self-Reliance" (1841) is full of verve and provocative lines that appeal to punk rockers and progressive educators alike. Extracted from their context, lines such as "Whoso would be a man must be a nonconformist" (29) or "A foolish consistency is the hobgoblin of little minds" (33) or "Trust thyself: every heart vibrates to that iron string" (28) have become a part of the American ethos, understood and used even by those unfamiliar with Emerson's great essay. Emerson sought to challenge his staid countrymen to cut ties with conformity and consistency. "I hope in these days we have heard the last of conformity and consistency," he claimed bluntly (35). Rather, Emerson argued, "Let us affront and reprimand the smooth mediocrity and squalid contentment of the times, and hurl in the face of custom, and trade, and office, the fact which is the upshot of all history, that there is a great responsible Thinker and Actor working wherever a man works; that a true man belongs to no other time or place, but is the centre of things" (35). Thus spoke Emerson, the great American apologist of individualism.

If all of this sounds rather self-centered, well, it is. Self-reliance (or what some of Emerson's peers called self-culture) is not a collective activity, but it does have a collective benefit. Emerson and his associates, those labeled Transcendentalists by their detractors, continually promoted means by which men and women could actualize their intuitive, spiritual capacities. They frequently referred to their pursuit of spiritual growth or unfolding as self-culture. The idea of self-culture or *Bildung* appeared in works of German philosophy that the Transcendentalists were reading with fervor (Kornfeld 19). The goal of self-culture, however, was far grander than personal improvement. The Transcendentalists sought to restore virtue to the broader, more holistic definition of ancient Greek culture when it denoted "human excellence" that included "the full flourishing of the whole human person" (Cafaro 538). Therefore, they promoted the consistent application of ethical standards personally and communally. Self-culture, then, paradoxically leads to ethical action. Reform of the self and reform of society were both prominent goals, but the latter depends on the former. As Len Gougeon succinctly explains, Emerson "felt . . . that the reform of society must always begin with the reform of individuals. Any effort to impose moral improvement on society through the passage of laws, restrictions, or prohibitions was doomed to failure because morality is a matter of the heart and all such impositions inevitably leave the heart untouched and unconverted" (xi).

That the idealism of the Transcendentalists flourished in the 1830s and the following decades before the Civil War is hardly surprising. Those decades were years when the nation seemed poised to realize all of its potential, and Transcendentalism was a religious and philosophical movement focused on potential. As the first historian of Transcendentalism, Octavius Brooks Frothingham, explained, this movement logically followed the general feeling of freedom of its context: "A feeling was abroad that all things must be new in the new world . . . . The popular faith in the capacities of men to make states, laws, religions for themselves, supplied the groundwork for the new philosophy" (106). Anything old, aristocratic, hierarchical, or coldly rational would have felt "disagreeable to people who, having just emancipated themselves from political dependence on the mother country, were full of confidence in their ability to set up society for themselves" (Frothingham 107). In New England, Transcendentalism naturally flourished at a time of national growth and transition.

That the flourishing of Transcendentalism seems natural is a testament to its lasting influence on American culture. Emersonian self-reliance is the heart cry of many American individualists. Perhaps what is lost among contemporary nonconformity, however, is the greater motivation of Emerson's doctrine of self-reliance, one of the great paradoxical contributions to American thought. Emerson did not advocate nonconformity for the sake of nonconformity. Rather, he believed true self-reliance was ultimately the only true solution to the evident ills of his age. Reformation was happening on a grand scale in antebellum America. Whether it would last depended on a reformation of the self.

Reformation of the Nation: Emerson's Historical Context

The antebellum era in which Emerson emerged as a leading public intellectual in New England was one of transition and enthusiasm. Likened to the development of a child, the nation in the decades leading up to the Civil War emerged from the birth pangs of the Revolutionary War as a baby nourished on the milk of European culture and ideas. Following the War of 1812, which concluded with General Andrew Jackson's victory at the Battle of New Orleans in 1815, the nation entered the early national period and began toddling toward the 1840s and 1850s when, as a vigorous youth, America stood poised to strut along the world stage. Indeed, the cockiness of adolescence characterized the nation in the late 1830s and early 1840s, the era in which John O'Sullivan christened American "The Great Nation of Futurity" in the *Democratic Review* in 1839 and introduced the phrase "manifest destiny" into the national lexicon a few years later. Emerson himself gave voice to the exceptionalism of the nation in the early 1840s. On February 7, 1844, he delivered a lengthy lecture titled "The Young American" marked by exuberance and enthusiasm for the probable future of the young American nation. With words reminiscent of O'Sullivan's "The Great Nation of Futurity," Emerson described the Puritans' decision to settle in the New World as "the simple acceptance of the plainest road ever shown men to walk in. It was the human race, under Divine leading, going forth to receive and inhabit their patrimony" (242). As the New Israel in the New World, America's forebears gladly possessed the new Promised Land.

The expanding boundaries of the new Promised Land at the outset of the nineteenth century was the most recognizable transition in antebellum America. That explosive growth commenced in 1803, the same year as Emerson's birth, with the Louisiana Purchase. Four decades later, the nation again extended its borders significantly through the annexation of Texas. In 1845, delegates from the Republic of Texas voted to seek admission into the United States after a decade of disputes with Mexico. A year later in April 1846, the United States and Mexico were embroiled in war that stemmed from a significant border dispute. President James K. Polk believed the southern border of Texas stretched to the Rio Grande River rather than the Nueces River, the river that demarcated the border between Mexico and the Republic of Texas. Mexico disagreed and could not be persuaded diplomatically to cede land between the Nueces and the Rio Grande. When Polk sent American troops to the Rio Grande, therefore, Mexico interpreted the action as one of aggression, and the Mexican-American War commenced in April 1846. Two years and thousands of casualties later, Mexico surrendered, and the United States increased its geographical territory by one-quarter (Delbanco 200–01).

As the antebellum era was a period of expanding borders, it was also the era of expanding opportunities. Freedom from the strictures and systems of Europe seemingly provided limitless opportunities for those willing to pursue them in America. In *Letters from an American Farmer* (1782), J. Hector St. John de Crèvecœur sought to describe the New World through letters to an imaginary recipient in the Old World. Addressing the question "What is an American?" in the third letter, Crèvecœur described Americans as possessing the freedom of self-determination: "The American is a new man, who acts upon new principles; he must therefore entertain new ideas and form new opinions. From involuntary idleness, servile dependence, penury, and useless labour, he has passed toils of a very different nature, rewarded by ample subsistence. This is an American" (70).

In the 1950s, critic R. W. B. Lewis described this self-determining figure as the American Adam. As Lewis explained, in the antebellum period in America a new ideal figure emerged, "a new kind of hero, the heroic embodiment of a new set of ideal human attributes" (5). That hero, whom Lewis called the American Adam, was "an individual emancipated from history, happily bereft of ancestry, untouched and undefiled by the usual inheritances of family and race; an individual standing alone, self-reliant and self-propelling, ready to confront whatever awaited him with the aid of his own unique and inherent resources" (5). Lewis's formulation of the American Adam was undoubtedly influenced by Emerson's own speaking and writing, especially the lecture "The Young American." In addition to this brief reference to the divinely orchestrated settling of the New World, Emerson proclaimed the exceptionalism of the nation. "It seems so easy for America to inspire and express the most expansive and humane spirit; newborn, free, healthful, strong, the land of the laborer, of the democrat, of the philanthropist, of the believer, of the saint, she should speak for the human race," he claimed. "America is the country of the Future . . . . It has no past: all has an onward and prospective look" (230). Given its geographic expansion, industrial development, and political confidence, America had become, in the words of historian James McPherson, "the *Wunderkind* nation of the nineteenth century" (6). Life in antebellum America was, indeed, full of promise and promising developments.

These confident pronouncements regarding the promise of the American experiment, however, belie a simultaneous anxiety about the detriments of American progress. Geographic expansion, for example, became increasingly controversial as the nineteenth century approached its middle age. While Alexis de Tocqueville certainly shared the enthusiasm of fellow Frenchman Crèvecœur in evaluating America, the former concluded the first volume of his influential two-volume study of antebellum America, *Democracy in America* (1835), with a reflection on the probable results of geographic expansion on "the white man, . . . man par excellence," and the two races "below him," namely "the Negro and the Indian" (317). What the two latter races shared in common, according to Tocqueville, was "their misfortunes . . . . Both occupy an equally inferior position in the land where they dwell; both suffer the effects of tyranny, and, though their afflictions are different, they have the same people to blame for them" (317). The native populations had largely been destroyed by westward expansion. Simultaneously, Tocqueville presciently predicted that westward expansion would enable slavery to proliferate and maintain its degrading effects. These fears were not unique to Tocqueville.

Emerson's prescient contemporaries understood that the addition of the massive geographical regions obtained through the Louisiana Purchase and the annexation of Texas would necessarily fuel debates about the plight of Indian populations pushed westward, a subject that Emerson's friend Margaret Fuller addressed in her travel narrative *Summer on the Lakes, in 1843*, and about the perpetuation of slavery. Westward expansion especially fomented strong emotions on both sides of the slavery debate. As historian Thomas Kidd asserts, "The question of *slavery on the expanding western frontier* . . . became arguably the most contested political issue in America from the 1810s to the 1850s" (*American History* 143, emphasis original). Emerson and many of his fellow Transcendentalists participated in this contest, especially in response to the dubious motivations of the Mexican-American War and after the passage of the Compromise of 1850.

Even in the enthusiastic lecture "The Young American," Emerson acknowledged that American progress would come at a price, something he discussed regularly in other lectures and writings. Coupled with the promise of the future were the painful, paradoxical realities of the present. In discussing the construction of the railroad, Emerson noted that this invention both introduced passengers to natural beauty and marred that beauty at the same time. Another painful, paradoxical reality was the effect of railroad construction on migrant laborers. On the one hand, "The Irish father and mother are very ill paid, and are victims of fraud and private oppression" (225). Further, "the labor done is excessive, and the sight of it reminds one of negro-driving" (224). On the other hand, these laborers "escape from the squalid despair of their condition at home, into the unlimited opportunities of their existence here," and this "must be reckoned a gain" (225). Similarly, in discussing trade, Emerson spoke largely of its benefits yet acknowledged its detriments, as well. Although many "rail at Trade," and intellectuals and philanthropists "have much harm to say of it," sage historians "will see that Trade was the principle of Liberty; that Trade planted

America and destroyed Feudalism; that it makes peace and keeps peace, and it will abolish slavery." Even so, "This is the good and this is the evil of trade, that it goes to put everything *into market*, talent, beauty, virtue, and man himself" (234, emphasis original). Progress in Emerson's antebellum era was fraught with complexity: two steps forward, one step backwards.

The shortcomings of the nation to live up to its ideals motivated Emerson and his associates to engage in reform efforts. As one early historian of Transcendentalism noted, "The Transcendentalist was by nature a reformer. He could not be satisfied with men as they were. His doctrine of the capacities of men, even in its most moderate statement, kindled to enthusiasm his hope of change" (Frothingham 153). That enthusiasm for change manifested itself in several spheres of society in Emerson's day.

At the height of Transcendentalism's influence (the 1830s–50s), the aforementioned significant political actions prompted national protest and reform efforts. Reform movements began more locally, too. Notably, Emerson in lectures such as "Man the Reformer" and "The Transcendentalist" and fellow Transcendentalist Henry David Thoreau in *Walden* championed the virtues of simple living within one's means. For others within Emerson's orbit, the emerging middle-class and its attendant materialism prompted communal associations such as Bronson Alcott's Fruitlands and George Ripley's Brook Farm. Among others, Alcott advocated for reform to education, as well. In his own way, Emerson addressed these issues and, in doing so, manifested the Transcendentalists' concern for reform no less than his associates even if they criticized him as too reluctant or passive in response to the ills of the age. For Emerson, however, the ills of the age stemmed from a graver disease to the individual. Reform must begin within the individual heart. This conviction compelled Emerson to advocate for reformation within religious practice and belief, the arena most adequate for an appeal to the human heart. Understanding the religious context of Emerson's day is vital to understanding Emerson himself and his legacy of self-reliance.

Reformation of the Congregation: Emerson's Religious Context

In the spring of 1840, a distraught churchgoer penned a letter to the *Christian Examiner* to express disappointment, perhaps even disbelief, over the preacher's negligence to lead the congregation at East Lexington in prayer on Sunday, April 12, 1840. "[T]he preacher's lips uttered no prayer," the letter reads, "and after the reading of a lecture, the congregation retired having had no worship" (qtd. in Grodzins 50). That preacher was Emerson. His avoidance of a public prayer, while it furrowed the brow of the author of this letter, was not necessarily surprising to those familiar with Emerson and his beliefs. Marianne Stevenson, for example, was also present that Sunday in East Lexington. While she admitted she lacked complete understanding of Emerson's beliefs, she saw a connection between those beliefs and his refusal to lead the congregation in prayer. She explained, "I see why he doubts whether he can speak to the in-dwelling Spirit, whether an address to him is not putting him farther off" (qtd. in Grodzins 50). Certainly, what is true for one person—addressing the in-dwelling Spirit admits separateness rather than essential unity—is also true of the people who sat before Emerson that Sunday—addressing the in-dwelling Spirit in public prayer separates the human listener even further than vocalizing personal prayer. There was also within Emerson a profound hesitancy *to put men further off from the Spirit* by means of his own influence. Given this understanding of Emerson's thought, one may readily grasp his hesitancy to practice public prayer. Emerson feared men and women would look outward at him rather than inward for enlightenment or instruction. Although one wave in a sea of large swells crashing onto and reshaping the shores of American religion, Emerson is rightly considered a significant contributor to religious reform.

In his history of the growth and transformation of American Christianity between 1775 and 1845, Nathan Hatch connects the proliferation of preaching and "insurgent" or "upstart" (4) denominations to geographical expansion, on the one hand, and the American democratic spirit on the other hand (5). He notes that "American Protestantism has been skewed away from central ecclesiastical institutions and high culture; it has been pushed and pulled into its present shape by a democratic or populist orientation" (5). As the population exploded during the seven decades following the Revolutionary War, people moved westward. As they moved "beyond the reach of any church organization" (Hatch 4), they founded denominations to their own liking. This democratization of American faith corresponded with the Second Great Awakening. "In the Second Great Awakening," Thomas Kidd explains, "new evangelical sects proliferated, and the leadership of the evangelical churches became even more 'democratized,' as more women, uneducated men, and African Americans found places of power and leadership" ("Introduction" 25). The second awakening, then, differed from the first in that the second championed the virtue and vernacular of ordinary religious people as opposed to learned and sophisticated clergy (Hatch 5). While Hatch and Kidd document the democratization of evangelical sects, a similar movement was afoot within Unitarianism.

Unitarianism experienced its own awakening in the 1830s. The liberal theology of Unitarianism emerged from late eighteenth-century disputes within orthodox Christianity over the nature and method of religious conversion. The context of these disputes was the First Great Awakening, a period of religious revival in New England that began in the late 1730s with renewed spiritual fervor in Jonathan Edwards's congregation in Northampton, Massachusetts. Edwards documented this revival in his book *A Faithful Narrative of the Surprising Work of God in the Conversion of Many Hundred Souls in Northampton* (1737). Historians have generally categorized the sides in these disputes as the New Lights and Old Lights, although there were more than two actual stances on the issue (Kidd, "Introduction" 2). The point of departure for these two groups was whether religious conversion was a matter of sensuous experience (New Lights) or rational assent (Old Lights). The vocal opponent of New Light revivalism was Charles Chauncy, a minister at Boston's First Church. Chauncy rejected the New Lights' emphasis on emotional responses that accompany conversion experiences. According to Chauncy, the emotional conversions that accompanied revivals such as the one Edwards described were fits of enthusiasm, a term that denoted "rational or emotional instability, and in religious contexts identified bodily fervor caused supposedly by divine inspiration" (Martin 200). Instead of highly emotional conversions, Chauncy contended a dispassionate conversion that is gradual and deliberate is as genuine as the conversions lauded by New Light evangelists (Marsden 269). In objecting to revivalism for its seeming basis in irrationality, Chauncy manifested his debt to John Locke, who contended that belief must, above all, be rational (Martin 200).

Unitarianism developed out of this dispute between the Old Light and New Light factions within the tradition of Puritanism. Anne C. Rose traces the development of this liberal offshoot of New England orthodoxy. "Unitarianism developed," she writes, "between 1790 and 1830 from a critique of Orthodox revivalism into a coherent value system. Unitarians stressed the importance of reason, intellectual freedom, and moral duty" (11). Unitarians inherited the emphasis on reason by way of Old Light Protestantism and John Locke's empiricism. Religion was eminently rational. In applying human reason to religion, Unitarianism challenged a number of tenets of faith and practice long held by orthodox Christian denominations. For example, they found no evidence for the trinity in their study of scripture and, consequently, rejected this fundamental doctrine of orthodox Christianity (Gura 23). This rational religion affected more than Bible study, however. As their forebears had vigorously opposed the emotionalism that characterized the First Great Awakening, the Unitarians opposed the Second Great Awakening on similar grounds. They "voiced their doubt of the lasting efficacy of emotional conversions without rational understanding, deplored the manipulative methods used by preachers to awaken sinners, criticized the demoralizing pessimism of the doctrine of total depravity, and denounced the competition for converts among evangelical sects as an antithesis of Christian toleration" (Rose 13). On these matters Unitarians seemingly agreed in the first two decades of the 1800s. By the 1830s, however,

Unitarianism itself became a house divided as had its theological predecessor.

The reasons for debate between conservative and liberal Unitarians were many, but one is especially noteworthy for its influence on Transcendentalism, a movement birthed out of liberal Unitarianism. More than other established and developing denominations, Unitarianism was regional. It flourished in Boston and smaller nearby towns, such as Concord, Massachusetts. Therefore, the transformation of Boston in the antebellum era had a profound influence on Unitarianism. As a port town rapidly growing and industrializing, Boston became a city with three distinct social classes with ever widening gaps among them. Although Unitarians tended to be either members of the elite wealthy class or the professional middle class, many of their fellow Bostonians inhabited the working class as skilled or unskilled laborers. That many Unitarians profited from the working class consequently spurred debates about the moral obligations of the religious elite or middle class to those beneath them (Rose 17–21). In tracing the awakening that occurred within Unitarianism in the 1830s, Anne Rose contends that a distinct "evangelical Unitarianism" emerged in response to the industrialization of Boston and its associated effects. Rose notes that *evangelical* when applied to Unitarianism does not reference proclamation of the Gospel, as it would in orthodox Christian denominations. Rather, the term applies to efforts of Unitarians "to seek heartfelt conversions as an antidote to the problems that came with socioeconomic change" (Rose 3). These evangelical Unitarians, or liberal Unitarians as they are more commonly known, sought to revitalize a denomination often oblivious to or uncaring about the plight of the working class, the poor, and oppressed groups. Unitarian divines such as William Ellery Channing and Theodore Parker were representative of this group within the larger denomination.

If the high-minded rationalism of Unitarianism inhibited compassion for the poor and oppressed, that same high-minded tradition inhibited the appeal of the religion to those outside of it. Unitarianism in the first half of the nineteenth century included vigorous debates about whether words possessed absolute or arbitrary meaning, whether scripture was a human or divine composition, and whether the meaning of scripture was literal or symbolic. To participate in such debates, many Unitarians pursued higher education at elite German universities (Gura 24–44). In such an environment, Unitarianism seemed a religion for the few rather than the many. The truth of a scriptural text, for example, could be understood only by one with specialized training. Although both conservative and liberal Unitarians were highly intellectual, the latter group challenged the rationalism of their conservative brethren. Truth was not apprehended solely through external data or sensory experience properly sifted by one's reason. Rather, truth could be intuited and was, thus, available to all rather than a select few. For some within Unitarianism in the 1830s, even the awakening fomented by liberal Unitarians did not go far enough in its efforts toward personal and social reform. From liberal Unitarianism, then, another group emerged with Emerson as its leading voice. These were the Transcendentalists.

Transcendentalism was foremost a religious reform movement within Unitarianism that sought to breathe life back into what Emerson called a "corpse-cold" denomination (*Journals* 9: 381). They believed so fiercely in individualism, however, that grouping them under such a label may be misleading. They themselves joked about being a group in which disagreement was one thing they held in common. They "unite to differ," James Freeman Clarke once quipped (qtd. in Gura 5). Similarly, James Elliot Cabot remarked that Emerson and his peers considered themselves not so much a group as a "changing body of liberal thinkers, agreeing in nothing but their liberality" (249). Emerson himself was notably vague when he described Transcendentalism as "Idealism as it appears in 1842" ("The Transcendentalist" 201). Despite the difficulties of definition, Emerson and his associates were similar enough in their thinking to constitute a movement. In general terms, the Transcendentalists hailed from Boston or nearby, had affiliation with Harvard College, and grew up within Unitarianism (Gura 5–6). Some remained Unitarians and comprised the liberal faction within the denomination. Others, such as Emerson, left the denomination formally even if they continued associating with liberal Unitarianism informally. Contention between Transcendentalists and conservative Unitarians arose from a fundamental disagreement over epistemology, the study of the nature and acquisition of knowledge.

To varying degrees, Transcendentalists rejected the empiricism (or sensationalism) of John Locke, a theory of knowledge esteemed by conservative Unitarians. The human mind according to Locke was a *tabula rasa*, a blank slate, without knowledge apart from sensory experience (*posteriori* knowledge). In contrast, Emerson and his coterie harkened back to Plato to assert that the human mind knows through intuition or apart from sensory experience (*priori* knowledge). Emerson categorized these two philosophies as Materialism and Idealism. To generalize, Locke and conservative Unitarians were Materialists. Emerson and his associates were Idealists. As Emerson himself described these two categories in "The Transcendentalist," a lecture he delivered in 1841, a Materialist's foundation is "experience" while an Idealist's foundation is "consciousness." Additionally, a Materialist "think[s] from the data of the senses" whereas an Idealist "perceive[s] that the senses are not final" but provide "representations of things." Last, a Materialist "insists on facts, on history, on the force of circumstances, and the animal wants of man" whereas an Idealist insists "on the power of Thought and of Will, on inspiration, on miracle, on individual culture." Both "modes of thinking are natural," Emerson concluded, "but the idealist contends that his way of thinking is in higher nature" (201). Although this passage retains some of the esoteric philosophizing the Transcendentalists themselves disliked when it appeared within Unitarianism, the distinction Emerson makes here is one that informed every area of his life as a leading American intellectual.

As an alumnus of Harvard and son of a prominent Unitarian minister, Emerson seemed destined for ordination and fruitful ministry within a Unitarian church. In March 1829 he was ordained in Boston's Second Church, but his commitment to Idealism, as he understood it then, required resignation from formal ministry. Just over three years later, on 9 September 1832, Emerson took his place behind the pulpit of Second Church in Boston to preach his final sermon as a Unitarian clergyman. As Emerson became a committed Idealist, he found the formalism of Unitarian worship increasingly distasteful.

In a sermon delivered 17 July 1831, Emerson addressed some of the "specific errors widely prevalent" among the respectable and religious ("Sermon CXXI" 65). Just as people can give themselves over too fully to their physical lives, the Church, Emerson argued, can focus too exclusively on physical reality: "It marks a very sensual state of the Church, when things are understood sensually, or by pictures addressed to the senses, and not spiritually" ("Sermon CXXI" 65). The Church's teachings on heaven and hell were two areas of doctrine that depended too much on appeals to the senses rather than the soul, according to Emerson. Many Christians, clergy and laity, "describe the happiness of heaven in language wholly got from the eye" ("Sermon CXXI" 65). Instead, Emerson asserted that "true heaven" is found in "the enlargement of this soul to the great and increasing capacity for virtue" ("Sermon CXXI" 66). If that is heaven, then hell is the soul's acclimation to and accommodation of vice. Damnation is not a physical sorting that results in the blessed being one place and the damned another. To be in hell is to possess a diseased soul overrun by vicious desires. Those twisted desires cannot be reformed through material means.

In his resignation sermon, Emerson explained why he could no longer administer the Lord's Supper and, thus, must resign from the pastorate. He argued against this ritual because the Lord's Supper fostered adoration of Christ rather than direct participation in the divine presence of God. Rather than deity worthy of worship, Christ is, according to Emerson, "an Instructor of man" whose teaching is worthy of emulation because he "teaches us how to become like God" ("Sermon CLXII" 75). Man becomes like God not by adoration of an external deity but by internal, unmediated communion with the divine presence of God suffused in creation, including the self. Emerson could not administer an ordinance that he thought fostered misplaced adoration. Although forms and rituals once had their place, Emerson suggested their usefulness had faded away as

Christianity had progressed. Indeed, Emerson contended that the deaths of Jesus, Paul, and numerous martyrs in church history were intended "to redeem us from formal religion, and teach us to seek our wellbeing in the reformation of the soul" ("Sermon CLXII" 76–77). Having reached such a conclusion, Emerson admitted that *he* could no longer administer the Lord's Supper.

Emerson's theological reformation is startlingly evident in a second (in)famous speech delivered to the graduating class of Harvard Divinity School on 15 July 1838. Within "The Divinity School Address," Emerson clarified and developed the ideas he had presented in "Sermon CXXI" and "Sermon CLXII" ("The Lord's Supper") and in *Nature*, a little book Emerson had published in 1836 that has become foundational to understanding his thought. If any of those graduates had read *Nature*, they would have been prepared for Emerson's salient point in "The Divinity School Address." *Nature* opened with a lament over retrospection. "Our age is retrospective," Emerson claimed. "It builds the sepulchres of the fathers. It writes biographies, histories, and criticism. The foregoing generations beheld God and nature face to face; we, through their eyes. Why should not we also enjoy an original relation to the universe?" (7). Yet "few adult persons can see nature," Emerson asserted. "At least they have a very superficial seeing" (10). Perhaps they see, but they lack vision. Perhaps they perceive the physical world but fail to intuit the way the physical world corresponds to metaphysical truth. Emerson, however, possessed such vision, something he had claimed in perhaps the most famous passage in *Nature*: "Standing on the bare ground,—my head bathed by the blithe air, and uplifted into infinite space,—all mean egotism vanishes. I become a transparent eye-ball; I am nothing; I see all; the currents of the Universal Being circulate through me; I am part and particle of God" (10). This original relation to God enjoyed by foregoing generations was also available to the graduates who sat before Emerson in 1838 if they would break free of the Materialism inculcated by the present Unitarian church. Jesus, Emerson revealed, was the one man "who saw with open eye the mystery of the soul. . . . Alone in all of history, he estimated the greatness of man. One man was true to what is in you and me. He saw that God incarnates himself in man, and evermore goes forth anew to take possession of his world. He said, in this jubilee of sublime emotion," Emerson continued, "'I am divine. Through me, God acts; through me, speaks. Would you see God, see me; or, see thee, when thou also thinkest as I now think'" ("Divinity School Address" 81). Note that Emerson did not call for a new religion (or Cultus as he called it within this address). Instead, he called for a reformation, a return to an original relation to the Universal Being (i.e., the Oversoul) just as Christ himself had. In this way, "The sublime is excited in me by the great stoical doctrine, Obey thyself. That which shows God in me, fortifies me. That which shows God out of me, makes me a wart and a wen" (82–83). He, thus, charged the graduates of the divinity school to seek original relation once again with the divine and to foster the same within their congregations through lively, creative preaching: "Yourself a newborn bard of the Holy Ghost,—cast behind you all conformity, and acquaint men at first hand with Deity. . . . By trusting your own soul, you shall gain a greater confidence in other men" (90). Paradoxically, these graduates were to inspire reform in their congregants by modeling such reform in their own spiritual lives. The congregants would become less dependent on the minister as they, too, turned to the still small voice within.

Reformation of the Self: Emerson's Paradoxical Contribution to Social Reform

In the era of Transcendentalism, Emerson endured criticism from friend and foe alike who argued self-reliance is selfishness writ large. Emerson's "Self-Reliance" is the supreme Transcendentalist expression of self-culture, but that essay garnered (and continues to garner) for Emerson a reputation as an advocate for "selfish solitariness" as one anonymous reviewer of his *Essays: First Series* (which includes "Self-Reliance") had put it (78). In short, critics would just as soon "hear that their friend was dead as that he was a Transcendentalist; for then is he paralyzed, and can never do anything for humanity" ("The Transcendentalist" 211). The fault of these critiques, Emerson contended, is that they too narrowly define service to society. What their opponents saw as a "retreat from work" was actually a demonstration of "the power to labor better and more availably than others" (211). As a leading intellectual within Transcendentalism, Emerson undoubtedly had his public lectures and writing in mind here. His written and spoken advocacy for self-reliance would far exceed the effects of momentary relief. In other words, the efforts of formal reform movements may meet an immediate need but fail to meet the remote need. Emerson was attempting to teach men to fish rather than treating them to one fish fry.

It should be noted that Emerson's doctrine of self-reliance did prompt him to condemn prevalent oppression in his day because he believed that people universally possessed worth that far exceeded most people's comprehension. To suggest, then, that Emerson was so preoccupied with himself that he was uncharitable or uncaring for others is to misread "Self-Reliance" and misunderstand the spiritual effects of self-culture. For Emerson, the great paradox central to his thought was his belief that societal reform starts with personal reform. Various institutions of society adhere readily to the status quo because the people behind those institutions cling to the status quo often out of a sense of duty to conformity and consistency. The antidote to conformity and consistency and, consequently, the catalyst to social reform is self-reliance. In the words of Emerson, "It is easy to see that a greater self-reliance must work a revolution in all the offices and relations of men; in their religion; in their education; in their pursuits; their modes of living; their association; in their property; in their speculative views" ("Self-Reliance" 44). Although this passage lacks the provocative tone of many memorable lines in "Self-Reliance," it suitably expresses what Emerson and his Transcendentalist peers' concerns were within their historical and religious context. Transcendentalism is rightly remembered as a religious upheaval within conservative Unitarianism, an upheaval that, in turn, sparked significant reforms in other realms of society and American letters.

Works Cited

Cabot, James Elliot. *A Memoir of Ralph Waldo Emerson*. Vol. 1. Houghton Mifflin, 1895.

Cafaro, Philip. "Transcendental Virtue." *The Oxford Handbook of Transcendentalism*. Edited by Joel Myerson, et al., Oxford UP, 2010, pp. 537–48.

Crèvecœur, J. Hector St. John de. *Letters from an American Farmer and Sketches of Eighteenth-Century America*. Edited by Albert E. Stone, 1782 and 1925, Penguin, 1981.

Delbanco, Andrew. *The War Before the War: Fugitive Slaves and the Struggle for America's Soul from the Revolution to the Civil War*. Penguin, 2018.

Emerson, Ralph Waldo. "The Divinity School Address." *The Collected Works of Ralph Waldo Emerson, Volume I, Nature, Addresses, and Lectures*. Edited by Alfred R. Ferguson and Robert E. Spiller, The Belknap Press of Harvard UP, 1971, pp. 76–93.

__________. *Journals and Miscellaneous Notebooks of Ralph Waldo Emerson*. Edited by William H. Gilman, et al., 16 vols. Harvard UP, 1960–82.

__________. *Nature. The Collected Works of Ralph Waldo Emerson, Volume I, Nature, Addresses, and Lectures*. Edited by Alfred R. Ferguson and Robert E. Spiller, The Belknap Press of Harvard UP, 1971, pp. 7–45.

__________. "Self-Reliance." *The Collected Works of Ralph Waldo Emerson, Volume II, Essays: First Series*. Edited by Alfred R. Ferguson and Jean Ferguson Carr, The Belknap Press of Harvard UP, 1979, pp. 25–51.

__________. "Sermon CLXII." *Transcendentalism: A Reader.* Edited by Joel Myerson, Oxford UP, 2000, pp. 68–78.

__________. "Sermon CXXI." *Transcendentalism: A Reader*. Edited by Joel Myerson, Oxford UP, 2000, pp. 62–67.

__________. "The Transcendentalist." *The Collected Works of Ralph Waldo Emerson, Volume I, Nature, Addresses, and Lectures*. Edited by Alfred R. Ferguson and Robert E. Spiller, The Belknap Press of Harvard UP, 1971, pp. 201–16.

__________. "The Young American." *The Collected Works of Ralph Waldo Emerson, Volume I, Nature, Addresses, and Lectures*. Edited by Alfred R. Ferguson and Robert E. Spiller, The Belknap Press of Harvard UP, 1971, pp. 222–44.

Frothingham, Octavius Brooks. *Transcendentalism in New England: A History*. 1876, Peter Smith/Harper, 1965.

Gougeon, Len. "Historical Background." *Emerson's Antislavery Writings*. Edited by Len Gougeon and Joel Myerson, Yale UP, 1995, pp. xi–lvi.

Grodzins, Dean. "Unitarianism." *The Oxford Handbook of Transcendentalism*, Edited by Joel Myerson, et al., Oxford UP, 2010, pp. 50–69.

Gura, Philip F. *American Transcendentalism: A History*. Hill and Wang, 2007.

Hatch, Nathan O. *The Democratization of American Christianity*. Yale UP, 1989.

Kidd, Thomas S. *American History, Volume 1*. B and H Academic, 2019.

__________. "Introduction." *The Great Awakening: A Brief History with Documents*. Edited by Thomas S. Kidd, Bedford/St. Martin's, 2008, pp. 1–27.

Kornfeld, Eve. *Margaret Fuller: A Brief Biography with Documents*. Bedford/St. Martin's, 1997.

Lewis, R. W. B. *The American Adam: Innocence, Tragedy, and Tradition in the Nineteenth Century*. U of Chicago P, 1955.

Marsden, George. *Jonathan Edwards: A Life*. Yale UP, 2003.

Martin, Ryan. "Enthusiasm." *The Jonathan Edwards Encyclopedia*, Edited by Harry S. Stout, et al., Eerdmans, 2017, pp. 200–02.

McPherson, James M. *Battle Cry of Freedom: The Civil War Era*. Oxford UP, 1988.

Rev. of *Essays* [First Series] by Ralph Waldo Emerson. *Emerson and Thoreau: The Contemporary Reviews*. Edited by Joel Myerson, Cambridge UP, 1992, pp. 77–79.

Rose, Anne C. *Transcendentalism as a Social Movement, 1830–1850*. Yale UP, 1981.

Tocqueville, Alexis de. *Democracy in America*. 1835. Edited by J. P. Mayer, translated by George Lawrence, Harper Perennial, 1988.

The Critical Reception of Ralph Waldo Emerson: A Longstanding American Commitment to Individuality and Freedom

Amy Leshinsky

Despite his place on numerous required reading lists for secondary schools in the United States, Ralph Waldo Emerson did not excel in school. Although he was privileged in the education he received, entering Boston Latin School in 1812 and enrolling at Harvard College five years later, he was "a slow learner and made no mark at Harvard as an undergraduate" (Franklin Park Coalition 3). In 1820, a year before graduating from Harvard, he received the Bowdoin Prize for an essay on "The Character of Socrates" and the Boylston Prize for public speaking. However, his performance at Harvard was stagnant; he did not gain admission into Phi Beta Kappa; and he did not graduate at the top of his class of fifty-nine. While his future seemed uncertain, in 1826 Emerson began to preach, and by 1827, he had preached forty-eight sermons. He would go on to preach more than one hundred sermons a year in subsequent years.

Sermons appealed to Emerson, in part, due to their ability to target a broader audience than the book industry. During the 1830s and 1840s when Emerson's seminal works appeared, the book industry saw a surge in interest due to increased literacy rates; however, there was a lack of centralization to provide writers with widespread exposure (Dowling 221–22). The lecture circuit, in contrast, had a longer reach due to daily and weekly published notices that were circulated throughout geographic regions. The press would advertise his speaking engagements prior to his lectures and publish reviews afterwards, which ensured his name was frequently in the press. Emerson wisely discerned that "the spread of his own reputation through lecturing was accountable not to the hundreds he had addressed at his orations, but to the tens of thousands who would read excerpts from those lectures in newspapers and magazines such as *The New Englander, The Springfield Republic, The Christian Enquirer,* and the *Atlantic Monthly*" (Dowling 225). Thus, Emerson was a savvy businessman with an ability to use the technology of the time to his advantage.

The critical reception of Emerson requires a unique lens, as the examination encompasses not only the spoken and written word but his physical attributes as well. First, this essay will explore the content, style, and diction of Emerson's works, as they relate to Transcendentalism and European influences. Second, Emerson's preferred genre and role on the lectern requires that his reception be not only considered as a critique of his written words but also his physical traits. For as much criticism and praise as he received for his writings and oratory skills, he received nearly as much on his physical aura and demeanor. Finally, with his passing in 1882, Emerson's reputation continued to expand. A quarter of the way into the twenty-first century, Emerson is one of the most well-known and frequently quoted American writers.

Reception of Emerson's Works During His Lifetime

Between 1828 and 1831, Emerson preached 100 sermons a year; therefore, his name was regularly in the press. Due to this constant publicity, Emerson and his works were subject to sustained human interest and critique. Critics provided mixed reviews of Emerson's speeches and writings, and discussion of his works would often center on the questionability of his language. Although some found beauty in the presentation of his thoughts, others found a disparate mix of unmarried images. Another point of contention with Emerson's works was the impact of European language and content on American vocabulary and values. For example, Francis Bowen in his review of "Nature" wrote with disdain concerning new language culled from German. Within a discussion of European influences, critics examined the sway of Thomas Carlyle, who Andrews Norton explained had great deficiency "in good sense, good taste and the soundness of principle" (34). However, despite criticism, Emerson remained steadfast in his values and commitment to writing, evidence of which can be found in his journals and written works like "Eloquence."

The style and quality of Emerson's rhetoric was a focus of criticism. Editor for the *Atlantic Monthly*, James Russell Lowell saw beauty in the presentation of Emerson's writing despite acknowledging that Emerson's oration was often disjointed. Within a letter to Charles Eliot Norton regarding "The Progress of Culture," Lowell wrote that Emerson's lecture "began nowhere and ended everywhere . . . [and] left you feeling that something beautiful had passed that way" (qtd. in Bosco and Myerson 54). In his book *My Study Windows*, Lowell's chapter on Emerson, "Emerson, the Lecturer," reinforced the charm of Emerson's language, calling him a poet who wrote in prose. However, not all found desirable qualities in what Reza Hosseini would later call the "fragmentary and unsystematic nature of his writing" and an anonymous review in *Knickerbocker* would call muddy (Hosseini 370; "The Method of Nature" 109). For example, Bowen in the *Christian Examiner* detailed frustration on what he deemed to be language defects in "Nature." Citing key lines from this work, such as "I expand and live in the warm day, like corn and melons," Bowen wrote that Emerson should know how to write better than offensive passages (Emerson "Nature"; Bowen 5). A similar conclusion was drawn by Samuel Gilman in his review of "Literary Ethics," where he found the ideas buried within "very involved and cloudy paragraphs" (56).

For contemporary critics from Emerson's day, the incorporation of untraditional and European-inspired phraseology was a point of contention. Writers from the Transcendental school, Bowen asserted, used words unnatural to American style. Language, he argued, drew from German, loading the writing with unfamiliar and peculiar nouns and adjectives. Regarding "Nature," he wrote that now "we speak of the *Infinite*, the *Beautiful*, the *Unconscious*, the *Just*, and the *True*. A new class of verbs also has been formed from the same or similar roots, such as *individualize, materialize, externalize*, &c" (8). The use of this language, he deemed, was an unwelcome addition to American language and literature. Andrews Norton expresses a similar argument in his review of the "Divinity School

Address," stating that within the lecture "our common language is abused . . . inversions, exclamations, anomalous combinations of words, unmeaning, but course and violent, metaphors abound, and withal a strong infusion of German barbarians" (34).

Although criticism often focused on disdain for German influence on American language, the content of Emerson's lectures and writings were challenged as well. The content of the "Divinity School Address" elicited some of the most caustic responses due, in part, to Emerson's alignment with Transcendentalism as well as his treatment of religion. Transcendentalism challenged religious groups at a time when controversy was ripe regarding biblical miracles and Christ (Myerson xi). In his review "The New School and Its Opponents," Theophilus Parsons wrote that in Andrews Norton's caustic review of the address, Emerson is treated "as if he were the head of this school in this country" (36). Parsons's point of contention with Emerson is his application of religion, as he "preaches a doctrine which leads man to worship his own nature and himself" (38). G. T. Davis's review of "The Divinity School Address" took similar concern with the "peculiar religious and philosophical views" (38).

Despite accolades afforded to Emerson in northern states, critics have documented the altered perspective of Emerson by southern critics. Critic Harold Bloom notes that while Emerson was controversial in his earlier years, he grew to be "universally accepted (except, of course, in the South) during his later years" (10). The southern press found Transcendentalism dangerous due, in part, to the threat it posed to the Southern slave-based economy, and while northern reviewers were not always favorable toward Emerson, southern reviewers afforded him little praise (Guinn 174). Although Emerson has been accused of racist views, his journals and antislavery writing "show he was deeply interested in the question of race" (Gougeon 197). His address "The Emancipation of the Negroes in the British West Indies" in 1844 was followed, the subsequent year, by an address that celebrated West Indian emancipation.

Despite criticism over his style and content, Emerson remained steadfast in his diligence and commitment to his ideas. His work, "Eloquence," describes the power of words and oration. He shares that "the eloquence of one stimulates all the rest" and suggests that words have the power to inspire and move others to speak (64). Although critics challenged his language, Emerson was steadfast in his beliefs about the power and beauty of language. Likewise, his journals indicate the publication of his works came with a meticulous combing of sentence structure. An entry from August 27, 1836 shares that the first proof of "Nature" arrived, and he would find peace in the maintenance of strong sentences. Several years later in 1841, he shared that "if I am born to write a few good sentences or verses, these shall endure and my disgraces utterly perish out of memory" (*Emerson in His Journals* 271). In addition to his commitment to his style and form, he was steadfast in his commitment to his beliefs. After this "Divinity School Address," which was steeped in controversy, Emerson remained unapologetic for his ideas. Three months after this address, he wrote: "And whilst I see this that you must have been shocked & must cry out at what I have said I see too that we cannot easily be reconciled for I have a great deal more to say that will shock you out of all patience" (*Emerson in His Journals* 201).

Reception of Emerson's Aura

The critical reception of Emerson would be incomplete without a discussion of his physical reception. He was a tall and slender man just shy of six feet, weighing 157 pounds, with sloped shoulders, and his contemporaries remarked on his physique in their biographies as well as their reviews of his speaking engagements (Wagenknecht 19). This is not atypical, as an interest in the physical appearance of an individual is "characteristic of a celebrity culture that seeks and even assumes intimacy with public figures" (O'Neill 249). The reception of Emerson's physical characteristics extends to his bright blue eyes, prominent chin, and tall frame; to his radiance at his sermons; to the melodic quality of his voice. Critics and peers would discuss not only his physical attributes, but his aura and spirituality.

However, not all were impressed by Emerson's physical qualities and spiritual aura, like David Scott who found him "severe, and dry, and hard" (Wagenknecht 19). In order to envision Emerson's presence, twenty-first-century readers rely on firsthand accounts by contemporaries as well as portraits of Emerson.

Physical descriptions of Emerson abound in criticism and biographies. For example, biographers and critics often refer to his New England figure with keen attention to his shoulders like Lowell who in his satirical poem published in *A Fable for Critics* refers to Emerson's "Greek head on right Yankee shoulders" (43). Two biographies published on Emerson during his lifetime also remark on his shoulders. In Oliver Wendell Holmes's biography, Holmes remarked that Emerson's "shoulders sloped so much as to be commented upon for this peculiarity" (360). Similarly, George Willis Cooke's biography, which had been published a few years prior, mentions Emerson's "more than medium height, small head, and shoulders remarkably sloping" (193). His sloping shoulders contributed to an aged appearance that occurred, in part, due to sickness. During his early years, he battled infections like rheumatism and experienced eye and lung trouble; however, despite hardships with health, wellbeing was a topic he frequently did not discuss (Wagenknecht 22).

Critiques often wrote his eyes provided insight into his soul and demeanor. Emerson's eyes were said to disclose "the secret of his character" (Bosco and Myerson xviii). Julian Hawthorne, son of American writer Nathaniel Hawthorne, shared that Emerson's eyes held the same piercing look as "an eagle on the perch" (Hawthorne 227). This description aligns with Emma Lazarus who makes reference to "eagle eyes" as well (qtd. in Wagenknecht 19). Cooke's biography draws a similar analogy and mentions Emerson's "keen eyes" (193). Walt Whitman, who visited Emerson on multiple occasions, maintained notes on their visit that details his impressions of Emerson mentally and physically. On an evening in September of 1881, he spent two hours during "a long and blessed evening with Emerson" where he could "just look squarely" at him (Whitman 81). Whitman found "a good color in his face, eyes clear" that evening, and the next day as well. He remarked that Emerson had "healthy color in the cheeks, and good light in the eyes" (Whitman 81). After Emerson passed away, Ednah Dow Cheney remarked on feeling pity for those who will never know him, hear his voice, or "look into his eyes, which always seemed to look into infinity and eternity" (113).

In addition to an evaluation of his shoulders and eyes, Emerson's aura was frequently discussed. Wagenknecht explains that on the lecture platform Emerson exhibited radiance, and Wagenknecht cites Rufus Dawes, a classmate of Emerson's who described him as "spiritual looking;" journalist Charles Taber Congdon, who described him as "the most gracious of mortals with a face of benignity;" and Nathaniel Hawthorne, who thought Emerson had a "pure intellectual gleam diffused about his presence like the garment of a shining one" (qtd. in Wagenknecht 20). Similarly, Holmes's biography shared that Emerson's expression was "calm, sedate, kindly, with a look of refinement" (360). Likewise, Cooke's biography shared that his personality "carries immense force, that molds and sways others, less by a dazzling brilliancy and the tremendousness of intellect, than by the persuasive might of a pure, unadulterated, and perfectly loyal nature, which never swerves, which goes steadily on to the goal it seeks" (193).

Emerson's voice aligned with beauty, musicality, and spirituality and was a contributing characteristic in depictions of his aura. Annie Sawyer Downs wrote in "Reminiscences of a Childhood in Concord in the 1840s" that Emerson's voice resembled an instrument and was "as nearly perfect as human limitations allow" and described his readings as "rhythmical pulsations of ordered thought" (14). Lowell, who attended many of Emerson's lectures, wrote that he was "one of the pioneers of the lecturing system" and "the charm of his voice, his manner, and his matter has never lost its power over his earlier hearers" (54). He would later write Emerson's "thrilling voice" was "charged with a subtle meaning and subtle music" (56). Listening to Emerson's lectures, he believed, was like being shipwrecked and finding unhoped for sustenance.

A large collection of portraits provides a way for twenty-first century readers to reflect on the physical attributes of Emerson.

An original portrait of Emerson, taken in 1848 by Southworth and Hawes, highlights "Emerson's serenity and inner light" through the photographer's "thoughtful and deliberate use of natural light" (Wilson 237). Gazing to the right, Emerson's face is aglow, highlighting his alertness, spirituality, and benevolence. In a subsequent daguerreotype profile taken several years later, Emerson looks to his left with a slight smile, showing that he is "a man of inner rather than outer vitality" (Wilson 238). A full portrait of Emerson, aimed to depict him as a lecturer, provides a greater understanding of his magnitude as a speaker. The photograph, which captures his hands clasped before his torso, highlights his frequently discussed sloping shoulders. This work, taken by James Wallace Black, conveys "the public demeanor of Emerson as observed by his audiences" (Wilson 242). During his lifetime, Emerson embraced the opportunity to be photographed, and the images that remain today continue to be examined in relation to the personal qualities shared from firsthand accounts of his life.

Reception of Emerson: Posthumous

Immediately following the death of Emerson, contemporaries discussed the source of his greatness, and speeches, obituaries, and biographies detailed his contributions to American thought. After the turn of the century, as Modernism became the defining literary movement, Lewis Mumford penned his influential work, *The Golden Day*. While this contribution, among others, kept Emerson's name circulating in the public and academic sphere, Harvard professor F. O. Matthiessen's work *American Renaissance: Art and Expression in the Age of Emerson and Whitman* contributed to a rebirth and appreciation of Emerson's works, and by the mid-twentieth century, Emerson was "at the center of American literature" (Johnson 272). As the twenty-first century approached, Emerson's prominence and popularity in the mainstream U.S. public enabled companies to use his name, works, and face to advertise products. With the turn of the century, Emerson remains a staple in American literature with works that still speak to the values of the American public.

Individuals and societies came forth after the 1882 passing of Emerson to offer respectful words. An obituary of Emerson was read before the American Philosophical Society by Charles G. Amos that shared Emerson "was one of the few Americans who have deservedly gained the name of philosopher" (503). Later that year, biographies would begin to appear like *Emerson at Home and Abroad* and *Emerson and His Views of Nature* by Moncure D. Conway. In the United States, emerging writings continued to share experiences, meetings, and criticism of Emerson. Sculptor Daniel Chester French reflected on his meetings with Emerson in his work, "A Sculptor's Reminiscences of Emerson." French shares that although many celebrities do not live up to their reputation, "Emerson seemed as great as he really was . . . whose presence was a benediction" (234). In addition to reflections on Emerson's influence and aura, reflections continued on his literary works. William James and Caroline Hazard write in "The Centenary of the Birth of Ralph Waldo Emerson" that Emerson was an artist and his medium, verbiage. The words that Emerson united formed "a chemical combination,—thoughts which would be trivial expressed otherwise are important through the nouns and verbs to which he married them" (qtd. in Bosco and Myerson 218).

In the following decades, and with a shift in literary movements, Emerson's works took on a new meaning for modernists and those in the era after the Great Depression. One primary critic, Lewis Mumford, defined Emerson's value in his work *The Golden Day*. This 1926 work defined "The Golden Day" as the time period of Emerson, Thoreau, and in part, Walt Whitman while rejecting the industrialism of the modern day. In the era after the Great Depression, Matthiessen's work *American Renaissance: Art and Expression in the Age of Emerson and Whitman* contributed to a renewed academic interest in Emerson. By the end of World War II, academic scholarship on Emerson blossomed. *The Report of the Committee on Trends in Research in American Literature, 1940–1950* found that Emerson served as the subject of university courses more than any other American writer and was "the focus on more dissertations than any other American author" (Fuller 274). Contributing further to a deepened understanding of Emerson was the 1982 release of his journals, making his private life more accessible. Fuller shares that Emerson was the “first ‘classic’ American author to have his letters published in a scholarly edition” (Fuller 275).

However, it was not just within academia that attention was paid to Emerson. Since his death, Emerson has been used to “sell everything from coffee and tea to greeting cards, collectible figurines, cigar boxes, United States postal stamps, and more” (Murphy 283). For example, a 1926 advertisement in the *Indianapolis Times* by Warren Emerson Cigar used Emerson in their sales pitch, which was a convenient association given his propensity to smoke cigars. Michael Weisenburg, writing for the Emerson Society, shared that “of all possible commodities cigars might well be the most fitting of consumables to associate with the Sage of Concord.” The advertisement highlights the Emerson Cigar, which was 10 cents for a Poet Size and 2 for 25 cents, Waldo Size, among other options. Nearly forty years later, in 1961, Emerson was featured in a full-page advertisement for John Hancock Mutual Life Insurance Company of Boston (Murphy 283). In 1989, shoe company Reebok created a campaign called “U.B.U.,” which *Chicago Tribune* writer Barbara Lippert called “a peculiar ad campaign that saluted American transcendentalism.” In one of the video advertisements, the “U.B.U” Reebok campaign showed images of individuals embracing an authentic self-like two individuals dressed as twins in oversized white jackets and matching red sneakers; a woman in a dress vacuuming a Persian style rug outside on the grass; and a sunbathing woman sitting on a multicolored boat playing a sousaphone, all while a speaker read excerpts from “Self-Reliance.”

At the turn of the twenty-first century, Emerson still makes headlines and continues to be a recognizable face in mainstream American society. For example, in 2003, Adam Cohen wrote an editorial in *The New York Times*, “Editorial Observer; It’s Emerson’s Anniversary and He’s Got Twenty-First-Century America Nailed.” Within the article, Cohen concludes that Emerson “still matters not because he has all the answers for how we should live, but because he so intriguingly reflects who we actually are.” More than a decade later, a 2018 article in *The New York Times* featured a photograph of Emerson's recognizable bust. The article, "Why the Hall of Fame for Great Americans Is 'At Risk,'" discussed the environmental pollutants destroying the statues located in a commemorative gallery of great Americans in the Bronx, New York. While more than 100 statues exist as part of this commemorative hall Abraham Lincoln and Booker T. Washington among them—Emerson's name begins the article and a picture of his bust depicted due to his recognizable features.

The first quarter of the twenty-first century continues to see Emerson in daily life: book clubs discuss his works, elementary schools contain his name, and quotations from his works can be followed on social media applications like *Instagram*. Independent filmmakers Michael Maglaras and Terri Templeton of 217 Films are set to premiere their documentary, "Ralph Waldo Emerson: Give All to Love" in 2023. Nearly two hundred years ago, Davis's review of "The Divinity School Address" attributed the popularity of Emerson to a craving in the American community for freedom, and he wrote that Emerson's work reflected "independence, to the homage he pays to the spirit of freedom" (40–41). Today, Davis's words still speak to the soul of the American people and their continued homage to Emerson is a reflection of a longstanding commitment to individuality and freedom.

Works Cited

Amos, Charles G. "Obituary Notice of Ralph Waldo Emerson." *Proceedings of the American Philosophical Society*, vol. 20, no. 112, June–Dec., 1882, pp. 498–503.

Barron, James. "Why the Hall of Fame for Great Americans Is 'At Risk.'" *The New York Times,* 5 Nov. 2018.

Bloom, Harold. "Introduction." *Modern Critical Views: Ralph Waldo Emerson.* Chelsea House Publishers, 1985.

Bosco, Ronald A. and Joel Myerson. "Introduction." *Emerson in His Own Time: A Biographical Chronical of His Life, Drawn from Recollections, Interviews, and Memoirs by Family, Friends, and Associates*. U of Iowa P, 2003.

Bowen, Francis. "Transcendentalism," *Christian Examiner* (Boston), 21 Jan. 1837, pp. 371–85.

__________. *Emerson and Thoreau: The Contemporary Reviews.* Edited by Joel Myerson, Cambridge UP, 1992, pp. 5–13.

Cheney, Ednah Dow. "From Concord Lectures on Philosophy . . . at the Concord School of Philosophy in 1882." *Emerson in His Own Time: A Biographical Chronical of His Life, Drawn from Recollections, Interviews, and Memoirs by Family, Friends, and Associates*, Edited by Ronald A. Bosco and Joel Myerson, U of Iowa P, 2003, pp. 111–15.

Cohen, Adam. "Editorial Observer; It's Emerson's Anniversary and He's Got Twenty-First Century America Nailed." *The New York Times*, 4 May 2003, www.nytimes.com/2003/05/04/opinion/editorial-observer-it-s-emerson-s-anniversary-he-s-got-21st-century-america.html.

Cooke, George Willis. *Ralph Waldo Emerson: His Life, Writings, and Philosophy.* Boston: James R. Osgood, 1882.

Davis, G. T. "Review of Divinity School Address," *Morning Post,* 31 Aug. 1838, p. 1, *Emerson and Thoreau: The Contemporary Reviews.* Edited by Joel Myerson, Cambridge UP, 1992, pp. 38–41.

Dowling, David O. "Publishers." *Ralph Waldo Emerson in Context.* Edited by Wesley Mott, Cambridge UP, 2014, pp. 221–29.

Downs, Annie Sawyer. "Reminiscences of a Childhood in Concord in the 1840s," *Emerson in His Own Time: A Biographical Chronical of His Life, Drawn from Recollections, Interviews, and Memoirs by Family, Friends, and Associates*. Edited by Ronald A. Bosco and Joel Myerson, U of Iowa P, 2003, pp. 12–15.

Emerson, Ralph Waldo. "The Divinity School Address," 1838. *Ralph Waldo Emerson: The Major Prose*. Edited by Ronald A. Bosco and Joel Myerson, The Belknap Press of Harvard UP, 2015, pp. 110–26

__________. "Eloquence." *Society and Solitude*, Cambridge, MA: The Riverside Press, 1870.

__________. *Emerson in His Journals.* Edited by Joel Porte, The Belknap Press of Harvard UP, 1982.

__________. *Literary Ethics.* Infomotions. 2000.

__________. "The Method of Nature." Infomotions, 2000.

_________. *Nature.* 1836. *Ralph Waldo Emerson: The Major Prose.* Edited by Ronald A. Bosco and Joel Myerson, The Belknap Press of Harvard UP, 2015, pp. 34–73.

_________. "Self-Reliance." 1841. *The Major Prose of Ralph Waldo Emerson.* Edited by Ronald A. Bosco and Joel Myerson, The Belknap Press of Harvard UP, 2015, pp. 127–51.

Franklin Park Coalition. "Ralph Waldo Emerson: The Schoolmaster of Franklin Park." Boston Parks and Recreation Department, 1980, www.franklinparkcoalition.org/wpcontent/uploads/2018/01/Ralph-Waldo-Emerson-The-Schoolmaster-of-Franklin-Park.pdf.

French, Daniel Chester. "A Sculptor's Reminiscences of Emerson," 1916. *Emerson in His Own Time: A Biographical Chronical of His Life, Drawn from Recollections, Interviews, and Memoirs by Family, Friends, and Associates.* Edited by Ronald A. Bosco and Joel Myerson, U of Iowa P, 2003, pp. 233–37.

Fuller, Randall. "Critics: 1948–2013," *Ralph Waldo Emerson in Context.* Edited by Wesley Mott, Cambridge UP, 2014, pp. 274–82.

Gilman, Samuel. "Ralph Waldo Emerson," Review of *Literary Ethics* by Ralph Waldo Emerson. *Southern Rose*, vol. 7, 24 Nov. 1838, pp. 100–06; *Emerson and Thoreau: Contemporary Reviews.* Edited by Joel Myerson, Cambridge UP, 1992, pp. 55–60.

Gougeon, Len. "Race," *Ralph Waldo Emerson in Context.* Edited by Wesley Mott, Cambridge UP, 2014, pp. 196–223.

Guinn, Matthew. "Emerson's Southern Critics, 1838–1862." *Resources for American Literary Study*, vol. 25, no. 2, 1999, pp. 174–91.

Hawthorne, Julian. "Personal Glimpses of Emerson," *Emerson in His Own Time: A Biographical Chronical of His Life, Drawn from Recollections, Interviews, and Memoirs by Family, Friends, and Associates.* Edited by Ronald A. Bosco and Joel Myerson, 1903, U of Iowa P, 2003, pp. 224–28.

Holmes, Oliver Wendell Sr. *Ralph Waldo Emerson,* Boston: Houghton, Mifflin, 1885.

Hosseini, Reza. "Emerson and the Question of Style." *Philosophy and Literature,* vol. 43, no. 2, 2019, pp. 369–82.

James, William, and Caroline Hazard. "From the Centenary of the Birth of Ralph Waldo Emerson," *Emerson in His Own Time: A Biographical Chronical of His Life, Drawn from Recollections, Interviews, and Memoirs by Family, Friends, and Associates*. Edited by Ronald A. Bosco and Joel Myerson, 1903, U of Iowa P, 2003, pp. 217–23.

Johnson, Glen M. "Critics: 1836–1948," *Ralph Waldo Emerson in Context.* Edited by Wesley Mott, Cambridge UP, 2014, pp. 265–73.

Lippert, Barbara. "After Emerson," *Chicago Tribune*, 3 Mar. 1989, www.chicagotribune.com/news/ct-xpm-1989-03-03-8903230968-story.html.

Lowell, James Russell. *A Fable for Critics.* Boston: Houghton Mifflin, 1890.

__________. "Emerson, the Lecturer." *My Study Windows*. London: Sampson Low, Son and Marston, 1871, pp. 274–81.

Matthiessen, F. O. *American Renaissance: Art and Expression in the Age of Emerson and Whitman*. Oxford UP, 1968.

Mumford, Lewis. *The Golden Day: A Study in American Experience and Culture*. Liveright, 1926.

Murphy, Jillmarie. "A National Icon," *Ralph Waldo Emerson in Context.* Edited by Wesley Mott, Cambridge UP, 2014, pp. 283–91.

Myerson, Joel. *Emerson and Thoreau: The Contemporary Reviews.* Cambridge UP, 1992.

Norton, Andrews. "The New School in Literature and Religion," Review of *Divinity School Address* by Ralph Waldo Emerson. *Daily Advertiser* (Newark, NJ), 27 Aug. 1838, p. 2.; *Emerson and Thoreau: Contemporary Reviews.* Edited by Joel Myerson, Cambridge UP, 1992, pp. 33–35.

O'Neill, Bonnie Carr. "Fame." *Ralph Waldo Emerson in Context.* Edited by Wesley Mott, Cambridge UP, 2014, pp. 248–56.

Parsons, Theophilus. "The New School and Its Opponents." Review of *Divinity School Address* by Ralph Waldo Emerson. *Daily Advertiser* (Newark, NJ), 30 Aug. 1838, p. 2.; *Emerson and Thoreau: The Contemporary Reviews.* Edited by Joel Myerson, Cambridge UP, 1992, pp. 36–38.

"The Method of Nature," Review of *Nature* by Ralph Waldo Emerson. New York: *Knickerbocker,* 18 Dec. 1841; *Emerson and Thoreau: The Contemporary Reviews.* Edited by Joel Myerson, Cambridge UP, 1992, pp. 109–10.

217 Films, "Announcing 217 Films' New Documentary 'Ralph Waldo Emerson: Give All to Love,'" *GlobeNewswire*, 6 July 2022, www.globenewswire.com/news. release/2022/07/06/2475395/0/en/Announcing-217-Films-New-Documentary-Ralph Waldo-Emerson-Give-All-to-Love.html.

Wagenknecht, Edward. *Ralph Waldo Emerson: Portrait of a Balanced Soul.* Oxford UP, 1974.

Warren Emerson Cigar Newspaper Ad. *The Indianapolis Times*, 23 Apr. 1926, *Chronicling America: Historic American Newspapers*, Library of Congress, chroniclingamerica.loc.gov/lccn/sn82015313/1926-04-23/ed-1/seq-28/.

Weisenburg, Michael C. "'a cigar had uses': Emerson as Advertising Icon." *The Transparent Eyeball*, Third Series, The Ralph Waldo Emerson Society, 25 May 2021, emersonsociety.org/the-transparent-eyeball/a-cigar-had-uses-emerson-as-advertising-icon/.

Whitman, Walt. "From Prose Works 1892 (1881–1882)," *Emerson in His Own Time: A Biographical Chronical of His Life, Drawn from Recollections, Interviews, and Memoirs by Family, Friends, and Associates*. Edited by Ronald A. Bosco and Joel Myerson, U of Iowa P, 2003, pp. 80–83.

Wilson, Leslie Perrin. "Portraits." *Ralph Waldo Emerson in Context.* Edited by Wesley Mott, Cambridge UP, 2014, pp. 233–47.

Emerson's "Hamatreya": A Critical History

Robert C. Evans

"Critical pluralists"—interested in multiple perspectives on any work of art—inevitably admire "critical variorum" editions, which bring many of those perspectives together in one place. Here I want to offer such an edition of one of Ralph Waldo Emerson's most interesting and effective poems: "Hamatreya."

Hamatreya

Bulkeley, Hunt, Willard, Hosmer, Meriam, Flint,
Possessed the land which rendered to their toil
Hay, corn, roots, hemp, flax, apples, wool, and wood.
Each of these landlords walked amidst his farm,
Saying, "'Tis mine, my children's and my name's.
How sweet the west wind sounds in my own trees!
How graceful climb those shadows on my hill!
I fancy these pure waters and the flags
Know me, as does my dog: we sympathize;
And, I affirm, my actions smack of the soil."

Where are these men? Asleep beneath their grounds:
And strangers, fond as they, their furrows plough.
Earth laughs in flowers, to see her boastful boys
Earth-proud, proud of the earth which is not theirs;
Who steer the plough, but cannot steer their feet
Clear of the grave.
They added ridge to valley, brook to pond,
And sighed for all that bounded their domain;
"This suits me for a pasture; that's my park;
We must have clay, lime, gravel, granite-ledge,
And misty lowland, where to go for peat.
The land is well,—lies fairly to the south.
'Tis good, when you have crossed the sea and back,
To find the sitfast acres where you left them."

Ah! the hot owner sees not Death, who adds
Him to his land, a lump of mould the more.
Hear what the Earth says:—

EARTH-SONG

"Mine and yours;
Mine, not yours.
Earth endures;
Stars abide—
Shine down in the old sea;
Old are the shores;
But where are old men?
I who have seen much,
Such have I never seen.

"The lawyer's deed
Ran sure,
In tail,
To them and to their heirs
Who shall succeed,
Without fail,
Forevermore.

"Here is the land,
Shaggy with wood,
With its old valley,
Mound and flood.
But the heritors?—
Fled like the flood's foam.
The lawyer and the laws,
And the kingdom,
Clean swept herefrom.

"They called me theirs,
Who so controlled me;
Yet every one
Wished to stay, and is gone,

How am I theirs,
If they cannot hold me,
But I hold them?"

When I heard the Earth-song
I was no longer brave;
My avarice cooled
Like lust in the chill of the grave.

Criticism from the 1960s

A critical variorum edition of any text traces, as fully as possible in the space available, the reactions a text has evoked from knowledgeable critics. One early helpful response to "Hamatreya" is an excellent example of source-study offered by Richard Bridgman in 1962. "Why," Bridgman asked, "did Emerson name his poem 'Hamatreya'?" He then explained that Emerson's "journals indicate that he drew [the poem's] basic ideas from . . . the *Vishnu Purana*, which featured a figured named 'Maitreya,'" a mere "novice asking his master conventional questions about the constitution of the world" (16).[1] Rejecting the idea that "Maitreya" and "Hamatreya" were synonyms, Bridgman instead suggested that Emerson derived the word "Hamatreya" from an ancient Greek word meaning "the ground" and a suffix ("treya") "denoting femininity" (16). Thus, "Hamatreya" means "approximately 'Earth-Mother,'" an explanation that "thoroughly suits a poem in which earth is explicitly feminine." But Bridgman also briefly suggested that "Hamatreya" might allude to "hamartia," ancient Greek for "error and sin" (16)—a suggestion convincingly developed by Alice Hall Petry in 1986. In the meantime, in 1963 Kiffin Ayres Rockwell argued that various sources might have led Emerson to create "a word meaning—for his purposes—'children of Father Sky / Mother Earth'" (24).

In 1967, Carl F. Strauch, valuably exploring the poem's themes, design, ironies, and speakers and offering detailed explication of its artistry, called it "Emerson's most sharply accentuated commentary on the physical sympathies between man and nature," arguing that the "picture of the Yankee farmland is bathed in a sinister atmosphere of Hindu illusion" (343). "There are," Strauch continued, "three speakers"—first "the Yankee landlord, materialistic and earth-bound," and secondly the earth, "a sub-divinity darkly primitive and universal." Emerson astringently contrasts "the blind ignorance of the landlord, unaware of ancient wisdom, and the freshly gained insight of the poet, who, as the third speaker, narrates the experience." The poem, Strauch continued, is "a pattern of ironies" including "the contrast between the flowing blank verse of the landlord's monologue and the cramped runic verse of the Earth-Song as well as the short verses of poetic insight at the close." The poem puns ironically in saying that the landlords can "'steer the plough, but cannot steer their feet / Clear of the grave.'" Irony, Strauch thought, appears again in "verbal paradoxes: since the 'hot owner sees not Death,' the poet, in his moral reflection, says, 'My avarice cooled / Like lust in tire chill of the grave'; and the moment of insight ends without typical Emersonian affirmations" (343–44). In the final four lines the poet's "complex vision . . . balances conflicting polar opposites. He is the interpreter and reconciler for both man and nature" (344). Such emphasis on reconciliation and harmony was common in formalist criticism of the postwar period.

Moham Lal Sharma, in 1968, once more tried (twice) to explain the poem's mysterious title, interestingly suggesting that "*hama* is a borrowing from the Sanskrit *ahama*, meaning 'I'" and perhaps also from "the Hindustani word *hama*, which means 'we,'" adding that the colloquial Hindustani usage "*treya*, or *tera*, of course, denotes 'thine,'" but that Emerson plays down "the idea of 'I' and 'mine' in the poem" itself, especially because he thought "I" and "mine" implied ignorance ("Emerson's 'Hamatreya'"; see also Sharma's "Emerson's Multilingual Coinage").

In 1969, Rex J. Burbank and Jack B. Moore, in a little-noticed but very insightful discussion of the poem's artistry, noted that it "begins most unpoetically, with a list of names common to New England," whereas the title "Hamatreya" might have led readers to expect "Oriental names like the names of kings Emerson found in his [Indian] source." Instead, he offers "jumbled together in rocky rhythm some dense, heavy sounding ('Bulkeley'), harsh, brittle

(‘Flint’) names” before shifting to “regular iambic pentameter” in line 2, which in turn is followed by “another miscellaneous group” in line 3 (112). Burbank and Moore called the items mentioned in that line

> mostly monosyllables which slow down the meter and [deliberately] do not flow gracefully . . . . The iambics of line two have been ignored rather consciously. Lines one and three employ parallel lists, but otherwise the poem has avoided internally balanced or symmetrical lines, smooth or metronomic rhythm, [and] poetic diction . . . . Even rime is absent.
>
> Yet the lines seem tied together by simply reporting observed fact. Line five breaks away from being outside reportage, however, and until line ten a sort of dramatic monologue that any of the possessors could have spoken is stated . . . [in which] the speaker . . . becomes increasingly patronizing in describing [how] “his” land flags (reeds) and water know him as his dog knows him. He is master, nature is his dog. The irony is devastating. (112)

Burbank and Moore thought that if the “opening lines had been generally objective, the later lines are quietly mocking.” Moreover, the language now

> becomes charged with shades of meaning. Puns are used; in line 12 ‘strangers’ can mean strangers to the original possessors of the land, or strangers to the land itself, or both; ‘fond’ can mean liking or foolish. As the dramatic monologue had emphasized the first person, the verse now plays with the third person, *they* and *their.* ‘Their furrows plough’ can mean the strangers plow [their] furrows . . . [or] plough the furrows that are Bulkeley’s or Hunt’s. As the mocking increases, imagistic and highly colloquial language . . . [describes] the kingly New England possessors: “Earth laughs in flowers to see her boastful boys.” (112–13)

Burbank and Moore offered the patient, microscopic attention to artistry typical of formalist criticism of the 1950s and 1960s, in which small details are thought to contribute to important meanings.

Indeed, their discussion of this poem concludes with the kind of assessment formalists routinely offered of all well-crafted writing:

> "Hamatreya" comprises in its relatively short compass a number of tones and styles, levels of diction and meters. All are carefully fused into a work of art with great integrity, but unity and form seem shaped not by pre-established design nor by art—though of course the poem is great art—but from some source internal to the poem or the poet. The poem has form, but not an obviously standard form. Its language levels do not operate against each other, but produce a language suitable for this particular poem. The poem does not appear to accept a form or language from without: both seem organic to the idea of the poem. (113)

Criticism from the 1970s

In 1974, Hyatt H. Waggoner offered an especially fine and thorough discussion of "Hamatreya." He admired its depth of sensibility and suggested that it showed Emerson's efforts to come to complex terms with the reality of New England's past, especially with the reality of the past of Concord, Massachusetts, where Emerson was now living and which his own ancestors had helped settle and develop. As Waggoner put it, "The *reality* of the past had to be reckoned with, and the attempt to reckon with it aroused the mixed feelings" evident in "Hamatreya" (148). Emerson was proud of Concord—both its past *and* its present—and felt that "without his ancestors there might have been no Concord, or . . . less reason for pride in its past" (149). Celebrating the town in a recent speech, he had praised his ancestor Peter Bulkeley ("the wealthiest and most important of the [town's] Founding Fathers and Emerson's Concord ancestor"), but he also, in revising "Hamatreya," listed Bulkeley first among the proud landowners the poem ultimately mocks.[2]

Postwar formalist critics often argued that the best poems were the most complex and ambiguous, and so it is not surprising when Waggoner writes that "[i]f Emerson had had no reason to feel personal pride in Concord's past and had not known its facts so well, 'Hamatreya' would have been a much weaker poem." Emerson's ambivalence, in other words, contributed to the poem's complex unity. Emerson "must have felt an estrangement [from his hometown] that was easy enough to ignore in the address but that in the poem, written a few years later, would find expression and exist in conflict with the attachment the poem also expresses, almost, but not quite, cancelling it out in the end" (150).

Waggoner thus intriguingly shows that formalists often combined historical knowledge with their interest in artistic details. Critics of formalism often mistakenly claim that formalists were uninterested in history, but Waggoner proves them wrong, as do many other examples. Noting that "Hamatreya" has almost nothing to say about the Puritan beliefs of Concord's early settlers, Waggoner comments that:

> As an interpretation of Concord's Puritan religious past, the poem is perversely ahistorical. And this despite the fact that both Old and New Testaments, as Emerson could not help knowing but apparently found it not to his purposes to remember, repeatedly rebuke the idea of man's "ownership" of God's creation, the earth, holding up in its place the ideal of "stewardship" and accountability, so that even if the religion of the forefathers was as superstitious and untenable as Emerson thought it to be, it could hardly be interpreted as exalting pride of ownership. (151–52)

Emerson, in other words, stacks the decks against Concord's Puritan founders, especially when implying that they were not themselves preoccupied with the reality and inevitability of death. Yet although Emerson ignores Puritan doctrines in favor of teachings from India, he nevertheless, by making the poem's landowners seem convincingly *real*, contributes to the poem's success (152). According to Waggoner, "The bravery the speaker has lost by the end of the poem turns out to have been more like bravado than like true courage. Its loss is necessary if there is to be a faith not based on delusion, as, in Emerson's view, that of the founding fathers was, but on truth as the earth speaks it" (152). Waggoner argued that the feeling underlying the poem's final four lines is "religious awe, or fear, but not despair. The speaker has lost the assurances that made the founders 'brave,' but, in the poem's terms, he is more truly religious than they. Emerson could not have said this in the address [celebrating Concord], but the poem says it" (153).

Discussing the poem's design and metrics, Waggoner particularly admired its "free use, and breaking, of traditional verse forms," noting that although "blank verse predominates in the opening section, the first and third lines subordinate the traditional form to the facts. . . . Neither line," he wrote, "can be scanned by any traditional prosodic system, and the poem is stronger for that fact. The blank verse is also broken," he added, "by two later lines, each of which deserves the special emphasis the breaking gives it: 'Clear of the grave' and 'Hear what the Earth says.'" The earth, he noted, "speaks in dipodic [two-foot] lines with irregular rhyme—in short, in no traditional poetic art form at all—announcing the verities in the simplest, most, direct way possible. If 'fact' had appeared to dictate the form of the poem's first and third lines, here it is artless, riddling 'wisdom' that seems in control" (153). According to Waggoner, the poem's "last four lines

> suggest both the dipodic tradition Emerson associated with the 'primitive' and 'bardic' and a free version of the Common Meter, which had roughly the same associations for him. Dipodics are suggested by the fact that there are only two strong stresses in each of the first three lines [of the final four]. Common Meter [is suggested] by the a-b-c-b rhyme scheme and by the longer, three-stress, last line. The final stanza is thus Emerson's 'invention,' dictated by the whole 'argument' of the poem." (154)

Ironically, what the settlers think they "'know' turns out to be illusory, and what they solemnly 'affirm' turns out to be true, but in a sense quite opposite from what they intend," so that

> when death has added the owner to his land, his decaying body becomes "a lump of mould the more." Only then does his "fancy" that he and the land have something in common, that they "sympathize," acquire any real truth. A lump of flesh in the grave may be said literally to "smack of the soil," as decay goes on, until finally it is

> inseparable from the soil, the two becoming one, though in a different sense from that imagined by the founders. (155)

Thus ends Waggoner's searching, multifaceted appreciation of "Hamatreya"—certainly one of the best readings the poem has ever received.

Another major response came from Albert Gelpi in 1975. Sounding initially like a formalist, Gelpi wrote that "'Hamatreya' strives for organic form . . . through variation of the dense and length" of its lines. He argued that the "second line, a perfect iambic pentameter, links possessors [in line 1] and products [in line 3], the names of the farmers as thick to the tongue and palpable to the hand as the crops they grow, so that the men and things seem identified. From the farmers' viewpoint," Gelpi continued,

> the list of names mirrored by the list of things exemplifies the physical contact between men and earth, but the ironic viewpoint which begins to emerge makes the proud possessors part of the land in a grisly sense which they do not comprehend. The next lines are strident with personal possessive pronouns: I, my, mine, me. . . . Beneath the onomatopoeic effects, the increasing irony lies in the fact that though the farmers claim reciprocal sympathy with their possessions, they actually think of themselves as superior as the master to his dog. The next verse paragraph demolishes the false pretensions, for those solid citizens are now very much of the land, six feet deep. (98–99)

This comment is then followed by Gelpi's argument that

> Earth has all along been the possessor, and men of any age are her immature children, The repetition of words ("earth," "proud," "steer," "not") and sounds ("flowers," "theirs"; "her," "earth"; "boastful boys"; "flowers," "proud," "plough"; "steer their feet clear") packs the lines with words like clods of earth. (99)

This is precisely the sort of detailed, nitty-gritty analysis formalists admire so much. Gelpi helps explain how and why the poem is so successful *as a poem* rather than as a mere statement of ideas. Thus, he notes that the "third verse paragraph tightens the ironic tension" in lines whose "thick, heavy words merely describe [the landowners'] burial plots." But at this point "a sudden shift in sound and meter marks a change in perspective. The lyric of the feminine Earth-Spirit has shorter lines chiming with sound effects to suggest, by contrast with the lumps of mould, the rhymes of the eternal feminine, who harmonizes life and death, Nature and Spirit" (99–100). Comments like these remind us that it was in the 1970s that a strong interest in feminist criticism really began to assert itself.

Continuing his perceptive commentary on metrics, Gelpi then wrote that "[a]fter hearing the Earth-Song, the chastened poet speaks for himself for the first time in a coda whose lines are reduced from the packed pentameters of the opening, yet have greater length and density than the airy, mostly two-beat lines of the Earth-Song" (100). Then, in a passage whose emphasis is more thematic, psychological, and apparently Freudian, Gelpi argued that the

> conflict between the ego and the life-process is concluded, if not resolved, in the last two lines: first, tersely ("My avarice cooled"), then with the solemn finality of the last line. The association of "lust" with "avarice" in the previously "hot owner" specifies the sinister suggestions of rape in "possessed" and "rendered to their toil" at the beginning of the poem; these pioneer settlers force the land to yield to themselves and their progeny—till the land, virgin despite her rape and fertile despite her virginity, absorbs them, frail husks of masculine ego, back into her womb. (100)

Here Gelpi combines formalist attention to detail with themes already common in psychoanalytic criticism since at least the 1920s and with themes increasingly common in feminist criticism of the 1970s and beyond. Indeed, combining twentieth-century Freudianism with ideas from the early nineteenth century, Gelpi asserted that the "imagery of Romantic poetry about Nature" suggests "that man's relationship with Nature is fundamentally psychosexual" (100).

Now, however, Gelpi also merges psychoanalytic criticism with historical commentary, arguing that the "frontier experience and the frontier mystique which so inform the American character" show (in a passage that adds touches of ecocriticism and Marxism to the theoretical mix) that in

> psychosexual terms the pioneers—their manhood challenged by the seemingly superior power of Nature in all its sublime height and depth and horizonless immensity, the virgin-mother turned destroyer as luring as she was deadly—turned destroyers in turn: possessing, raping, razing, gauging their proof of manhood in patriarchal, contractual terms of dollars and cents.
>
> But in the end, "she" triumphed, such was the poet's vision. The combat was mortal because, in rejecting "her" and exploiting "her" for profit, men destroyed themselves; their avarice cooled with their lust in the chill of the womb-grave. (101)

This combat set "the masculine world of economics and law against the feminine world of nature and metaphoric vision" (101). Then, in language that can simultaneously sound Freudian, Jungian, and feminist, Gelpi contends that

> Emerson in his most unguarded moments knew that as a man his responsibility and opportunity led him not to contend with, but to live, with "her"—that is, with nature, with the intuitive, the instinctual, the pre-verbal and supra-verbal. He knew the feminine Earth-Spirit, and his masculine obeisance to her. Emerson assimilated her meaning deeply enough to be able to translate her inexpressible song. In the poem, Emerson sees life from her perspective and not from that of the vainglorious men; he sings not a masculine or patriarchal consciousness but a feminine or matriarchal consciousness. (101–02)

By closely attending to meter and sound effects, Gelpi looks back to the formalism of the 1940s–1960s; by employing both Freudian and Jungian ideas, he looks back to theories influential since at least the 1920s; by exploring relations between "patriarchy" and nature, he exhibits the kind of feminism that was beginning to take hold in the 1970s; and by commenting about man's destruction of nature, he not only echoes Romantic ideas but also foreshadows our present concern with "ecocriticism." His is a rich essay indeed.

In 1975, an essay by Richard Tuerk thought "Hamatreya" revealed "that Emerson's concept of the relation between man and the universe is not blandly optimistic" (a charge often leveled against him) "and that he could grapple with the dangers inherent in man's precarious position in an apparently hostile universe." Tuerk believed the poem conveys "an overwhelming sense of inescapable alienation" (28), showing that "living is a constant dying, a tending back to the soil, with no hope of rebirth," unlike the hope implied in the *Vishnu Purana*. Comparing this work to other poems by Emerson, Tuerk concludes that in "Hamatreya" the "interaction between man and his universe produces loss as he returns to the earth," not any kind of cosmic consolation (30).

Criticism from the 1980s

In 1986, R. K. Gupta argued that although Emerson had read widely in Indian texts during 1845 (the year before composing "Hamatreya"), before that year his "published writings . . . show little influence that can be conclusively established as specifically Indian." But in 1845, from among many other passages from Indian writings he copied into his journals, he recorded the much-discussed passage from the *Vishnu Purana* to which "Hamatreya" alludes (33). Giving his poem an American locale, Emerson drew on the Hindu passage throughout his text to imply "an important theme in Hindu scriptures—that of fundamental unity behind the illusions of the phenomenal word" while also suggesting another prominent Indian idea, "that of the immortality and indestructability of the human soul"—an idea he had treated in various other writings (34).

Also in 1986, Alice Hall Petry, surveying commentary on the poem's title, suggested that Bridgman, in 1962, while offering the most convincing explanation of its meaning, had not taken his argument far enough (47–48). Petry suggested that "Hamatreya" not only means "Earth-Mother" but elaborately plays "on the word 'hamartia,'" so that Emerson faults Concord's founders "less as historical personages than as symbolic materialists," thereby alluding to Aristotle's concept of *hamartia* as the "first criterion for a 'tragic hero'" (49). For Aristotle, *harmartia* suggested a tragic error or tragic flaw, usually involving hubris or pride, especially pride that involves ignoring a divine warning (49). Therefore, to do full justice to the poem, one needs to see that the first section emphasizes *hamartia* whereas the second section stresses the "Earth-Mother" idea. The whole poem manifests "Emerson's considerable fondness for word-play and the Greek language," and the poem's title "does double-duty, referring simultaneously" to the poem's "two very different halves." Petry concluded that "ultimately the Yankee orientation (which insofar as it is tragic is Greek) does merge into the all-encompassing Hindu one (in which there is no possibility of tragedy), as the farmers become part of the feminine earth. In the final analysis, the bivalent title . . . underscores this merging" (51).

Finally, in 1987, Mularam Joshi, in a passing reference to the poem, called it probably Emerson's "best instance of acclimatising Oriental doctrine in a Yankee setting" while also noting that this "doctrine is also substantially that of [Emerson's key idea] of 'The Over-Soul,'" which he had already developed "before reading the *Vishnu Purana*" (18).

Criticism from the 1990s

Richard O'Keefe, in a significant article from 1992, wrote that "Hamatreya" has "remained to a surprising degree unread," even by critics "who interest themselves in Emerson's verse" (1). Commenting on its themes, he called it "no celebration of the Transcendentalist self, but rather a chilling evocation of the self's *angst* confronting mortality" before he then contended, in a formalist assessment, that the text "merits by now an appreciation of its strength as a *poem*, before we can begin to appraise its value as a *philosophical* poem." Focusing particularly on its meter(s), he said "Hamatreya" could be read "as a powerfully imaginative poem using a perfectly traditional scansion" reflecting models resembling Milton's (1). O'Keefe thought the "difficulty that [Hyatt] Waggoner and others have had with the poem's arrestingly dramatic first few lines suggest a failure to recognize technical sophistication"—a claim he buttressed by showing how closely some of Emerson's meters resembled some of Milton's in *Paradise Lost*.

Responding to some passing comments made by R. A. Yoder in 1978, O'Keefe asserted that "Yoder is probably correct about [an] Anglo-Saxon [metrical] influence on the half-lines of the 'Earth Song,'" but O'Keefe thought Yoder had failed "to observe that this middle section . . . contains [the poem's] least interesting lines," so that when "Emerson shifts from the 'spoken' iambic pentameter" in the first section "to 'sung' half-lines, he creates an unpleasant, 'sing-songy' effect." Yet this effect, O'Keefe suggested, was deliberate and was not the result of Emerson's technical incompetence: "the Earth is a jingle woman because her song is a *taunt*. Earth in this poem is Nature as Bitch Goddess. Her half-lines are crafted to be rhythmically irritating because so is their message" (2). But O'Keefe thought "Emerson's conclusion returns us to musical as well as philosophical excitement. If he skillfully captured our attention at first by surprising our ears, he provides us with an even more satisfying metrical effect in his last lines, to make us remember them":

> ˘ / ˘ ˘ /
> My avarice cooled
>
> ˘ / ˘ ˘ / ˘ ˘ /
> Like lust in the chill of the grave.
>
> Suddenly, in this complex, highly crafted piece of verbal music, we have a series of anapests [˘ ˘ / = an anapest], in fact three of them in two very short lines. (2)

"Those three terminal anapests," O'Keefe dramatically concluded, "with their senses falling on *cooled*, *chill*, and *grave*, are shivers." Meanwhile, in a brief reference to "Hamatreya" from 1993, Lawrence Buell noted that it featured one of the few "shifts of speaker that occur occasionally, very occasionally, within Transcendentalist poems" (115).

In 1995, O'Keefe offered an especially extensive and important assessment of the poem. Reflecting the interest in "deconstruction" common in critical theory since the mid- 1970s, O'Keefe asserted that if ever "a poem . . . looked 'deconstructed' on the printed page, that poem must surely be . . . 'Hamatreya'" (14). Whereas formalists emphasize the complex unities of literary texts, deconstructors do the opposite, arguing that works of literature can never be completely unified or stable in meaning but are, instead, unstable and, therefore, open to endless reinterpretation. Calling attention to the "two radically asymmetrical sections" of "Hamatreya," O'Keefe not only emphasized differences in meters but also noted the existence of "lines of quotation in both parts (speakers within speakers)"—one more way Emerson complicates his text. But even these quotations are asymmetrical: "The number of lines outside of quotation marks is also unbalanced: fifteen in the first part, only four in the second" (14). Thus Emerson, instead of imposing some neat design, did the opposite. Moreover, even the "blank verse Emerson employs in his first part is unorthodox, at times daringly contrapuntal, creating a conversational voice much more modern than Coleridge's 'Conversation' poems and prosodically more modern than [Robert] Frost's blank verse" (14).

Thus, the "whole poem" both looks and sounds like two different poems. Some lines in section 1 "are so colloquial that they push the iambic pentameter almost (but not quite) beyond the limits of scansion," as in the first line. Yet, "much of the 'Earth-Song' is so sing-songy that it seems to burlesque the lyric mode" (15). O'Keefe thus used formalist close reading to undermine the usual formalist concern with unity and coherence. Even the poem's title, he showed, had elicited multiple interpretations, making that title apparently "contradict itself" (16).

But O'Keefe's interest in complexity continued, as when he argued that a "superficial reading of 'Hamatreya' renders the landowners the villains" and makes "the poem a simplistic denunciation of private property in favor of existential claims for Nature." He noted, for example, that the poem is sometimes presented as "simply pro-environmental, anti-capitalist propaganda."

But Emerson, O'Keefe asserted, "is not exactly anti-capitalist" (16)—one more example of O'Keefe's tendency to reject simple, "obvious," "stable" interpretations. "Hamatreya," he maintained, is too structurally and rhetorically complicated to be read merely as a question-and-answer, an error (the landlords) corrected by the Earth-Song." As other critics have pointed out, Emerson had already mentioned the names of the Puritan landowners from line 1 in his "highly favorable . . . patriotic and eulogistic speech," and "[i]t is the anonymous speaker of the first section . . . who mocks [the Puritan] founding fathers (before the earth does later), not Emerson. But who," O'Keefe asked, "is this speaker?" He then continued:

> Is, in fact, the anonymous speaker of the poem's beginning the same as the anonymous speaker who ends the poem after Earth's song is finished? Since he mocks the "fond" and "Boastful" landlords for their avarice . . . , it is unsettling to discover him confessing avarice himself at the end . . . . Or is the terminal anonymous speaker not the same one as the one at the beginning? The poem itself does not provide an unambiguous answer to this question. (17)

O'Keefe's analysis complicates nearly every aspect of the poem—or, more accurately, reveals all the complications he thinks are already inherent in the text itself. Instead of looking for coherence and finding it (as formalists tend to do), O'Keefe looks for incoherence and also finds it (as deconstructors tend to do). Thus, it is not surprising to find him asking (and then answering) yet another question: "What does 'Hamatreya' say about ownership in the face of mortality? It does not say one thing, but several things, *in unresolved contraries*" (my italics emphasize the typical deconstructive phrasing). But more complexities soon appear: the Earth "is certainly as 'boastful'" as the landlords; the poem's "second section . . . in no way erases the first"; the landlords speak 105 words, the Earth speaks 117 (not some neatly balanced figures); and, furthermore,

> each section betrays an internal dialogue within itself: the first, between the landlords and their skeptical, critical chronicler; the second, between the Earth and the acquiescent commentator who

> has, however, in acquiescing to Earth's wisdom, also discovered his common bond with the rest of the human community. . . . If the last speaker is the first speaker, he has gone through a spiritual transformation effected by his listening to both the boasts of the landlords and the scorn of the Earth. . . . Assuming the final speaker to be the same as the first, there are only three voices. Through the collision of the opposing messages of the landlord and of the Earth, a dialectical demonstration, the speaker has achieved the concluding level of awareness that he lacked at the beginning. (18–19)

Yet O'Keefe emphasizes *further* complexities, noting that although Waggoner considered "Hamatreya" one of "Emerson's 'three greatest' poems," and that although Waggoner thought that Emerson's poetry in general did not lend itself well to formalist analysis, Waggoner himself had used such exploration to analyze "Hamatreya" (19). O'Keefe saw "Hamatreya" as "a single, short, concentrated example of an essential pattern of Emerson's thought, namely dialectical organization" (19). "There seems," O'Keefe continued, "to be always a push, in Emerson's thought, through contradictions toward *qualified* affirmation. *But the contradictions must be dealt with first*" (my italics highlight O'Keefe's "deconstructive" tendencies; 20). In fact, O'Keefe mentions one more "contradiction": just before writing "Hamatreya," Emerson himself became a landowner. Therefore, the "contradictions are not just in the text; they are in Emerson. The text profoundly reveals them" (20).

O'Keefe concludes that

> [a]s dialectical organization, Emerson's "Hamatreya" retains enormous vitality as a poem. Part of that vitality stems from the fact that it resists simple or single interpretation. It is ornery but open. It resists and teases our aesthetic. It combines solidity with fluidness. Its earth is both the farm and the grave. The last word in this poetic debate between commodity and nature is simply the last word of the poem. The grave reminds us that, no matter who is speaking the line, whatever voice representing whatever value, human existence itself ends its dialectic in a synthesis of silence. (20–21)

If Waggoner's reading of "Hamatreya" is a superb formalist interpretation, O'Keefe's is a superb deconstructive reading. Yet even O'Keefe, by emphasizing poetic vitality and ultimate synthesis, ends on a note most formalists would welcome: an emphasis on complex *unity*.

In 1999, Saundra Morris briefly suggested that "Hamatreya," like Emerson's "The Sphinx," treats "death as a contest between a man and a powerful mythic female figure; contains imbedded interrogation and interpolated voices, including than of a captious female figure; couches enigmas in elliptical and convoluted wordplay that centers upon pronouns"; and "culminates in a question that is actually a riddling paradox." And Morris added yet another possible reading of the title, suggesting that it conflates "'Hamadryad,' or 'wood-nymph,' and 'Maitreya,' perhaps to represent a bonding between two of [Emerson's] own seemingly opposite loves—American nature and Eastern philosophy" (226).

Criticism from the Twenty-First Century

Commentary on "Hamatreya" during the 2000s has not (with one exception) been especially detailed. In 2003, Paul Scott Derrick thought the Earth-Song "signifies an identification with nature" of the sort Isaac achieves in Emerson's "The Old People" (125). In 2004, M. Jimmie Killingsworth called "'Hamatreya' . . . almost certainly a source for [Walt] Whitman's 'operatic' poems," suggesting in particular that "Emerson's 'Earth-Song' anticipates the song of Whitman's 'mockingbird'" (112) and adding that Emerson's "poet does not find consolation in the earth's song but rather humility and even fear." Comparing and contrasting "Hamatreya" with William Cullen Bryant's "Thanatopsis," Killingsworth contended that in responding to the idea of Earth as man's "ultimate home or resting place, the grave of humankind," Bryant "treats this realization with stoic acceptance, Emerson with Romantic awe and irony" (113). Both poets, according to Killingsworth, "participate in the pastoral tradition, the literature of agricultural people who lay claim to the earth only to be claimed by it." In addition, Killingsworth linked

"Hamatreya" to the ancient tradition of *ubi sunt* [where are?] poetry, which asks: Where are all the people and things now that once seemed so powerful but that now have altogether vanished (113)?

In 2005, John R. Eperjesi, reflecting recent disdain for western imperialism and the consequent rise in "postcolonial" literary studies, sarcastically argued that "Emerson was critical of British violence against people who had yet to see the light of civilization. America is great, according to Emerson, because we aren't nasty and short like the colonized or mean and brutish like the colonizers. America simply brings sweetness and light, in the form of reason and democracy." But Eperjesi contended that "it would not be long before Emerson would be knocked off his high horse and discover that maybe everything didn't revolve around the enlightenment project," a project emphasizing reason above all else. In 1830, according to Eperjesi, Emerson began to read "ancient Indic, Chinese, and Persian" texts that directly influenced "Hamatreya," which delivers "a very clear lesson to American readers." Eperjesi also claimed that "Hamatreya" was partly a response to recent economic events, for "the [financial] Panic of 1837 had made Emerson suspicious of the vacuous materialism and vain individualism that was coming to define the [President Andrew] Jackson era" in American politics (37). "Hamtreya," in other words, was rooted (for Esperjesi) as much in the real world of financial collapse as in the vagaries of eastern mysticism.

In 2008, Robinson Blann compared Emerson's text to Shelley's famous lyric "Ozymandias," arguing that Emerson, like Shelley, condemned human vanity but did so "in a more detailed and dramatic manner." Blann found it noteworthy that "in 1876 Emerson revised" the poem's first line to include Bulkeley, his ancestor, so that "the focus of the poem's lesson bears even more directly on Emerson than it did before the name change," thus increasing "the poem's predominant tone or irony by subtly inserting a private irony directed at himself" (26). But Blann cautioned that "Emerson (or the first-person persona) is not really of the same ilk" as the "boastful boys," and that it is in fact "the difference between them and him—

between their levels of perception of Nature—that actually causes the poem to function as it does" (27). According to Blann, the poem's "tripartite" structure emphasizes three speakers: the "landlords," the "Earth," and the first-person narrator: "The 'landlords' have two pompous speeches" that are "interspersed with the stolidly ironic commentary of the narrator," who eventually and "appropriately approximates [the Earth's] direct and forceful rhythm, symbolically acknowledging the higher truth of her message." Emerson applies "Reason to Nature in order to break through to the Over-Soul and apprehend the higher, unseen things of that World Spirit." He satirizes "the materialistic, mundane-thinking town fathers and their equally acquisitive offspring" who are Emerson's own "bragging agrarian neighbors" (27). Ultimately, the Emersonian persona "has lost any remaining admiration for his 'brave' (l. 52) ancestor from whom he derived his own feeling of bravery and pride" (29), and "the reader realizes that the meaning of the poem is not simply provincial in scope, but universal": Emerson "allows his readers to make the same moral movement from Concord to Hamatreya that his persona does" (30).

Teresa Gibert, in 2009, called "Hamatreya" one of Emerson's "most popular poems," reviewed some standard ideas about the work, and identified the word "Hamatreya" with the name "Maitreya" from Emerson's Indian source—an identification disputed by many earlier critics (194). "In the last stanza," she wrote, "Hamatreya speaks about himself," but then she interestingly added that "Maitreya in Hindu scripture could not have come to the conclusion Hamatreya comes to," because the "Emersonian, Transcendentalist view of nature 'does not correspond to the Hindu way of thinking,'" which places much less emphasis on nature than Emerson and "Hamatreya" do (195).

In another reflection of "postcolonial" ideas, Nicholas Birns in 2019 emphasized that the poem's landowners are Whites "who do not really own the land" they have "stolen and conquered from indigenous people" (193). According to Birns, "Emerson was, as far as a white person in his day could be, an advocate of native rights." Therefore, "American indigenous people can never be presumed to be absent when Emerson discusses American nature," and indeed the "two 'Indians'—Asian Indian and the American Indian—coexist in 'Hamatreya'" the way they do in "Walden," by Henry David Thoreau (194).

Finally, in a 2023 reference work, Prentiss Clark briefly reviewed previous responses to "Hamatreya" while also suggesting (perhaps unfairly to the critics surveyed here) that the poem "has yet to receive more rigorous attention"—a view that anyone who has read, for instance, the discussions by Waggoner and O'Keefe may dispute (118).

Conclusion

By surveying criticism of "Hamatreya" from the 1960s to the early 2020s, I have tried to bring together, in one place, the best that has been thought and said about one of Emerson's very best poems. I have also tried to indicate the various theoretical approaches (whether formalist, thematic, historical, feminist, psychological, economic, deconstructive, postcolonial, ecocritical, and so on) that appear—sometimes separately but often in combination—in various critics' attempts to make sense of the poem. I have, in other words, tried to present a dialog, rather than a monolog, about the poem's artistry and meanings and thus pay tribute not only to the work itself but also to the thoughtful responses it has elicited over the past sixty years.

Notes

1. For the full text of this passage, and of the poem itself, see the citation of Emerson below.
2. In a note, Waggoner comments: "Apart from Bulkeley, it is not clear what principle led Emerson to select just *these* names from the much longer list of founding fathers given in the address. It seems to me very possible that it was Emerson's much-maligned poetic 'ear' that guided him in selecting names for the sound of them. There is assonance in Bulkeley and Hunt and in Willard and Flint; alliteration

in *H*unt and *H*osmer; and a kind of 'rhyming' for which there is no name in Flint and Hunt." (149–50n). In paying such close attention to sound effects, Waggoner practiced good formalist principles.

Works Cited

Birns, Nicholas. *The Hyperlocal in Eighteenth- and Nineteenth-Century Literary* Space. Lexington Books, 2019.

Bridgman, Richard. "The Meaning of Emerson's Title, 'Hamatreya.'" *Emerson Society Quarterly*, no. 27, 2nd Quarter 1962, p. 16.

Buell, Laurence. "The American Transcendentalist Poets." *The Columbia History of American* Poetry. Edited by Jay Parini, Columbia UP, 1993, pp. 97–110.

Burbank, Rex J., and Jack B. Moore. *The Literature of the American Renaissance*. Charles E. Merrill, 1969.

Clark, Prentiss. *Ralph Waldo Emerson: A Companion*. McFarland, 2023.

Derrick, Paul Scott. "*We Stand Before the Secret of the World": Traces Along the Pathway of American Romanticism*. Publicacions de la Universitat de València, 2003.

Emerson, Ralph Waldo. "Hamatreya." www.bartleby.com/370/14.html.

Eperjesi, John R. *The Imperialist Imaginary: Visions of Asia and the Pacific in American* Culture. Dartmouth College P, 2005.

Gelpi, Albert. *The Tenth Muse: The Psyche of the American Poet*. Harvard UP, 1975.

Gibert, Teresa. *American Literature to 1900*. 2nd ed., Editorial Universitaria Ramón, 2009.

Gupta, R. K. *The Great Encounter: A Study of Indo-American Cultural* Relations. Abhinav Publications, 1986.

Joshi, Mularam. *Emerson: The* Poet. Mittal Publications, 1987.

Killingsworth, M. Jimmie. *Walt Whitman and the Earth: A Study in Ecopoetics*. U of Iowa P, 2004.

Morris, Saundra. "'Metre-Making Arguments': Emerson's Poems." *The Cambridge Companion to Ralph Waldo Emerson*. Edited by Joel Porte and Saundra Morris, Cambridge UP, 1999, pp. 218–42.

O'Keefe, Richard R. *Mythic Archetypes in Ralph Waldo Emerson: A Blakean Reading*. The Kent State UP, 1995.

_________. "Scanning 'Hamatreya': Emerson as Miltonic Prosodist." *Emerson Society Papers*, vol. 3,

no. 2, 1992, pp. 1–2.

Petry, Alice Hall. "The Meeting of the Twain: Emerson's 'Hamatreya.'" *English Language Notes*, vol. 23, no. 3, Mar. 1986, pp. 47–51.

Rockwell, Kiffin Ayres. "Emerson's Hamatreya—Another Guess." *Emerson Society Quarterly*, no. 33, 4th Quarter, 1963, p. 24.

Sharma, Mohan Lai. "Emerson's HAMATREYA." *Explicator*, vol. 26, Apr. 1968, item # 63.

_________. "Emerson's Multilingual Coinage 'Hamatreya.'" *Word Study*, vol. 44, no. 2, Dec. 1968, pp. 6–8.

Strauch, Carl F. "Emerson and the Doctrine of Sympathy." 1967. *Critical Essays on Ralph Waldo Emerson*. Edited by Robert E. Burkholder and Joel Myerson, G. K. Hall, 1093, pp. 326–45.

Tuerk, Richard. "Emerson's Darker Vision: 'Hamatreya' and 'Days.'" *American Transcendental Quarterly*, no. 25, Winter 1975, pp. 28–33.

Waggoner, Hyatt H. *Emerson as Poet*. Princeton UP, 1974.

Ralph Waldo Emerson's Influence on Margaret Fuller's "Woman Thinking"

Christopher Allan Black

As a philosophical guide who helped her to develop into a self-sufficient intellectual woman, Ralph Waldo Emerson played a crucial role in the ability of Margaret Fuller to promote female education, stress the need for women's equality, and advocate for the right of women to become self-reliant, equal participants in American democracy. Fuller learned the principles of Transcendental self-culture from her father Timothy, Emerson, and her study of the German philosopher Johann Wolfgang von Goethe. However, for Fuller truly to become an independent, self-reliant woman, she had to challenge and adapt the belief of influential thinkers like Emerson that men were the only individuals within American society who could advocate for themselves as self-made men.

From an early age, the Transcendental feminist reformer was motivated to develop both intellectually and spiritually as a self-sufficient woman. Sarah Margaret Fuller was born in Cambridgeport, Massachusetts on May 23, 1810, to Margaret Crane Fuller, a local schoolteacher in Canton, and Timothy Fuller, a prominent Republican politician first elected to the House of Representatives in 1818. Timothy and his wife Margaret Crane were determined that their daughter would have a first-rate education. When she was six, Timothy began teaching his daughter Margaret English and Latin grammar. Instruction in Greek, French, and Italian soon followed. The Fuller's bright and precocious daughter benefited from an introduction to literature, language, and cultural studies that was equal to the preparation that any young man in the nineteenth century would have had who was preparing for college. At fourteen, Margaret was sent to a school for women, but she had difficulty acclimating herself to the less rigorous aspects of the school and the domestic expectations for young ladies finding her classmates cliquish and dull. Her experience with nineteenth-century female domestic education as an impressionable young woman caused Fuller to come to the realization that she wanted more out of life than being a subservient housewife. Returning home to Boston, Margaret became determined to become an educated independent public intellectual. Fuller continued her studies with her father who encouraged the bright young woman to become a writer. Fuller's first publication "In Defense of Brutus," an article on the often-maligned leader of the plot to assassinate Julius Caesar, appeared in the *Boston Daily Advertiser and Patriot* in 1834. Following her first successful publication just a year later in 1835, Timothy Fuller died, suddenly forcing Margaret to find a way of earning a living for her now destitute family.

Although Fuller struggled to make enough money to support herself and her family, she was determined to maintain her intellectual independence and continue the self-education that her father had instilled in her. Believing that she could further her education by becoming a schoolteacher like her mother before her, Fuller opened a school for girls and young women in Boston. She proved to be a popular teacher, but Fuller found her work in the classroom frustrating and intellectually limiting. Following Timothy Fuller's example, Margaret hoped to teach young women to advocate for their ability to become self-made individuals who could pursue careers outside the domestic sphere. However, the nineteenth-century New England educational system would not allow women the type of intensive classical liberal arts education from which she had benefited in studies with her father.

After failing to connect with young women in the classroom, Fuller decided to take her father's advice and became a social reformer, activist, and writer. Margaret Fuller's belief in the ability of women to become self-reliant came from her reading and interpretation of the German philosopher Goethe who had also inspired Emerson's own belief in Transcendental self-culture. Studying legends and ballads, Fuller learned about the German tradition of respect for women. According to Carol Strauss Sotiropoulos "Germany did not need to learn a high view of woman, it was inborn in that race. Woman was to the Teuton warrior his priestess, his friend, his sister, in truth, a wife. . . The idea of woman in their literature is expressed both to a greater height and depth than elsewhere" (82). Fuller incorporated this cultural perception of German womanhood through her discussions of Goethe's female characters, praising Goethe as the champion of women. Because of his emphasis on women as the self-reliant equals of men, every work by and about Goethe fascinated Fuller. Fuller observed that "Goethe, proceeding on his own track, elevating the human being, in the most imperfect states of society, by continual efforts at self-culture, takes as good care of women as of men" (Sotiropoulos 82). The women Fuller cites in her critique are both real (Goethe's Mother, his sister, Duchess Amelia, Lili) and fictional characters. Fuller's assessment of Goethe's high regard for women can be attributed in part to her misperception of his character. This misperception of Goethe's character helps us to understand Fuller's misimagined Germany. Had Fuller been able to travel to Germany to conduct onsite research for the Goethe biography she had once began to write, she might have encountered uncomfortable aspects of Goethe's position on civic and women's rights. Sotiropoulos observes, "Further, if she had access to his review of novels by three women writers, she might have been disturbed by his condescending dismissal of women writers as dilletantes" (Sotiropoulos 82). Even with his antiquated views of gender roles in society, Fuller still viewed Goethe as the greatest champion of natural rights and self-reliance for women.

Fuller was not entirely unaware that Goethe had disparaged the character of women. In her preface to her translation of Johann Eckermann's *Conversations with Goethe in the Last Years of His Life* (1850), Fuller declares that she had not omitted anything "which would cast either light or shade on his character" (Fuller, *Conversations with Goethe XXV_XXVI*). In reality, Goethe like Emerson may have been a traditional male who did not truly believe in equal rights and democratic equality for women. However, what the educated female Transcendentalist did take from Goethe just as she had done in her reading of Emerson was his belief in the importance of self-culture to the development of the independence of men. It was through her reading of Goethe that Fuller developed her belief in the importance of self-reliance towards promoting the independence and education of women.

Moreover, through her reading and study of German philosophy, Fuller developed the idea of a space for women where they would debate the critical issues of their day and advocate for their rights as full human beings. David Robinson argues that Fuller's embracing of the concepts of transcendental self-culture came through her participation in the public lecture circuit and the lyceum. According to Robinson, "Margaret Fuller came to an understanding of her era by a route akin to Emerson's—through the performance of public speaking in a venue that she had largely engineered herself" (27). Although Fuller's experiment in public conversations for women resembled Emerson's self-reinvention as an independent lecturer, the Conversations that Fuller and Elizabeth Palmer Peabody developed were extraordinarily innovative because they attempted to radically apply the concept of self-reliance to challenge the traditional roles of women in society. Christina Zwarg asserts that the function of the Conversations was "to break through the deeply entrenched barrier between the male public sphere and the female domestic sphere" (163). The conversations would bring women together for public discussion of literary and philosophical subjects. The female lyceum enabled women to pursue what Zwarg refers to as "the association between conversation and feminist agency" (163). In the same manner as Emerson's public lectures, Fuller's conversations drew from the established forms of discourse such as the sermon and the increasingly popular lyceum lectures held in New England. The conversations were also rooted in the important women's traditions of the European literary salon of Madame de Stael, the New England reading societies, and female academies that had their roots in the mid-eighteenth century. Fuller's friend and mentor Eliza Farrar Fuller had experienced firsthand a woman with the qualities of a de Staël. Fuller hoped that the Conversations would cultivate critical thinking in women that in turn would promote feminist self-agency.

The Transcendental feminist hoped that communally gathering in the open but focused environment of the Conversation groups would "help women to ascertain what pursuits are best suited to us in our time and state of society, and how we may make best use of our means for building up the life of thought upon the life of action" (Robinson 28). The Conversations and their emphasis on the application and reflection of self-culture resulted in a call for interrogation of the "foundations of patriarchal society" (Robinson 28). Fuller and Peabody believed that a universal call to reflect and converse about broad subjects such as the "departments of thought and knowledge or literature and the arts in endless profusion" would ultimately lead to a class of educated and thoughtful women to reflect on their place in American democratic society (Robinson 28). She encouraged women to reflect on such critical questions as "What were we born to do? How shall we do it? Fuller had repeatedly confronted the axiom of patriarchal society "I think therefore I am a man" (Robinson 28). Fuller came to see herself as a representative woman who had struggled openly with a barrier that most intellectual women had struggled with inwardly.

However, advocating for and representing the aspirations of women was not synonymous with thinking and speaking for them. In a period in which evangelical preachers, political orators and male lyceum lecturers employed the public platform to proscribe social roles to women, Fuller as an advocate and teacher attempted to resist imposing hierarchies on her disciples. Fuller asserts "I am so sure that the success of the whole depends on conversation being general that I do not wish any one to join who does not intend, if possible, to take an active part" (Robinson 28). This pedagogical emphasis on individual participation and free self-expression draws from Fuller's reverence for Goethean creative activity as the sustaining purpose of the soul "a vitality that cannot be achieved or sustained in a state of reception only" (Robinson 28). Commenting on the very first Conversation meeting, Peabody asserted that Fuller resisted the notion that she was to teach anything to her female disciples. Fuller "merely meant to be the nucleus of conversation and give her own best thoughts of others" (Robinson 28). The overriding principle of the Conversations was to model for her audience the difficult task of public self-expression on intellectually challenging questions.

Elizabeth Palmer Peabody recounted an exchange during the Conversations that demonstrates Fuller's awareness of the connection between Emersonian Transcendentalist self-culture and women's rights. "Ellen Hooper asked if she thought that there was any quality in the masculine or in the feminine mind that did not belong to the other?" (Robinson 28). Fuller's emphatic response confirmed her progressive comprehension of the importance of this question to the perception of gender and the question of women's rights. According to Peabody, "Margaret said no—she did not—and therefore she wished to see if others fully admitted this. Because if all admitted it, it would follow of course that we should hear no more of repressing or subduing faculties because they were not fit for women to cultivate" (Robinson 28). Fuller's answer to this question led to the belief that opportunities for intellectual study and work should be equally available for women. Fuller believed that whatever faculty we felt stirring within us, that we should consider a principle of our perfection and cultivate it to the best of our abilities.

Fuller's belief in the ability of women to develop their skills to equally participate in vocational careers along with men is opposed to Emerson's belief that the true fulfillment of women comes from laboring in the domestic sphere. In his 1855 lecture "Woman" Emerson asserts that "Plato said, Women are the same as men in faculty, only less in degree. When women engage in any art or trade, it is usually as a resource, not as a primary object. The life of the affections is primary to them, so that there is usually no employment or career which they will not with their own applause and that of society quit for a suitable marriage" (2). Emerson argues that the strength of women comes from their sentiment and that they cannot fully participate in the intellectual work of men because they have not obtained the same level of mastery in the arts and sciences. Carolyn R Maibor observes that "Emerson acknowledges that [women's lack of knowledge in the arts and sciences] is likely due to opportunities of education and position. He celebrates however what women have achieved in their own sphere" (188). For Emerson, women's confidence in themselves comes from their ability to nurture children and support the aspirations of their husbands.

However, according to Fuller the idealization of the domestic sphere does not take into account the limiting environment of the home that denies women educational opportunities. Emerson believed that "the misunderstanding between the sexes created in part by their separation into distinct spheres [would] erode naturally" (Maibor 192). Fuller rejected this belief and advocated for women to have full access to the social, educational, and political institutions of the patriarchy. Len Gougeon correctly observes that Emerson's "Woman" has been a problematic argument for feminist advocates and scholars because in the lecture "his emphatic support for the principles of women's rights is matched by equally strong reservations about the wisdom of fully exercising those rights" (580). Emerson insists that women have sympathetic and sentimental qualities that are naturally vulnerable to the competition and self-deprecation of political and social institutions. However, Fuller argues that women should have the choice to participate in the social institutions outside their home environment. Women should not excuse themselves from any duty on the basis "that it was not for women to do on an intellectual ground." (Simmons 215). Fuller declared through the focus on self-culture in the Conversations that women were entitled to full opportunity and encouraged them to exercise their innate faculties and powers responsibly.

Although Fuller had learned a great deal about the Transcendental philosophy of self-culture from her reading of Goethe and her application of the ideology of self-reliance in facilitating the Conversations with her friend Peabody, Fuller still longed for an intellectual guide that would help her to develop as a fully self-reliant intellectual woman and advocate for woman's natural right to equality. Fuller gravitated toward Emerson and the Transcendentalists because she believed that they alone could provide a solution to her personal identity crisis. As Henry Warfel observes, Fuller wondered "how she a woman fettered by the conventionalities, might make her life rich, full, and meaningful" (577). Initially she had sought assistance in achieving this goal from Harriet Martineau, but their plans for an educational tour of Europe had been complicated by the death of Fuller's father. Fuller's philosophical queries remained unresolved. She was unwilling to remain confined and isolated in a mental prison of her own and society's making. Fuller sought another human being who might direct her future footsteps into proper paths. Warfel observes that this was "a romantic notion perhaps, yet it arose from a fundamental psychological need. In 1833, Fuller had written to James Freeman Clark, "How often have I thought, if I could see Goethe, and tell him my state of mind, he would support and guide me! He would be able to understand" (577). In 1835 Fuller writes in her journal:

> I sigh for an intellectual guide. Nothing, but the sense of what God has done for me, in bringing me nearer to Himself, saves me from despair. . .I had hoped some friend would do—what none has ever yet done—comprehend myself. I have had some hope that Miss Martineau might be this friend but cannot yet tell. She has what I want—vigorous reasoning powers, invention, clear views of her objects—and she has trained to the best means of execution. Add to this, that there are no strong intellectual sympathies between us, such as would blind her to my defects (Warfel 577).

Although Martineau was educated like Fuller, she was untrained in the Transcendental concepts of self-reliance and self-culture that Emerson and his colleagues promoted. Martineau was too much of a conformist. Having failed to acquire self-comprehension from Martineau, Fuller turned more eagerly toward Emerson in the hope that she might attain the orientation this fearless theological rebel demonstrated. Emerson's "calm enunciation of principles, his steady view of life, his insistence upon individual self-sufficiency, his personal integrity, and above all his luminous seminal thought—these qualities which she had found in his sermons led her to believe that he alone was her fit counsellor" (Warfel 577). Unlike Martineau who provided the cultural and intellectual training that Fuller already possessed from her studies with Timothy Fuller and her reading of Goethe, Emerson provided the spiritual Transcendentalism that Fuller needed and desired.

In one of her brief letters, Fuller explained in simple terms why she had specifically sought out Emerson's counsel. "It is partly because yours is an image in my oratory. . .and I must pray" (Warfel 577). Before Emerson and Fuller formally met, she knew the philosopher and minister as prolific public speaker. Unlike the other philosophers she had studied including Goethe, there was nothing that Emerson had written that she could have read other than local interest pieces in the media summarizing his lectures. However, she had been personally affected by his rhetorical power as a speaker. In her later years, Fuller told Clarke that Emerson's

> influence has been more beneficial to me than that of any American [Goethe came first for her] and that from him I first learned what is meant by the inward life. . .That the mind is its own place was a dead phrase to me till he cast light upon my mind. . .It would take a volume to tell what this one influence did for me, but perhaps I shall some time see that it was best to be forced to help myself (Richardson 239).

Much like Goethe, Fuller viewed Emerson as a type of saint or holy priest in a confessional that she might turn to gain a sense of release from emotional pressure. Fuller had learned from her reading of Francis Bacon that "no receipt opened the heart but a true friend, to whom you may impart griefs, joys, fears, hopes, Suspicions, counsels, and whatsoever lieth upon the heart to oppress it in a kind civil shrift or confession" (Warfel 578). The individual to whom Fuller desired to unburden herself could not simply be a mere casual friend. Fuller desired and needed a spiritual advisor to assist her in the development of her own philosophy of life and the development of self-identity. However, although Fuller initially believed that she needed Emerson's tutelage and counsel to grow and develop intellectually and spiritually in the end Fuller gained less from Emerson than either Henry David Thoreau or Walt Whitman. In reality, Fuller provided him with more instruction in self-reliance than any of the other Transcendentalist colleagues of their time.

In 1836 Fuller finally gained the introduction to Emerson that she had been seeking. After several years of mutual friends including Martineau insisting that they should meet, Fuller came to visit the Emersons at their home in Concord for a period of three weeks on July 21. Emerson had read Fuller's translation of Goethe's *Torquato Tasso*, and in early 1835 he became eager to meet her. Fuller traveled to Concord from Groton, Massachusetts where she had been living with her mother and her younger siblings. In October of the following year, her father had passed away from cholera. During their first meeting, Emerson and Fuller connected through their mourning of the loss of close relatives. Jeffrey Steele notes that "Like Emerson Fuller when they first met was mourning the death of a beloved relative whose passing left a significant void in her life" (125). Emerson was searching for a replacement for his lost brother Charles, and Fuller eventually came to see Emerson as a substitute for her departed father. While Emerson was reluctant to become a surrogate father to Fuller, the father of the Transcendental movement did provide the young female intellectual an environment in which she could challenge herself.

Fuller was 26 and Emerson was 33 when they first met; Emerson and Fuller were almost completely formed intellectually. They had both scanned life and settled its main problems. From the beginning of their relationship, Fuller deliberately challenged Emerson's "conception of himself primarily it seems because she embodied a style of being that he admired but could not completely fathom" (Steele 126). Warfel astutely observes that Fuller "disturbed Emerson's equanimity as no one else had done except possibly his aunt Mary Moody Emerson" (Warfel 591). During their visit, Goethe's writings were discussed and debated early on. Emerson and Fuller were two of a minority of Goethe readers in America. Emerson thanked Fuller for sending him her translation of *Tasso,* however he refused to grant Goethe the high literary honors that Fuller had bestowed upon him. Emerson claimed that "Goethe lacked dependence upon soul; he was devoted to truth for the sake of culture and not to pure truth" (Warfel 580). Fuller challenged Emerson's view arguing that "Goethe was the greatest liberating personality of the nineteenth century, the only writer who freed his readers from the tyranny of the narrow ideas of the time" (Warfel 580). They discussed the great intellectual group of overseas writers who were making philosophical inroads in America. They expressed their admiration for Thomas Carlyle who had introduced both to a study of German literature. Emerson discussed his meeting with William Wordsworth who at the time was becoming fully appreciated in America. Lastly of major importance was their discussion of religion and the difficult situation the Unitarian Church found itself in that became the initial problem of the Transcendental Club.

For Fuller the most tangible outcome of the three-week visit was her introduction to Amos Bronson Alcott. Following her meeting with Alcott, Fuller was recommended by Emerson to teach at the school he was establishing in Boston where she would teach Latin and French as well as report via stenography the conversations between Bronson Alcott and his pupils. All this ideological and intellectual exposure to the Transcendentalists and their innovative methods of spiritual education contributed greatly to Margaret's personal growth as a writer and thinker. This invitation by Emerson into the Transcendentalist Club provided Fuller the agency and self-confidence that she would need when Emerson asked her to become the editor of *The Dial*.

The founding of *The Dial* in 1840 marked not only a significant cultural moment in America, but also provided an important platform for Fuller to apply Emerson's concept of self-reliance to the status of women. Emerson's description of the intellectual community that would support the new journal is notable for its egalitarianism. Robinson observes that "*The Dial* was not to be seen, Emerson urged, as a coterie journal. Its potential devotees are of all constitutions and conditions he wrote describing a varied and by no means privileged *Dial* public" (30). Emerson's catalogue of the economic and class status of Transcendental souls resembles the inclusivity of Whitman in *Leaves of Grass* (1855). Like Whitman would attempt nearly a decade later, Emerson and Fuller hoped that *The Dial* would provide a public forum that would open the "clogged channels of expression that characterized the New England intellectual culture at this juncture" (Robinson 31). Too much concerning pressing social issues and the struggle for republican natural rights and equality was going unsaid. For Fuller, *The Dial* would provide a forum in which she would employ and adapt the Emersonian concept of self-reliance to promote the need for women's equality and become the philosophical inventor of the antebellum women's rights movement.

In Emerson's essay on Self Reliance the founder of Transcendentalism promotes individuality, nonconformity, and spiritual development of the individual soul. These concepts promote a radical breakaway from traditional social roles. In a utopian egalitarian republican democracy these concepts should apply equally to both women and men. In "Self-Reliance" Emerson writes "The sentiment they instill is of more value than any thought they may contain. To believe your own thought, to believe that what is true for you in your private heart, is true for all men—that is genius. Speak your latent conviction and it shall be the universal sense for always the inmost becomes the outmost—and our first thought is rendered back to us by the trumpets of the Last Judgment" (596). In the opening to his essay, Emerson proposes radical individualism and encourages the individual to break away from the institutions of society that oppress him. However, during his time this philosophical emphasis on nonconformity and breaking free of perceived oppression could only be applied to the station of men. Emerson asserts that "Whoso would be a man must be a nonconformist. He who would gather immortal palms must not be hindered by the name of goodness but must explore if it be goodness. Nothing is at last sacred but the integrity of our own mind. Absolve you to yourself and you shall have the suffrage of the world" (598). In this passage, Emerson discusses individual rights and suffrage, but this can only be applied to men. Although Margaret Fuller philosophically endorsed these principles, in reality she knew that they could only be applied to men.

Fuller in part used her position as editor of *The Dial* to challenge Emerson's view that self-reliance could only be applied to men. Stanton and her coauthors in their *History of Women's Suffrage* claimed that Fuller had been the precursor to the women's rights movement that began in 1848 as a result of her publication in Emerson's journal of "The Great Lawsuit: Man Versus Men Woman Versus Women" that would ultimately result in the publication of *Woman in the Nineteenth Century*. According to Phyllis Cole, Fuller challenged Emerson's definition of exclusively male self-culture "by offering a vindication of women's right to think." Beginning with the publication of "The Great Lawsuit" a critical distinction between Emerson and Fuller's concept of self-reliance began to emerge. Fuller in stark contrast, to Emerson according to C. Michael Hurst "believes that an individual lacks the autonomy to fully author his or her own destiny" (80). For Fuller, an individual's spiritual progress and development is not completely within his or her control. Self-reliance is determined particularly for women in part by the influence of social forces upon the individual. In contrast, the Emersonian male subject can maintain full control over "the consummation of its spiritual transcendence" (Hurst 8). For men, external social relationships are merely obstacles that block one from achieving self-reliance if one chooses to allow them to. According to Emerson, it is up to the self-reliant individual to reject and shun even fathers, mothers, wives and brothers if they become obstacles. Hurst asserts that "In the Emersonian scenario, all agency remains with an unassailable subject who completely controls the actualization of his or her own destiny" (8). Because self-culture in American society highly favored men social institutions do not take into account the social oppression of gender roles that inhibited women's ability become fully self-reliant.

In "The Great Lawsuit" Fuller argues that the only way for women to be able to challenge patriarchal authority that limits their ability to become self-reliant is to advocate for themselves in the courts and invoke legal complaint to sue for their divine inheritance. The title of the 1843 essay in *The Dial* featured the allusion to legal complaint extending the metaphor "by telling of a human inheritance lost and now, despite delays for lack of counsel to plead the cause pursued to higher courts for recovery" (Cole 16). Fuller presents herself as the needed legal counsel to defend women's cause of regaining their self-reliance that was their natural right to independence. In the conclusion to the essay, Fuller becomes the independent Virgin mother of a renewed humanity who would be able to assume her self-reliant inheritance. Cole observes that the principal irony of "The Great Lawsuit" was that Fuller proposed a means of "public remediation to which in 1845 women had no access" (Cole 17). A single woman like Fuller could theoretically have exercised legal authority but in practice especially in the absence of wealth or status single women were absorbed back into dependent status so much so that they were dead to the law. In "The Great Lawsuit" Fuller attempted to fulfill Mary Wollstonecraft's vision of a revolution in female manners in which women's lost dignity was restored and to make them an equal part of the human species.

If "The Great Lawsuit" exposed the social instructions that limited women's access to becoming independent, educated, and self-reliant, *Woman in the Nineteenth Century* (1845) analyzes the challenges of improving the relationship between men and women. In their current social status Fuller maintains that the repressed role of women limits the development of social harmony. As a result of their oppression women only achieve discounted value at best. Fuller asserts that the imbalance between the sexes does not allow for the concept of social harmony. Fuller argues that social harmony for women is not merely the ability to coexist in the same sphere with men, nor is it a parasitic relationship. Harmony involves a symbiotic relationship in which the strengths of one gender complement the strengths of the other. Fuller writes, "I lay no especial status on the welfare of either. I believe that the development of the one cannot be affected without that of the other" (1). A sense of duty rather than personal satisfaction motivates most women. Fuller admires women who pursue traditional domestic functions however these duties must be sought out with zeal. According to Fuller "these functions must not be a drudgery or enforced necessity, but a part of life" (20). Women assume these traditional domestic roles without questioning their interest in performing these tasks. When women fail to express their personal needs and desires to their spouses, they leave their partners to believe that they are happy in the traditional domestic role. Because women have been raised to be dependent on others, they cannot truly achieve self-reliance until they learn to rely on themselves. Developing the ability to rely on themselves, women will acquire the ability to live in harmony with me. Fuller asserts

"I have urged upon the sex self-subsistence in its two forms of self-reliance and self-impulse. . .then, if she finds what she needs in man embodied she will know how to love and be worthy of being loved" (96). Without a clear sense of self a woman cannot truly appreciate her interactions with others—especially men. After women learn their own innate self-worth then will she only be of value to society.

Emerson's concept of self-reliance was important to Fuller's development as a Transcendental advocate for women's rights and equality because it provided a utopian model of individual agency and social reform that women could strive for. However, for Emerson self-culture was reserved specifically for men. Through her reading, translation, and application of Goethe along with her application of Emersonian self-reliance in "The Great Lawsuit" and *Woman in the Nineteenth Century* Fuller successfully demonstrated that women could advocate for their natural right to equality and citizenship in a democratic republic. Although, self-culture could be abused if women were forced into accepting social roles and obligations that traditionally fell to males. "In other words, Emerson did not feel that the best women would want to participate in the sordid game of politics and certainly, should not be compelled to do so by the democratic obligations of citizenship" (Gougeon 578). Fuller advocated for the right of women to become full self-reliant citizens in order that they could make their own representative decisions unhindered by the influence of patriarchy. Fuller's application of Emersonian self-reliance to the position of women provided the catalyst for the Transcendentalists support for women's rights and the successful development of the suffrage movement of the 1850s.

Works Cited

Cole, Phyllis. "Fuller's Lawsuit and Feminist History." *Margaret Fuller and Her Circles*. Edited by Brigette Bailey. U of New Hampshire P, 2012, pp. 15–31.

Emerson, Ralph Waldo. "Self-Reliance." *The Norton Anthology of American Literature Vol. 1 Beginnings to 1865*. Edited by Robert S. Levine 1841. W. W. Norton, 2017, pp. 496–612.

__________. “Woman, Lecture 1855.” *American Transcendentalism Web* Virginia Commonwealth U, 10 Mar. 2023. archive.vcu.edu/english/engweb/transcendentalism/authors/emerson/essays/woman.html.

Fuller, Sarah Margaret. *Conversations with Goethe in the Last Years of His Life, Translated from the German of Eckermann*. Hillard, Gray, 1839.

__________. “The Great Lawsuit: Man Versus Men Woman Versus Women.” *The Norton Anthology of American Literature Vol. 1 Beginnings to 1865*. Edited by Robert S. Levine 1843. W. W. Norton, 2017, pp. 806–810.

__________. *Woman in the Nineteenth Century*. 1845. Dover, 2012.

Gougeon, Len. “Emerson and the Woman Question: The Evolution of His Thought.” *The New England Quarterly*. vol 71. no. 4 Dec. 1998, pp. 570–92.

Hurst, Michael C. “Bodies in Transition: Transcendental Feminism in Margaret Fuller’s *Woman in the Nineteenth Century*.” *Arizona Quarterly*. vol. 66, no. 4, Winter 2010, pp. 1–32.

Maibor, Carolyn R. “Working Girls: Emerson on Female Self Self-Reliance and Vocation.” *Arts, Literatures, and Civilizations of the Anglophone World*. vol 12, 2002, pp. 187–197.

Richardson, Robert D. *Emerson: The Mind on Fire*. U of California P, 1995.

Robinson, David M. “The Movements Medium: Fuller, Emerson, and the Dial.” *French Revue of American Studies*. Vol. 140, no. 3, 2014, pp. 24–36.

Simmons, Nancy Craig. “Margaret Fuller’s Boston Conversations: The 1839-1840 Series.” *Studies in the American Renaissance*. Edited by Joel Myerson. U of Virginia P, 1994, pp. 195–226.

Sotiropoulos, Carol Strauss. “Fuller, Goethe, Bettine: Cultural Transfer and Imagined German Womanhood.” *Toward A Female Genealogy of Transcendentalism*. Edited by Jenna Argersinger and Phyllis Cole. U of Georgia P, 2014, pp. 81–102.

Steele, Jeffrey. “Transcendental Friendship: Emerson, Fuller and Thoreau.” *The Cambridge Companion to Ralph Waldo Emerson*. Edited by Joel Porte and Saundra Morris. Cambridge UP, 1999, pp. 121–140.

Warfel, Henry R. "Margaret Fuller and Ralph Waldo Emerson." *PMLA*, vol 50, no. 2, June 1935, pp. 576-94.

Zwarg, Christina. *Feminist Conversations: Fuller, Emerson, and the Play of Reading*. Cornell University Press, 1995.

CRITICAL READINGS

Emerson's Polarity of Loneliness and Friendship

Susan L. Dunston

> There must be very two, before there can be very one.
>
> (Emerson, *CW* 2:123)
>
> It takes two to know one.
>
> (Gregory Bateson, qtd. in Nachmanovitch 21)

Emerson was a sought-after companion, and he loved and cared for his family and relatives. He was a generous neighbor and an engaged citizen who advocated social justice and reform. He had numerous friends on both sides of the Atlantic with whom he had lively conversations, long walks, and voluminous correspondence. He mentored many younger writers. Even in his old age, he began mentoring the young Emma Lazarus who was to write "The New Colossus," the poem featured on the pedestal of the Statue of Liberty. After his death, mourning friends such as James Elliot Cabot elaborated his reputation as a serene, kindly sage whose lifelong friendships and sweet smiles evidenced his equanimity. Social bonds were important to him. But as a youth, struggling with grief and self-doubt and trying desperately to formulate his identity and purpose in life, Emerson took refuge in solitude even as he suffered from loneliness. Throughout his life, he valued his solitude and protected it from the press of friends and society. He did not join reformist groups even though he actively and publicly protested injustices, including the Cherokee removal of the late 1830s, slavery, and the oppression of women. Nor did Emerson accede to the urgings of close friends to join their experimental utopian communes such as Brook Farm. Though he wrote that he "wished to be convinced, to be thawed" to join their venture, he wrote with wry humor "I do not wish to remove from my present prison to a prison a little larger," determined that his "solitude" was more "beneficent than the concert of crowds" (*JMN* 7:407–08). As his choice of "thawed" suggests, he characteristically accused himself of cool detachment and doubted his capacity for personal relationships. His self-assessment in his early twenties that "What is called a warm heart, I have not" (*JMN* 2:241) seemed accurate at times to him later in life as well. In 1839 and 1840, when he was seeing a great deal of Margaret Fuller and her friends, he still called himself "cold" and lamented his "icy barriers" (*JMN* 7:273, 509).

Emerson grew up chronically lonely and suffered the terrible losses of his father and siblings, and later the deaths of his first wife and first-born child. The tensions and nexus formed by loneliness, loss, and friendship marked his life through what he called his "unpleasing boyhood" and adolescence, his health crisis in the mid 1820s, his intense and brief first marriage, his second marriage and fatherhood, his friendships and professional life, and his old age (*JMN* 2:309). Coming into his own as an internationally known poet, philosopher, lecturer, essayist, and public intellectual entailed dealing with how to transform deep-seated loneliness into the productive solitude that makes creative and generative connections possible. That process of transforming became his life-long practice. It permeates his published work and is the essence of all that is useful in those texts for readers today: Emerson exemplifies a way of thinking and being toward "each and all" of us flourishing in the "fluid and volatile" universe that is our home (*CW* 9:14; 2:179).

Hardship, Self-Doubt, and Despondence

As Evelyn Barish details in her study of Emerson's earliest years, *Emerson: The Roots of Prophecy*, Emerson's childhood and adolescence were traumatically shaped by the death of his father shortly before Emerson's eighth birthday and by the pressure of family tradition. Emerson's father, William Emerson, was a Unitarian clergyman descended from generations of ministers. The weight of family precedent was considerable, and the Emerson boys were expected to become clergymen as well. By the time Emerson was born, William held a prestigious position as the pastor of Boston's First Church, which had been established in 1630 under the leadership of John Winthrop. By Emerson's account, his father was an emotionally distant parent. His mother, Ruth Haskins Emerson, was also sparing in displays of affection, though she worked unstintingly to provide for her family. She was a strict disciplinarian who saw her parental duty as instilling "active and all-controlling consciences at the earliest possible age" (Barish 20). After William's death, his sister, Emerson's aunt Mary Moody Emerson, assisted Ruth with the children, especially with respect to the boys' educations. She was an eclectic reader and imaginative writer who by turns championed, prodded, encouraged, and criticized young Emerson. He and she shared a lively rapport, and he appreciated her influence, writing in his journal "A good aunt is more to a poet than a patron" (*JMN* 4:371).

Emerson was five when his father became ill, and the tension in the household must have been profound. Emerson had already lost a brother, John Clarke, who died about a month before Emerson's fourth birthday. A sister, Phebe, died before his birth. And now there was grave concern for William's health. Years later, Mary wrote to Emerson that his father's death was "preceded by a lingering disease of long endurance and of a kind w'h deadened almost every affection" (qtd. in Barish 43). William's death left Ruth to provide for their children—William, Ralph, Edward, Robert Bulkeley, Charles, and infant Mary Caroline. Mary Caroline died at age three just before Emerson's eleventh birthday. Bulkeley's mental illness and developmental delays required family support, intervention, and financial assistance throughout his lifetime. With Ruth and Mary, the Emerson children had to contend with their grief, the disruption and danger of the War of 1812, and financial distress. Barish notes that "poverty threatened constantly, hunger sometimes, and bankruptcy at least once" (54).

Emerson's memories of his father were few and largely negative. At forty-six, he wrote to his brother William "I have no recollections of him that can serve me. I was only eight years old when he died, & only remember a somewhat social gentleman, but severe to us children" (*Letters* 4:179). Yet, his father's death impacted Emerson's development deeply. Barish details the long-lasting effects: the ever-present absence of his father; the pressure to someday fill the pulpit; the confused mix of grief, anger, and guilt; childhood poverty with hunger both literal and metaphorical; and the duty to provide financial support for the educations of his younger brothers. As Stephen Nachmanovitch, an improvisational musician whose method and philosophy of creativity are strikingly similar to Emerson's observes, "disappearance is full of content" (197). Not surprisingly, Emerson recoiled. "As a child," Barish writes, he "responded to the catastrophe of his loss by withdrawal . . . he tended to avoid interaction," thus creating "a distance, or space around himself" (30, 9). Unlike Emerson's self-assessment that he had not a warm heart, however, Barish argues that "although shy, he was far from cold; what he did feel was a profound inhibition in his capacity to express love or gain it" (92). More self-aware by 1840, he wrote in his journal that he was "cold because I am hot,–cold at the surface only as a sort of guard & compensation for the fluid tenderness of the core" (*JMN* 7:368).

Of necessity, Ruth aimed to get the boys graduated from college and self-supporting as soon as possible. Emerson and his older brother William each entered Harvard at fourteen. The weight of the name Emerson and all it meant to Ruth was upon them. Ruth wrote to Emerson's older brother William when he began at Harvard "should you not be *all* you *ought and all I wish* I should be *very unhappy*—Let your whole life reflect honour on the name you bear" (qtd. in Rusk 42). Emerson reacted by claiming his own identity and space in which to develop it. When he entered Harvard in October 1817 he was, at fourteen, younger than the average age of his fellow students. Looking back in 1834, he described that time as "a crisis . . . the passage from the Unconscious to the Conscious; from the sleep of the Passions to their rage; from careless receiving to cunning providing; from beauty to use; from omnivorous curiosity to anxious stewardship" (*JMN* 4:348). He would later criticize the educational system and its pedagogy in "The American Scholar" (1837) and complain in his journal that "We are shut up in schools & college recitation rooms for ten or fifteen years & come out at last with a bellyfull of words & do not know a thing" (*JMN* 7:238). At Harvard he was a middling and quietly nonconformist student who pursued his own reading outside the syllabus and what he called "my immoderate fondness for writing" (*JMN* 2:238). He struggled with his feelings for a fellow student, Martin Gay, with whom he exchanged glances but did not speak. By graduation he had read more widely than most of his classmates (Rusk 84). As Barish points out, his "real achievement during this difficult decade [between his father's death and graduating from Harvard] was the invisible but profound one of constructing an inviolable and private space in which his mind could grow" (54). Haltingly, over five years from age thirteen onward, he renamed the "me" who was emerging from "Ralph" to "Waldo." He protected his space in which to develop as "Waldo" "from the demands of competition and his mother's emphasis on constant productivity" with habits that would become lifelong elements of his character: "good-natured humor and cheer," an "intense inner life" marked by "freedom of imagination and an independent taste for speculation" (Barish 61) and, most importantly, his own creative reading and writing. These capabilities added to his resilience in the difficult years immediately following his father's death and in the hard times to come: the life-threatening bout with tuberculosis that prompted his trip to the warmer climate of St. Augustine, Florida in 1826, the excruciating deaths from tuberculosis of his first wife (at nineteen after a marriage of less than seventeen months) and his younger brothers Edward and soon after Charles (at the ages of twenty-nine and twenty-seven), the loss of his first-born son Waldo who died of a fever at five years old, and the enormous national tragedies of slavery and civil war.

Emerson's youthful struggles did not end with his graduation from Harvard at eighteen. Soon he was teaching at his brother William's school for girls to help support the family. Biographer Ralph Rusk writes that he "was terrified at entering a girls' school and was troubled by what he later called 'the infirmities of my cheek,' 'occasional admirations of some of my pupils,'" and the need to discipline as well as teach (Rusk 90). Feeling awkward and embarrassed much of the time, he found himself "brooding over the problem of society and solitude and debating it with Aunt Mary" (Rusk 92). He ate so little that Mary was to blame his "fasts" along with school teaching for the eye affliction that was to trouble him as a divinity student (qtd. in Rusk 111). The editors of his journals, which he began writing while at Harvard, note the "extremes of the anguish," "the darker shades of doubt and pessimism," and the "frustration, bad health, and loneliness, his anguish of spirit in the early years" he confided to these pages (*JMN* 1:*xxvii*). At twenty-two, he wrote "My external condition may to many seem comfortable, to some enviable but I think that few men ever suffered more genuine misery than I have suffered" (*JMN* 3:13).

Unquestionably the blows dealt to Emerson by circumstance were severe, but this response of misery and frustration could be self-defeating. His self-assessment of his sociability in an 1824 journal entry was glum. Comparing himself to others, he concluded he had "a signal defect of character which neutralizes in great part the just influence my talents ought to have," the "bitter fruits" of which "are a sore uneasiness in the company of most men & women, a frigid fear of offending & jealousy of disrespect, an inability to lead & an unwillingness to follow the current conversation, which contrive to make me second with all those among whom chiefly I wish to be first" (*JMN* 2:238–39). Out of this period came his 1824 poem "Good-bye," the earliest poem he included in collections of his poetry, though in 1839, he described it as one of his "juvenilities" marked by "a slight misanthropy, —a shade deeper than belongs to me" (*Letters* 7:333). "Good-bye" begins by rejecting society and its conceits: "Good-bye, proud world! I'm going home: / Thou are not my friend, and I'm not thine" (*CW* 9:75, lines 1–2). He bids good-bye "To crowded halls, to court and street; / To frozen hearts and hasting feet," vowing to go "home" to "A secret nook in a pleasant land" where he will be "safe in my sylvan home" (*CW* 9:75, lines 11–12, 14, 17, 23). The poem's emotional expression of disdain is not particularly mature or compelling, nor is the withdrawal from society to rural solitude imagined with great confidence. As Albert J. von Frank comments in his editorial headnote, the poem "seems to mask a sense of disappointment . . . and . . . thwarted professional ambition" (Emerson *Major* 30). The extremity of scorn for society seems also to mask a longing for the intimacy, love, and friendship that Barish identifies as his "deepest needs" (192). But Emerson was soon to start transforming the bitter taste of loneliness into something far sweeter and more fruitful.

From Brooding to Serenity: Transforming Loss and Loneliness into Productive Solitude

The fear of failing socially can be paralyzing and isolating, but as Barish notes, Emerson's "achievement began when he . . . made of his isolation a useable freedom" (9). He used that freedom to develop his sense of self and to find his own way into intimacy and friendship, learning that vulnerability goes hand in hand with invigoration. By his late twenties and early thirties, he looked to nature, not institutional or familial authority, as the standard of truth, beauty, and moral behavior. From then onward, as Robert Richardson writes, Emerson always "held up his doings—his writing and his life—to the great standard, that is, to nature," including his "doings" with respect to social interactions, personal relationships, and solitude (5). By the time of his second marriage to Lidian Jackson in 1835, Emerson equated "safe in his sylvan home" with a home full of friends. He and Lidian settled in rural Concord, their "nook in a pleasant land," and within a few years, with their own growing family, they were hosting a variety of visiting relatives, friends, and protégés.

The safe, sylvan home Emerson envisioned in "Good-bye" ultimately turned out to entail not withdrawal from society to solitude, but rather an ecological relationship between the two. Emerson desired and experienced both, and he came to understand their symbiotic relation as natural and generative. His poem "Each and All," composed in the mid to late 1830s, describes the physical and moral relationships by which all beings have identity and value. The solitary walker/observer/thinker is both witness to and participant in a "web of relation" (*CW* 6:20).

> Little thinks, in the field, yon red-cloaked clown,
> Of thee from the hill-top looking down . . .
> Nor knowest thou what argument

Thy life to thy neighbor's creed has lent.
All are needed by each one;
Nothing is fair or good alone . . .
As I spoke, beneath my feet
The ground-pine curled its pretty wreath,
Running over the club-moss burrs;
I inhaled the violet's breath;
Around me stood the oaks and firs . .
Beauty through my senses stole;
I yielded myself to the perfect whole.

(*CW* 9:14–15, lines 1–2, 9–12, 40–44, 50–51)

Biology describes the necessity of each and all as ecology; environmental ethics rests on the premise of the earth as an ecosystem rather than a set of resources; feminist theory describes personal identity as relational rather than autonomous; Yogic tradition describes the reciprocity of breath (and Emerson read with admiration ancient Hindu texts in translation). There is resonance with all of these in "Each and All."

In the essay "Fate," Emerson, taking his cue from nature, writes "relation and connection are not somewhere and sometimes, but everywhere and always" (*CW* 6:17). He would have immediately understood the Buddhist monk Thich Nhat Hanh's concept of "interbeing" (13). In Emerson's view, as in nonhuman nature, so in human nature. "The laws of friendship are . . . of one web with the laws of nature," and neither society nor solitude is fair or good alone (*CW* 2:117). In *Representative Men* (1850), he writes "We have social strengths. Our affection towards others creates a sort of vantage or purchase which nothing will supply. I can do that by another which I cannot do alone. I can say to you what I cannot first say to myself" (*CW* 4:4). Yet solitude is also requisite: "in the solitude to which every man is always returning, he has a sanity and revelations, which in his passage into new worlds he will carry with him" (*CW* 3:49). The language of nature and ecological interbeing in "Each and All" has its prose counterpart in the essay "Friendship" where he describes friendship as "a new web of relations" (*CW* 2:115). As in "Each and All," in "Friendship" solitude and society are needed by each other: "The soul environs itself with friends, that it may enter into a grander self-acquaintance or solitude; and it goes alone for a season, that it may exalt its conversation or society" (*CW* 2:116–17). One "season" prompts the desire for the other, thus maintaining the tension between the two moods. "I chide society, I embrace solitude," Emerson writes, but "I awoke this morning with devout thanksgiving for my friends, the old and the new" (*CW* 2:114).

"Each and All," like the famous transparent eyeball passage in *Nature*, describes a joyful, invigorating experience of interbeing, but by that same dynamic we are also vulnerable to unpleasant surprise. Our relationality exposes us to uncertainty, loss, and loneliness. The grief-wracked poems Emerson wrote in his journals in the weeks after his wife Ellen's death are stark with such lines as "And now I am alone / Unheard I moan / . . . She comes not even to my dreams / O Ellen" (*Major* 259, lines 16–17, 21–22). But in that loneliness, Emerson made the solitary and life-changing trip to Europe that resulted in his revolutionary 1836 book, *Nature*. After his young son's sudden death plunged him into grief yet again, Emerson asked "Shall I ever dare to love any thing again" (*Letters* 3:8). But in "Experience," the essay in which he writes of Waldo's death "now more than two years ago," he again transformed grief and loneliness into a productive solitude and regained the footing to move onward: "Never mind the ridicule, never mind the defeat: up again, old heart" (*CW* 3:29, 49). Later, in the essay "Fate" he declared that "every calamity is a spur and valuable hint" (*CW* 6:19). Emerson learned "to integrate death into living" (Lorde 11). As a result, loss for Emerson, as Karen Sánchez-Eppler notes, "will always be an opportunity for production and renewal" (81). Loss did not invalidate close connections to others but instead moved him forward in an evolving "web of relation" (*CW* 6:20), and he was thus able to affirm that "life is a series of surprises, and would not be worth taking or keeping, if it were not" (*CW* 3:39).

Selecting Friendships

Though, as the volume of his correspondence illustrates, Emerson had many warm friendships, he desired quality, not quantity, in friendship. The warp and weft of friendship ought to weave "the tough fibre of the human heart," not "a texture of wine and dreams," he writes in "Friendship" (*CW* 2:117) "Real" friendships, he continues, "are not glass threads or frostwork, but the solidest thing we know" (*CW* 2:118–19). The brief poem "Forbearance" describes many of his own aspirations in friendship as well as what he valued in a friend, especially the quality of respect for others–for each and all.

> Hast thou named all the birds without a gun?
> Loved the wood-rose, and left it on its stalk?
> At rich men's tables eaten bread and pulse?
> Unarmed, faced danger with a heart of trust?
> And loved so well a high behavior,
> In man or maid, that thou from speech refrained,
> Nobility more nobly to repay?
> O, be my friend, and teach me to be thine!
>
> (*CW* 9:163, lines 1–8)

Emerson identified the two key elements to friendship as "truth" and "tenderness" (*CW* 2:119, 120). The "paradox" of real friendship for Emerson lies in what he finds most requisite in a friend: "Let him not cease an instant to be himself" (*CW* 2:120, 122). The "delicious torment" of a friend is that "the only joy I have in his being mine, is that the *not mine is mine*" (*CW* 2:117, 122). Friendship, like the interbeing described in "Each and All," is a matter of unity in variety–unity that nourishes rather than erases what is different about individuals. By Emerson's reckoning, friendship is "an alliance of two large formidable natures, mutually beheld, mutually feared" who "recognize the deep identity which beneath these disparities unites them" (*CW* 2:123). Friendship entails the dual capacity to acknowledge and yield tenderly to another, despite fear and vulnerability, yet also to bring oneself whole, entire, and honest to another. As the poem "Étienne de la Boéce" admonishes, "I serve you not, if you I follow, / Shadowlike, o'er hill and hollow" for "When the pilgrimage is done, / . . . I am bitter, vacant, thwarted, / And your heart is unsupported" (*CW* 9:158, lines 1–2, 5, 7–8). "The essence of friendship is entireness"; it is possible when both parties act from self-restraint *and* self-respect (*CW* 2:127).

Emerson considered not only which society to keep, but also how long to keep it. "Society we must have," he writes, and he eagerly sought friendship, but not merely "because I do not wish to be alone" (*CW* 7:7). In his view, the right society is that which augments each party. When a social circle or a friend no longer enlarges either party, he saw moving on as a natural evolution. The society of institutional religion, for example, was not a long-lasting choice for him. After teaching to support his younger brothers' educations, he entered the newly created Harvard Divinity School in 1825 as he was expected to do. The profession offered a living, and a few weeks after his December 1828 engagement to Ellen, he became colleague pastor of Boston's Second Church and was later promoted to pastor. However, as Barish notes, although he was "nurtured in the heart" of Unitarian culture, he was "not of it," and by age seventeen he already "felt and rejected the strictures it imposed upon his native bent" (104). After Ellen's death, he acted on his long-standing reservations about organized religion and resigned from Second Church in 1832, noting in his journal "I have sometimes thought that in order to be a good minister it was necessary to leave the ministry" (*JMN* 4:27). In "Circles," published in 1841, he explicitly connects personal growth with successive friendships: "A man's growth is seen in the successive choirs of his friends. For every friend whom he loses for truth, he gains another" (*CW* 2:182).

Dynamic Balance

Emerson suggests that the tension between solitude and society is not a dilemma to settle but rather something we experience again and again. All the elements—we, solitude, and society—are in motion, "fluid and volatile" in what Nachmanovitch calls the "loop of mutual attention" so essential to successful improvisation (Emerson *CW* 2:179; Nachmanovitch 94). Emerson's essay "Society and Solitude" is the lead essay and title of his 1870 book, published shortly before his sixty-seventh birthday. It was the last book he was able to assemble by himself before the dementia and aphasia that shaped his final years interfered with his writing and lecturing. When the essay first appeared in *The Atlantic Monthly* in 1857, the title was inverted—"Solitude and Society"—a telling artifact of the topsy-turvy experience and relationship of the two. Throughout the essay, Emerson keeps the tension between solitude and society in play. He never prescribes an optimal ratio or settles on a static balance.

The essay begins like a fable: "I fell in with a humorist, on my travels," a man so awkward and ill at ease in society that he "left the city; he hid himself in pastures" (*CW* 7:1). When the man bought a home, he planted trees and hedges all around to "conceal himself" (*CW* 7:1). The similarity to the "sylvan home" Emerson imagined in "Good-bye" is uncanny. The "humorist" is such a caricature, the consummate social misfit, that the fable seems a fiction of Emerson's good-natured humor. From this seemingly tongue-in-cheek opening, Emerson keeps the tension between solitude and society in play by moving back and forth between the benefits and drawbacks of each. No statement on either is final. Solitude appears to be our fate ("the dearest friends are separated by impassable gulfs"), but this "is so against nature, such a half-view, that it must be corrected" (*CW* 7:4, 5). Drawing an analogy between solitude and nudity, Emerson writes "A man must be clothed with society, or we shall feel a certain bareness and poverty" (*CW* 7:5). We must "be dressed in arts and institutions, as well as body-garments" (*CW* 7:5). The image recalls Emerson's impoverished childhood days and the embarrassment of being taunted by schoolmates for having to share one coat between himself and his brother (Rusk 55). There is "that necessity of isolation which genius feels" (*CW* 7:3). To "the culture of the world, an Archimedes, a Newton is indispensable" so nature "guards them" with the penchant for solitude, with "a certain aridity" (*CW* 7:3). But his humor at play again, he reminds us that "If these had been good fellows, fond of dancing, port, and clubs, we should have had no 'Theory of the Sphere,' and no 'Principia'" (*CW* 7:3). Their accomplishments notwithstanding, "the capital defect of cold, arid natures is the want of animal spirits," the "genial heat" that is stimulated "by the friction of society" (*CW* 7:6). The solitary genius is also short on the forbearance Emerson values and can be overbearing. If he does "affect to be a good companion," it is because "he means and needs to impose his system on all the rest" (*CW* 7:4). We need the society of others as a corrective, Emerson suggests. Rapidly he ticks off the benefits of social interaction for all our endeavors. With others, "we are capable of energy and endurance"; together, people are capable of "performance they can rarely reach alone"; and "both for the vehicle and for the aims of fine arts, you must frequent the public square" (*CW* 7:5). Although he was always protective of his own space and time to write, Emerson names "the people" as "the writer's home" much as Nachmanovitch names "other human beings" as "the key to creativity" (*CW* 7:5; Nachmanovitch 20). To be productive, solitude needs what Emerson calls the "magnetic experiment" of conversation (*CW* 7:7). As he wrote in his journal, conversation gave him "self-possession" that was not otherwise possible: "a new nimbleness—almost wings" (*JMN* 7:176). But he is quick to destabilize his comments about the need for social interaction, cautioning that "people are to be taken in very small doses" (*CW* 7:6). Too much society inevitably requires conventions and courtesies that compromise our integrity. It seems neither solitude nor society is entirely good or fair: "If solitude is proud, so is society vulgar" (*CW* 7:6).

In the case of society and solitude, "here again, as so often, Nature delights to put us between extreme antagonisms, and our safety is in the skill with which we keep the diagonal line," remaining with "our head in the one, and our hands in the other" so that we can "keep our independence, yet . . . not lose our sympathy" (*CW* 7:7). His poem "The Apology" exemplifies the "diagonal line" plotted on two axes: independence from others and relation with others. Emerson simultaneously invokes a solitary ramble through woods and meadow and an empathic defense of solitude to those who might take offense at his withdrawal. It is a poem addressed truthfully and tenderly to friends.

> Think me not unkind and rude,
> That I walk alone in grove and glen;
> I go to the god of the wood
> To fetch his word to men.
> Tax not my sloth that I
> Fold my arms beside the brook;
> Each cloud that floated in the sky
> Writes a letter in my book.
> Chide me not, laborious band,
> For the idle flowers I brought;
> Every aster in my hand
> Goes home loaded with a thought. (*CW* 9:221, lines 1–12)

The poem's apology and assurance that he will return with a gift of inspired words are exactly what he writes about the point of solitude at the end of "Experience": that we will carry the "sanity and revelations" we discover in solitude into new worlds, not metaphorically but practically and generously, in the conviction that "there is victory yet for all justice" (*CW* 3:49). The moral import of "Each and All" is that "weal does not exist for one, with the woe of any other" (*CW* 10:449).

Onward from Emerson

In "Circles" Emerson reminds "the reader that I am only an experimenter . . . an endless seeker" (*CW* 2:188). "Society and Solitude" is the work of an experimenter who seeks endlessly and without the need for, or an expectation of, a conclusive or ideal balance between the two. Drawing on his own needs for friendship and solitude, Emerson makes no final claim about either except that each necessitates the other. Instead, he explores and experiments by thinking in "aversion" not only to social expectations, but also to his own thoughts and assumptions (Cavell 36). Keenly attuned to his surroundings and experience, his thinking is provisional, his conduct improvisational. Thus, Emerson leaves himself, and his readers, room to draw new circles of wider acquaintance and insight. If Emerson is a teacher, he illustrates Nachmanovitch's idea that a teacher's job is "to encourage students to have the gumption to do what is theirs to do" (67).

As Barish notes, Emerson's writings are "so delicately tuned to the uncertainties of being in our unanchored and disorderly culture that we go on reading him" (253). Emerson turned toward, not away from, his experiences and surroundings however surprising, unanchoring, or disorderly they were. Insofar as an individual is able, he noticed, regarded, and yielded himself to the whole, thus finding the personal integrity essential for leaving space for readers to find their own. Emerson sought to be of use to others. In fact, as Lawrence Buell writes, "more than any other major writer, Emerson invites you to kill him off if you don't find him useful" (192). He never wanted a flock of followers. As Richard Poirier observes, Emerson is "forever trying to liberate himself and his readers from the consequences of his own writing" (27). He never wanted to lose the freedom to change his mind because he knew his knowledge, like anyone's knowledge, is at best partial. He acknowledged that "I know better than to claim any completeness for my picture. I am a fragment, and this [essay] is a fragment of me" (*CW* 3:47). As a seeker and experimenter, Emerson put himself on the page with entire truth and with tenderness for his readers' own searching and innovating.

Works Cited

Barish, Evelyn. *Emerson: The Roots of Prophecy*. Princeton UP, 1989.

Buell, Lawrence. *Emerson*. The Belknap Press of Harvard UP, 2003.

Cavell, Stanley. *Conditions Handsome and Unhandsome: The Constitution of Emersonian Perfectionism*. U of Chicago P, 1990.

Emerson, Ralph Waldo. *The Collected Works of Ralph Waldo Emerson*. Edited by Alfred R. Ferguson, et al., 10 vols., The Belknap Press of Harvard UP, 1971–2013.

__________. *The Journals and Miscellaneous Notebooks of Ralph Waldo Emerson*, Edited by William H. Gilman, et al., 16 vols., Harvard UP, 1960–1982.

_________. *The Letters of Ralph Waldo Emerson*, Edited by Ralph L. Rusk and Eleanor M. Tilton, 10 vols. Columbia UP, 1939–1995.

_________. *The Major Poetry*, Edited by Albert J. von Frank, The Belknap Press of Harvard UP, 2015.

_________. "Solitude and Society." *The Atlantic Monthly*. Dec. 1857, www.theatlantic.com/magazine/archive/1857/12/solitude-and-society/376145/.

Lorde, Audre. *The Cancer Journals*. Aunt Lute, 1997.

Nachmanovitch, Stephen. *The Art of Is: Improvising as a Way of Life*. New World Library, 2019.

Poirier, Richard. *Poetry and Pragmatism*. Harvard UP, 1992.

Richardson, Robert D. *First We Read, Then We Write: Emerson on the Creative Process*. U of Iowa P, 2009.

Rusk, Ralph L. *The Life of Ralph Waldo Emerson*. Charles Scribner's Sons, 1949.

Sánchez-Eppler, Karen. "Then When We Clutch Hardest: On the Death of a Child and the Replication of an Image." *Sentimental Men: Masculinity and the Politics of Affect in American Culture*. Edited by Mary Chapman and Glenn Hendler, U of California P, 1999, pp. 64–85.

Thich Nhat Hanh. *The Art of Living: Peace and Freedom in the Here and Now*. HarperCollins, 2017.

Moral Sentiment and the Salvation of Spirituality in Emerson's "Divinity School Address" (1838)

Trevor B. Williams

Ralph Waldo Emerson's (1803–82) association with Transcendentalism is well-known through his published essays and lectures, but one of his most controversial ruminations on American spirituality was expressed in his "Divinity School Address" on July 15, 1838. This address, offered to the graduating students and faculty of Harvard Divinity School, provoked backlash from several leaders in the Unitarian movement and other Christian groups because of its negative assessment of traditional Christianity (Buell 31). Emerson denied the divinity of Jesus while affirming his capacity to morally instruct human beings and help them participate in the divine structure of the universe. Brett Malcolm Grainger points out that Emerson's earlier (and also famous) 1836 essay "Nature" shows his affirmation that the "image of nature as a mirror of divinity—external divinity reflecting the inner divinity of the soul, offered Emerson a pathway to retain an enchanted universe at a time when mechanistic scientific models threatened to drain the magic from the universe" (Grainger 24). However, Emerson gradually evolved on these issues, and we see the emergence of his Transcendentalist philosophy during his short tenure as a junior pastor in Boston. For him, traditional Christianity had compromised the authentic teachings of Jesus, replacing them with a ritualistic system of superstition and violence. His critique of religion relied on the notion that humans possess a spiritual *intuition*, a natural knowledge of God's power within them and the world. The moral/religious sentiment, Emerson claimed, was in danger of being obscured by the rigidity of organized religion, because people had become addicted to secondary accounts of religious experience.

Emerson's "Divinity School Address" helps contextualize his transcendental writings, showing that despite his weighty critiques, he did, in fact, retain some value for organized religion. Regardless of his ultimate limitations from the standpoint of contemporary scholarship and his socio-theological context, his fears about the decay of Christian teaching demonstrates a remarkable historical prescience about the future of Western spirituality and the challenges of secularization. Emerson, in my view, wondered if people would forget their innate ability to spark a new revelation through their *religious sentiment*, and that because of this erosion, some would not only give up on organized religion but on spirituality itself. Emerson's address to Harvard Divinity School intended to inspire students and faculty to look to the divine power of their own souls and access the spiritual resources unmediated by tradition or historic Christian doctrine about Christ. This historical observation offers contemporary students and scholars an insightful parallel with the way many religious people (rightly or wrongly) interpret the spiritual significance of secularization. In this sense, Emerson's insight is useful for those in the New Age movement as well as those who continue to value organized religion. His contributions to American spirituality can especially help us to evaluate the sources of religious formation and clarify what is at stake in human reflections on the divine. This chapter, therefore, begins with a description of Emerson's spiritual and literary writings that help contextualize his approach to religion before turning directly to the "Divinity School Address."

The Unitarian Church, Transcendentalism, and the Frailty of Institutions

Unitarianism is a branch of Christian theology that emerged in Europe and subsequently found its way into North America during the 1700s. It denies the doctrine of the Trinity and the deity of Christ affirmed by Protestant, Catholic, and Orthodox segments of traditional Christianity. In this regard, Emerson was already engaged in a radical religious movement that was trying to think through Christian doctrine in ways divergent from previous tradition. Like many Protestant denominations, the Unitarian movement was interested in recovering a more "primitive" set of Christian doctrines, believing that the message of Jesus and the early Christian community had become corrupted over time. The Unitarian denomination did not fare well in Europe because of established churches like Anglicanism and Catholicism, but in North America, it gradually rose to become an incredibly powerful and influential group. This power largely emerged from its connection to influential congregations throughout New England and a long-time association with Harvard Divinity School that continues to the present day. One of the most important reasons for its capacity to influence the political and social policies of the day was that it also provided a religious alternative to the evangelical tendencies of the First and Second Great Awakenings. The Second Great Awakening occurred from 1790–1840 and should be considered here because it coincides with Emerson's lifetime.

Unitarian churches were often associated with rationalism and participate in the American reception of Enlightenment beliefs about miracles and science. They believed that humans "could live productive lives through education. With effort and foresight human history could become a story of moral progress rather than an upending cycle of war and suffering" (Butler, et al. 167). It should be noted, however, that one should not confuse this iteration of Unitarian belief with the Unitarian Universalists of contemporary times, as the movement has undergone significant institutional change. The association with Harvard Divinity School still remains, but its progressive leanings evident in early parts of its history have increased exponentially, making it an institution that often includes self-identified pagans and other non-Christian individuals. Emerson's contributions to Transcendentalism marked his unique voice in the competitive environment of American religion, for he was not simply influenced by Christianity but also by "an early American intrigue with Asian philosophy" (Lippy 97) that is also evident amongst the "spiritual but not religious" segment of contemporary spirituality as well as New Age movements. Emerson did not think about religion in a purely abstract way; he had years of experience working and preaching in the context of Unitarian institutions. For example, he was the junior pastor of Boston's Second Church from 1829–32, which though being a relatively short pastoral assignment, embodies his point of contact with Christians of the time. He was ordained in January 1829 with his struggle over the Last Supper occurring during the same period, pushing him to think through his critique of religious institutions as not meeting the needs of his contemporaries (Richardson 88).

Emerson's Transcendentalist beliefs included "the idea of a universal spirit or mind, whose presence infiltrated every aspect of reality from the natural world to human life. There was a correspondence between this single spiritual essence and everyday life, known more by intuition than traditional religion based on revelation and sacred texts like the Bible" (Lippy 97). He began to sharpen this approach to spirituality during his tenure as a junior pastor in Boston. In this context, therefore, I offer two examples of this development. First, Emerson preached "Sermon CLXII: The Lord's Supper" in 1832, making his objections to the ordinance of the Lord's Supper public (not all communions use "sacrament" language). His motivation was based on his private reading of the Bible and his advocacy for more fluid ecclesial practices. For him, the freedom of Christ means that believers need to be highly suspicious of any claim to a permanent (or, read negatively, static) attachment to rituals. He claims that there is no evidence that the New Testament places the Lord's Supper in such a place, and that a static outlook on rituals distract from Christ's true message. Emerson expands upon his theological background in relation to this claim, expressing that the effect of baptism wraps "Jesus with an authority which he never claimed and which distracts the mind of the worshipper . . . I am so much a Unitarian as this, that I believe the human mind cannot admit but one God, and that every effort to pay religious homage to more than one being goes to take away all right ideas" (Emerson, "Sermon CLXII," 8). Emerson held to a kind of orthodoxy that denied the divinity of Jesus but that underscored his role as stoking the fires of human activity. He stressed that Jesus is the mediator between God and humanity (1 Timothy 2:5) only to the extent that he is "the Instructor of Man. He teaches us how to become like God. And a true disciple of Jesus will receive the light he gives most thankfully, but the thanks he offers and which an exalted being will accept are not compliments, commemorations—but the use of that instruction" (Emerson, "Sermon CLXII," 8). In this specific account of Christian belief, Emerson was not alone or unique.

His moral interpretation of Christianity is comparable to thinkers like Immanuel Kant (1724–1804) and Friedrich Schleiermacher (1768–1834). Both appeal to the moral formation of religion against Christianity's traditional focus on doctrine and liturgical rituals. For Schleiermacher, the appeal to morality as the essence of Christianity supported his defense of religion against the ferocity of Enlightenment critiques. Emerson held a similar view but framed his belief in a less defensive posture. He continues, adding, "It is of the greatest importance that whatever forms we use should be animated by our feelings; that our religion through all its acts should be living and operative" (Emerson, "Sermon CLXII," 9). For Emerson, not only is Christianity principally concerned with morality, the activity of humans in the world, but actions themselves must contain a fluidity that incorporates change and walks in step with human progress. Emerson claims that, in Christianity, what

> I revere and obey in it is its reality, its boundless charity, its deep interior life, the rest it gives to my mind, the echo it returns to my thoughts, the perfect accord it makes with my reason, the persuasion and courage that come out of it to lead me upward and onward . . . Freedom is the essence of Christianity . . . Its institutions should be as flexible as the wants of men. That form out of which the life and suitableness have departed should be as worthless in its eyes as the dead leaves that are falling around us. (Emerson, "Sermon CLXII," 10)

The Unitarian church refused to dispense with the Lord's Supper and so Emerson felt that his process metaphysic compelled him to resign. It is in this spirit, then, that I point to a second source that attests to his aggressive program of spiritual reform, the 1837 lecture titled "The American Scholar," which took place at Harvard College a year before the "Divinity School Address." The content of this document illuminates what he will have to say about the institution of the Christian church and his fear that authentic spirituality was dying out.

Emerson's lecture addresses what it means to be a scholar, and it speaks poetically about the value of books and learning for the human spirit in what he calls "Man Thinking." For him, institutions—not specifically the church—must continually seek renewal by fostering the active soul. He indicates that books are meant to provide thought, not to stifle or replace it, for "The one thing in the world of value, is, the active soul,—the soul, free, sovereign, active. This every man is entitled to; this every man contains within him, although, in almost all men, obstructed, and as yet unborn" (Emerson, "The American Scholar," 95–96). Emerson thus proposes that human beings have a naturally direct or unmediated connection to the divine, which is a belief that runs counter to the integral approach to mediation in traditional Christianity and even the ongoing institutional attachments pertaining to the Unitarian church. In Emerson's words, "The soul active sees absolute truth; and utters truth, or creates. In this action, it is genius; not the privilege of here and there a favorite, but the sound estate of every man" (Emerson, "The American Scholar," 95). The problem with many institutions is that they stifle this genius and essentially clog up the human mind with the genius of the past. This presents an inauthentic mediation that fixates the soul on an insight that is not active and so ceases to be truly spiritual. Emerson specifies that "Genius creates. To create,—to create,—is the proof of a divine presence. Whatever talents may be, if the man create not, the pure efflux of the Deity is not his;—cinders and smoke there may be, but not yet flame" (Emerson, "The American Scholar," 96). He does not see this spiritual activity as being restricted to a secular sphere set apart from the sacred; rather, he thinks it is the obligation of all human thought.

This insight is pivotal for understanding Emerson's evolution toward the spirituality we see expressed in the "Divinity School Address." Many of Emerson's theological arguments were welcome in the Unitarian church of the time, but his views on the Lord's Supper represent his increasing tendency to emphasize the active soul against "static" doctrinal and institutional practices. For him, it is the role of Christian religion (not just the Unitarian church) to point to Jesus as one who preached on the greatness of humankind. This proclamation is not a directive toward the worship of Jesus himself but is a moral imperative to cultivate the active soul in an unmediated, direct way. Indeed, "Everyone, Emerson insisted, must make their own decisions about what was true about God, humans, and the world. In the grand tradition of American individualism Emerson concluded that the only valid authority was the authority of each person's private judgment" (Butler, et al., 264). He hoped that his audience would cease looking to the experiences of others to vivify their lives and, instead, look to their souls. Grainger points out that this message greatly contributed to the religious movements of the time, for Emerson's "declaration of religious independence helped to inaugurate what Robert C. Fuller has called the 'Great Metaphysical Awakening,' a period of creative spiritual tumult in early America stretching from the 1830s to 1860s that produced not only the elite currents of Transcendentalism but the more populist movements of mesmerism, spiritualism, and New Thought" (Grainger 24). This movement overlaps with and follows the Second Great Awakening, which only serves to highlight the incredible influence of Emerson and his peers.

"The Divinity School Address" (1838)

Emerson's "Divinity School Address" is a speech directed to a graduating class at Harvard Divinity School, which includes future ministers of Unitarian churches, in addition to other Christian groups of the time. As I noted earlier, this address was controversial, but it was received negatively by some of the leaders in the Unitarian movement, not necessarily because Emerson denied the divinity of Christ but because he brought his individualist approach to religion to bear on Christian institutions. The whole opening argument of the "Divinity School Address" sets forth his conception of the moral sentiment that is accessible to every human being through intuition. This sentiment is also used in concert with the term "religious sentiment" as both signify how humans have direct access to the Laws of Nature and their Divine establishment. He contends that,

> The child amidst his baubles, is learning the action of light, motion, gravity, muscular force; and in the game of human life, love, fear, justice, appetite, man, and God, interact. These laws refuse to be adequately stated. They will not by us or for us be written out on paper, or spoken by the tongue. They elude, evade our persevering thought, and yet we read them hourly in each other's faces, in each other's actions, in our own remorse. the moral traits which are all globed into every virtuous act and thought,—in speech, we must sever, and describe or suggest by painful enumeration of many particulars. (Emerson, "The Divinity School Address," 111)

However, Emerson's mastery of language here also evidences the limits he ascribes to it, for the sentiment of the divine that can be intuited directly from experience cannot be mediated to and by others. For his audience at Harvard, this argument about mediation was a major point of controversy. Emerson also integrates it into his defense of spirituality.

The moral/religious sentiment is, for Emerson, the "essence of all religion" (Emerson, "The Divinity School Address," 111) and this compels him to speak plainly about what he perceived to be the shortcomings of traditional Christianity (or at least what he encountered in American religion). Emerson's argument about sentiment depends on a framework of immutable laws that structure and enliven nature, but at the same time, the form and representation of these laws are always in process, which means they cannot be frozen in amber by human beings (they are infinite qualities of nature and so have an endless number of potential forms). To do so, for Emerson, is to fall short of an embrace of humanity. He argues that "the soul first knows itself. It corrects the capital mistake of the infant man, who seeks to be great by following the great, and hopes to derive advantages from another,—by showing the fountain of all good to be in himself, and that he, equally with every man, is a door into the deeps of Reason" (Emerson, "The Divinity School Address," 113). The soul must be independent if it is to be great, which for Emerson, represents one of the primary teachings of Jesus. For Emerson, the "temple" of this religious sentiment remains open for all people but is "guarded by one stern condition; this, namely; It is an intuition. It cannot be received at second hand . . . the absence of this primary faith is the presence of degradation" (Emerson, "The Divinity School Address," 114). In the centuries following his life of instruction and moral formation, Emerson believed that Jesus' followers froze his words and reduced them to something so dead that they are now poisoning the well of contemporary spirituality. Emerson adds that "because the indwelling Supreme Spirit cannot wholly be got rid of, the doctrine of it suffers this perversion, that the divine nature is attributed to one or two persons, and denied to all the rest, and denied with fury. The doctrine of inspiration is lost . . . Miracles, prophecy, poetry, the ideal life, the holy life, exist as ancient history merely" (Emerson, "The Divinity School Address," 114).

Emerson is interested in countering the poisonous degradation of spirituality and human intuition by trying to spark a new approach to inspiration. In this regard, he directs his attack against two errors that he associates with historical Christianity, which are crucial to articulate, for him, because he is addressing future ministers who will have important opportunities to enact his vision of Christian religion. The first of these errors is that the church has engaged in the "exaggeration of the personal, the positive, the ritual. It has dwelt, it dwells, with noxious exaggeration about the *person* of Jesus" (Emerson, "The Divinity School Address," 115). This observation is a stark reminder of Emerson's earlier protest against the Lord's Supper. He felt that there was an excessive focus on Jesus, not his teachings or attempt to direct humanity toward the truths of the soul, but on the individual in what Emerson sees as a kind of false deification, an absurd directive that also places the font of revelation in *the other*. For Emerson, this path is a kind of fraud; it declares that "You shall not be a man even. You shall not own the world; you shall not dare, and live after the infinite Law that is in you, and in company with the infinite Beauty which heaven and earth reflect to you in all lovely forms; but you must subordinate your nature to Christ's nature; you must accept our interpretation; and take his portrait as the vulgar draw it" (Emerson, "The Divinity School Address," 116). The "vulgar" substance of preaching, in this case, pertains to the proclamation from the pulpit that is not sufficiently refined in its rhetorical sophistication and that simultaneously fails to instruct the congregation to seek the religious sentiment that is directly available to their souls. In contrast, the "divine bards" help ease people to a "true conversion" for "a true Christ, is now, as always, to be made, by the reception of beautiful sentiments" (Emerson, "The Divinity School Address," 116).

The second error is connected to the first in that it concerns the "Moral Nature, that Law of laws, whose revelations introduce greatness . . . Men have come to speak of the revelation as somewhat long ago given and done, as if God were dead. The injury to faith throttles the preacher; and the goodliest of institutions becomes an uncertain and inarticulate voice" (Emerson, "The Divinity School Address," 117). By looking to Jesus as a divine figure and establishing institutions to mediate Christian revelation, historical Christianity, for Emerson, is complicit in the decline of spirituality itself. Our contemporary language about "secularization" and disaffiliation would fit in here, with the marked decrease in religious participation often being attributed to mutations of Christianity, not merely a result of external sources of thought and belief (Casanova 1–20; Taylor 146–220, 299–380). Emerson's concern about religious disaffiliation is historically interesting in that his "Divinity School Address" was given at the very end of the Second Great Awakening, which was, as we saw, a period of intense religious revival in the United States that ended in 1840. This highlights certain features about Emerson's audience in the Boston community and *intelligencia*, showing a kind of elitist disconnect with the rapid increase of Church membership in the Western frontier and American South. The Second Great Awakening inspired diverse new forms of Christian institutions and belief systems, from the apocalyptic (Second Adventists), to reform movements (Methodism), and everything in between (Restoration Movement). Overall, they not only represent the beginnings of what would become modern evangelicalism in the United States—far removed from the Unitarianism of Emerson and his audience at Harvard—but also transformed "mainline" traditions.

Emerson's concern about the stagnation of revelation, however, builds upon his previous observations about inspiration. He makes a gesture to his audience's future vocation as ministers, telling them that

> To this holy office, you propose to devote yourselves. I wish you may feel your call in throbs of desire and hope. The office is the first in the world. It is of that reality, that it cannot suffer the deduction of any falsehood. And it is my duty to say to you, that the need was never greater of new revelation than now. From the views I have already expressed, you will infer the sad conviction, which I share, I believe, with numbers, of the universal decay and now almost death of faith in society. The soul is not preached. The Church seems to totter to its fall, almost all life extinct. (Emerson, "The Divinity School Address," 118)

This statement represents Emerson's core concern in the "Divinity School Address." He offers this message to future ministers so as to avoid the continuation of this spiritual decline, which is most obvious in his plea for them not to "suffer" falsehoods. Emerson hopes that their preaching will solve the "famine" in their respective churches and embody his notion that it is "the expression of the moral sentiment in application to the duties of life" (Emerson, "The Divinity School Address," 118). For him, the American tradition of preaching does not follow this same tack, and thus fails to communicate the Law that stands at the center of Emerson's system. He says that "the pulpit in losing sight of this Law, loses all its inspiration, and gropes after it knows not what. And for want of this culture, the soul of the community is sick and faithless" (Emerson, "The Divinity School Address," 121). This line of argument is continued further as Emerson turns to summarize his findings about the two errors, saying that, in both, he finds "the causes of that calamity of a decaying church and a wasting unbelief" (Emerson, "The Divinity School Address," 122). The desiccation of religious sentiment leads to overall cultural decay, but more devastating, for Emerson, is that this rot is centered around the individual and diminishes her capacity to have fulfilling experiences with these societal forms.

This observation about the rise of unbelief is the most important concern that Emerson expresses in the "Divinity School Address." It is paradoxical for two reasons: first, in his time, this observation would typically end with a rousing call to return to church and embrace the message of historical Christianity, that Christ is the incarnate Son of God who was crucified to redeem humanity. However, contrary to this Gospel, Emerson directs his audience's attention to the notion that it is in "the soul" that "redemption be sought. In one soul, in your soul, there are resources for the world" (Emerson, "The Divinity School Address," 122). Human individuals are where the life of churches emerges, because "When a man comes, all books are legible, all things transparent, all religions are forms. He is religious . . . the stationariness of religion; the assumption that the age of inspiration is past, that the Bible is closed; the fear of degrading the character of Jesus by representing him as a man; indicate with sufficient clearness the falsehood of our theology" (Emerson, "The Divinity School Address," 122). For him, "The imitator dooms himself to hopeless mediocrity. The inventor did it, because it was natural to him, and so in him it has a charm. In the imitator, something else is natural, and he bereaves himself of his own beauty, to come short of another man's. Yourself a newborn bard of the Holy Ghost,—cast behind you all conformity, and acquaint men at first hand with Deity" (Emerson, "The Divinity School Address," 123). Second, Emerson's message does not then lead to other solutions of his time, for he rejects the call to create new forms, new churches, or even the embrace of secular movements like France's "Goddess of Reason." Instead of such proposals, Emerson tells the graduating class at Harvard to "let the breath of new life be breathed by you through the forms already existing" (Emerson, "The Divinity School Address," 125). In this way, Emerson once again makes a surprising move, as he does not posit a radical overthrow of the Christian church itself but a kind of reinterpretation, revision, and, in his view, resurrection.

Reflection and Conclusion

Emerson's efforts to revive American spirituality at Harvard Divinity School aroused shock and condemnation from many Christian leaders, both in his own Unitarian church and outside of it. There are aspects of his address that, for many Christians today, are controversial, such as his denial of Christ's divinity and assigning of salvation to a purely moral or pedagogical frame. However, what is truly controversial about this address is its indictment of Christian institutions themselves and his effort to go much further than many of his Unitarian contemporaries. His Transcendentalist vision of human spirituality continues to influence reflections amongst those who identify as "spiritual but not religious" and, in the end, the Unitarian church whose pulpits he had once occupied. The continued advance of secularization in these institutions (and in his other inheritors) makes one question the ultimate effectiveness of his proposal, but it is fascinating that he was also so prophetic about the direction of American spirituality. He earnestly believed that people were failing to truly embody the traditional Christian forms of religion and so were becoming blind to the reality of religious sentiment that was native to them. This calamity, as he saw it, meant that churches were not helping people to truly connect to the font of their being, which was, paradoxically, the true source of the church's life. Thus, for Emerson, by denying the necessity of the individual and her religious experience, churches were bringing death upon themselves. Perhaps it would not happen right then and there, as he saw it, but it would indeed occur should the trajectory remain unimpeded.

The unity of Emerson's theological writings spanning from the "Lord's Supper," "American Scholar," and "Divinity School Address" highlights his lamentation that institutions were failing people. Emerson suggests that this is evident in the church as it forces rituals on people that do not have a tangible purpose in Unitarian practice, in schools that place books above experience, and in historical Christianity itself as it denies the font of its own existence. For Emerson, one cannot live through the life of another. This prohibition does not just include living through the life of Christ in place of one's own but is also entirely applicable to the whole constitution of human experience. Books, sermons, and other forms of communication should never *replace* religious experience itself; they should only supplement it and enhance its positive trajectory through education. In this sense, Emerson shows himself to be deeply concerned with trends of religious disaffiliation, and this poses a few notable insights for Western spirituality and its historical significance. He knew that religious rites, rituals, and doctrines need to have connective tissue with lived experience. His conviction on this is largely what contributed to his struggle over the "Last Supper" and his gradual shift away from Unitarian doctrine, but it is a perennial insight for religious people and for those who identify as "spiritual but not religious." Emerson understood this connection within the framework of Transcendentalist belief and sought to apply his conclusions with consistency and rigor. At the same time, we also learn that his fears about the waning of religious belief did not represent the entirety of the American religious landscape, for the nation was swept up in a period of intense revival and spiritual innovation. It is also plausible to wonder if Emerson's individualist approach to spirituality contributes to the very problem he hopes to alleviate. This could occur by limiting the potency of common grammars or belief systems that sustain fruitful communication between spiritual practitioners (especially intergenerationally). Overall, Emerson's insights about religious sentiment, intuition, and the frailty of institutions continue to strike a chord with readers who appreciate the historical significance of his spirituality and its relevance today.

Works Cited

Buell, Lawrence. *Emerson*. The Belknap Press of Harvard UP, 2003.

Butler, Jon, et al. *Religion in American Life: A Short History.* Oxford UP, 2011.

Casanova, José. *Public Religions in the Modern World*. The U of Chicago P, 2012.

Emerson, Ralph Waldo. “The American Scholar.” *The Major Prose*, Edited by Ronald A. Bosco and Joel Myerson, The Belknap Press of Harvard UP, 2015, pp. 91–109.

__________. “The Divinity School Address.” *The Major Prose*. Edited by Ronald A. Bosco and Joel Myerson, The Belknap Press of Harvard UP, 2015, pp. 110–26.

__________. “Sermon CLXII: The Lord’s Supper.” *The Major Prose*. Edited by Ronald A. Bosco and Joel Myerson, The Belknap Press of Harvard UP, 2015, pp. 1–12.

Grainger, Brett Malcolm. “The Place of Nature in Metaphysical Religion: A Brief History.” *The Future of Metaphysical Religion in America*, Edited by Mark Silk and Christopher White, Springer International Publishing, 2022, pp. 17–42.

The King James Bible Online. (1 Timothy 2:5), www.kingjamesbibleonline.org/1-Timothy-2-5/.

Lippy, Charles H. *Introducing American Religion*. Routledge, 2009.

Richardson, Robert D. *Emerson: The Mind on Fire*. U of California P, 1995.

Taylor, Charles. *A Secular Age*. The Belknap Press of Harvard UP, 2007.

Emerson's Transcendental Antislavery Writings

Len Gougeon

Introduction

Emerson's antislavery writings are an important but often neglected element of his canon. The reason for this is that until recently most scholars assumed that Transcendentalism, because it emphasizes self-reliance, tended to discourage social engagement in favor of a serene individualism. This is somewhat ironic in the light of Emerson's declaration in "Man the Reformer" (1841) that every man is born "to be a Reformer, a Remaker of what man has made; a renouncer of lies; a restorer of truth and good" (CW 1:156). The truth is that, rather than discouraging social engagement, Transcendentalism demanded active participation in social reform. Historically, Transcendentalists contributed to many social reform movements, especially antislavery.

American Transcendentalism was the product of many influences. Three stand out. The first is German Idealism, based largely on the writings of Immanuel Kant and Johann Wolfgang von Goethe. Emerson and other New England Transcendentalists acquired their initial knowledge of Kant through an English Romantic, Samuel Taylor Coleridge. Coleridge's *Aids to Reflection* (1825) blended Kantian philosophy with the ideas of various seventeenth-century British philosophers who emphasized, like Kant, the importance and validity of intuitively perceived, abstract truths or ideals. This belief was central to the movement, to the point that Emerson declared in his 1841 lecture "The Transcendentalist" that "What is popularly called Transcendentalism among us, is Idealism" (CW 1:201).

New England Transcendentalists were predisposed to embrace idealism through the second major influence on the movement, Puritanism. The early Puritan settlers of New England were high-minded idealists who were determined that their new civilization would be "as a city upon a hill," a moral exemplum to the rest of the world. Puritans were persecuted in England because they placed the authority of their personal perception of spiritual truth above that of the Church of England, of which the reigning British monarch was the head. They wished to "purify" that church to bring it into alignment with their view of Christianity. Their religious independence made these Puritans natural revolutionaries and reformers. They brought this spirit to America.

The third influence on American Transcendentalism was Asian philosophy. Emerson and others in his circle developed a strong interest in Indian, Chinese, and Persian literature and thought in the 1840s. The Hindu sacred texts were a major influence. Emerson was especially taken with the classics, the *Bhagavad-Gita* and the *Upanishads*. These works emphasize the oneness of life that derives from the universal spirit or world soul that was believed to be the source of all life and all truth. Emerson referred to this life force as "that Over-Soul, within which every man's particular being is contained and made one with all other" ("The Over-Soul" CW 2:160). This concept of spiritual unity is reflected in Emerson's assertion in "Self-Reliance" (1841) that "All men have my blood, and I have all men's" (CW 2:41) and in "Compensation" (1841) where he states, "The heart and soul of all men being one . . . . I am my brother, and my brother is me" (CW 2:72). Transcendentalists believed that this idea was articulated by the Founding Fathers in the Declaration of Independence, which proclaims the "self-evident" truth that "all men are created equal." This belief in the spiritual unity and equality of all people became the political and moral cornerstone of Emerson's Transcendentalism, and it lies at the heart of his enduring opposition to slavery. In an early journal entry, he observed that "Democracy/Freedom has its root in the Sacred truth that every man hath in him the divine Reason." That is "the equality & the only equality of all men," and "because every man has within him somewhat really divine therefore is slavery the unpardonable outrage it is" (JMN 4:357).

Emerson and the Antislavery Movement

In the same year that Emerson inscribed these thoughts on democratic equality, he became actively involved in the antislavery movement. His first antislavery speech was an address on the abolition of slavery in the British Empire. American abolitionists celebrated this historic development every year as a way of encouraging their own government to follow suit. In "The Emancipation of the Negroes in the British West Indies" (1844), Emerson applauded "the arrival in the world of men such as Toussaint, and the Haytian heroes, . . . [and] the leaders of their race in Barbadoes and Jamaica" (AW 31). These militant Black leaders were key figures in a successful Haytian revolt against their European overlords. Emerson believed their example pointed the way to the future freedom of the Black race in America. "The anti-slavery of the whole world," he insisted, "is dust in the balance before this,—is a poor squeamishness and nervousness: the might and the right are here: here is the anti-slave: here is man: and if you have man, black or white is an insignificance" (AW 31). Emerson emphasized the self-reliance and personal courage of the West Indian slaves who were willing to fight for their freedom. "They won the pity and respect which they have received by their powers and native endowments," he stated. "I think this a circumstance of the highest import. Their whole future is in it" (AW 30). The reason this circumstance was so important to Emerson was because he believed personal courage was essential in the work of reform. As he declared in "Self-Reliance" (1841), "God will not have his work made manifest by cowards" (CW 2:28). Every individual must embrace those personal values that give meaning, purpose, and dignity to life. For Emerson, "Nothing is at last sacred but the integrity of your own mind" (CW 2:30). It is this personal sense of integrity and self-worth that determines the individual's relationship with society. Personal integrity must be maintained at all costs, even in the presence of violent opposition because "Nothing can bring you peace but yourself. Nothing can bring you peace but the triumph of principles" (CW 2:51).

For Emerson, self-reliance was an essential prerequisite for social reform. You must believe in yourself before you can believe in a cause beyond yourself. This point is often missed by critics who view Emerson's emphasis on self-reliance as antithetical to collective social action. Emerson saw no such contradiction. In his "Lecture on Slavery" (1855) he made this point clear. "But whilst I insist on the doctrine of the independence and inspiration of the individual," he declared, "I do not cripple but exalt the social action. . . . A wise man delights in the power of many people" (AW 103). This collective "power" was especially important in a democracy where "what great masses of men wish done, will be done" (AW 28).

In 1845, Emerson spoke again on the anniversary of West Indian emancipation. He used the occasion to excoriate the racism and vile bigotry conveyed by what is referred to today as the infamous "*n-word*." "What is the defense of Slavery," he asked. "What is the irresistible argument by which every plea of humanity and reason has hitherto been borne down?" (AW 36) The argument could be summed up in one detestable word, "*Niggers!*—a word which . . . is reckoned stronger than heaven" (AW 36). "They who say it and they who hear it think it the voice of nature and fate" proclaiming a "hopeless inferiority of the colored race" that renders all the arguments of the reformer moot (AW 36). Such hateful racism struck at the very heart of Emerson's Transcendental belief in the spiritual unity and equality of the human family. "This damnable atheism," he declared, violated "the sentiment of right," and the moral order of the universe (AW 37). Emerson was staunchly opposed to the racist theories of his day, on both moral and scientific grounds. He was convinced, long before Darwin, that we all evolved from the same source and that we all shared the same spiritual identity. He also believed that the universe was inherently moral at its core and any theory of law or science that attempted to visit upon any particular group of people a damning determinism was clearly out of sync with scientific truth and moral law. As he stated in his earlier Emancipation address, "the civility of no race can be perfect whilst another race is degraded" (AW 32).

Emerson's resistance to slavery became more militant throughout the 1840s. He accepted invitations to speak at antislavery gatherings despite growing opposition to the movement. Southern cotton was a source of profit for Northern textile manufacturers and these "gentlemen of property and standing," as well as many others who profited from the institution of slavery indirectly, were determined to resist any movement that threatened their prosperity. Sectional tensions grew following the Mexican War (1846–48), which added a vast, new territory to the nation. The question now arose, would the new states carved out of this territory be slave or free? Congress attempted to address the situation with "The Compromise of 1850," which consisted of five pieces of legislation.

The Fugitive Slave Law, passed in September of 1850, was one of them. It required that citizens of the Free States cooperate with authorities in the arrest and detention of fugitive slaves. It also mandated substantial fines and imprisonment for those who aided in their escape. Before the passage of this law, fugitives who made it to a Free State like Massachusetts, often with the help of the Underground Railroad, were protected by the state's "Personal Liberty Law" that guaranteed their freedom. The new Federal law voided such protections and made all citizens potential slave catchers. Not surprisingly, this caused an uproar among Northerners, many of whom had previously been indifferent toward slavery. Emerson was outraged by the measure. Such an atavistic development challenged his faith in moral progress. In his journal, he questioned how such a "filthy enactment" could have been "made in the nineteenth century, by people who could read & write" (JMN 11:412). Like other persons of conscience in the North, including both average citizens and active reformers, he vowed, "I will not obey it, by God" (JMN 11:412). At first, he was confident that the law simply could not be enforced. But after several attempts were made to do so, even in Boston, the birthplace of the abolition movement, it was clear that Federal authorities had every intention of enforcing it. Emerson responded by calling for civil disobedience in a letter published in William Lloyd Garrison's antislavery newspaper, *The Liberator* (18 April 1851). "At this moment," he wrote, "it seems imperative that every lover of human rights should, in every manner, singly or socially, in private and in public, by voice and by pen—and, first of all, by substantial help and hospitality to the slave, and defending him against his hunters,—enter his protest for humanity against the detestable statue of the last Congress" (AW 51).

Initially, a group of activists known as the Boston Vigilance Committee had prevented the rendition of fugitive slaves from the city. However, not long after Emerson's letter appeared, a seventeen-year-old Black boy, Thomas Sims, was seized by authorities in Boston. After a brief hearing and under heavy guard, he was returned to his "owner" in Savannah, Georgia, where he was publicly whipped. The South had its first victory. Emerson's fellow townsmen asked him to speak on the growing crisis. He obliged and delivered his "Address to the Citizens of Concord on the Fugitive Slave Law," on May 3, 1851. It was a dramatic and fiery piece wherein Emerson invoked Transcendental principles in addressing what was fast becoming a major social and political crisis. Earlier, in "Self-Reliance," he had criticized American society as being "a joint-stock company in which the members agree for the better securing of his bread to each shareholder, to surrender the liberty and culture of the eater. The virtue in most request," he noted, "is conformity" because conformity always protects the status quo (CW 2:29). People who value material comfort more than social justice, in Emerson's view, do so because they lack moral and spiritual substance. Their "reliance on Property" erodes the dignity of life, as they "measure their esteem of each other by what each has, and not by what each is" (CW 2:49). Slavery was a toxic by-product of this corrosive materialism. It literally defined certain people as property and seduced ostensibly moral citizens into tolerating a grossly immoral institution like slavery because it was both legal and profitable.

In his first address on the Fugitive Slave Law, Emerson showed how this morally abhorrent law was a reflection of the corruption that inevitably follows when society values profit over principle. "Boston, spoiled by prosperity, must bow its ancient honor in the dust, and make us irretrievably ashamed," he declared. Recent events clearly demonstrated that self-reliance, the key to moral conduct, was subverted as prominent citizens willingly cooperated in the re-enslavement of Thomas Sims. "[T]he whole wealth and power of Boston . . . are thrown into the scale of the crime; and the poor black boy, whom the fame of Boston had reached in the recesses of a rice-swamp . . . on arriving here, finds all this force employed to catch him" (AW 56). The entire society was tainted in this shameful rush to placate the slaveowners. "Every liberal study is discredited. . . . The college, the churches, the schools, the very shops and factories are discredited; real estate, every kind of wealth, every branch of industry, every avenue to power, suffers injury, and the value of life is reduced" (AW 55).

Fortunately, there were still some moral people who saw the evil that so many others were willing to shut their eyes to. These were individuals in whom humanity's natural "moral sentiment" had not been repressed. This force was empowering to any individual open to it. Emerson invoked this force when he assured his listeners that the Fugitive Slave Law would not stand because "it is contrary to the primal sentiment of duty" and, therefore, all moral people are "found to be [its] natural enemies" (AW 58). This concept of moral law, he showed, had been acknowledged throughout history by such famous jurists as Cicero, Edward Coke, and William Blackstone, all of whom held that "immoral laws are void" (AW 59). In light of all this, Emerson declared, "If our resistance to this law is not right, there is no right" (AW 57).

Among those prominent citizens who supported the Fugitive Slave Law was Massachusetts' own Senator Daniel Webster, one of the most respected men in America at the time. Webster had presidential ambitions, and he was willing to sacrifice morality to win Southern support. He claimed to be a patriot and, in his speeches, frequently invoked the example of the Revolutionary Founding Fathers. Emerson knew better. He declared that Webster's actions showed that he was no revolutionary reformer. He was, in effect, little more than a "white slave," an obedient servant of a corrupt status quo and a conservative defender of what is, rather than a crusader for what should be. "In Massachusetts, in 1776," Emerson declared, "he would, beyond all question, have been a refugee. He praises Adams and Jefferson; but it is a past Adams and Jefferson that his mind can entertain. A present Adams and Jefferson he would denounce" (AW 67). In this moment of crisis, Webster had failed as a leader because "he has no moral perception, no moral sentiment" (AW 67), which, for a Transcendentalist, was an unpardonable sin. Webster claimed that he supported the Fugitive Slave Law because he wished to preserve the Union but, as Emerson pointed out, "as soon as the Constitution ordains an immoral law, it ordains disunion" (AW 67). Unjust laws can only bring chaos and conflict. Therefore, he declared, "this law must be made inoperative. It must be abrogated and wiped out of the statute book; but whilst it stands there, it must be disobeyed" (AW 71).

In the mid-1840s, at the same time Emerson was attacking the institution of slavery, his journals show that he was following the debate on the question of Negro inferiority. It was around this time that "scientific racism" emerged, offering a variety of theories regarding the origins and evolutionary potential of various racial groups. All of these theories ultimately favored the Caucasian as the most advanced race and the Negro as the least. Emerson, however, insisted in his address that these theories of deterministic racial inferiority were inconsistent "with the principles on which the world is built" (AW 86–87). He rejected them outright. Emerson believed that the universe was inherently moral and that physical laws reflected moral laws. These laws were intuitively perceived as "moral sentiments," even by the uneducated. Emerson's moral sentiments told him that racial inequality was neither the law of God nor the law of nature.

Emerson delivered his second address on the Fugitive Slave Law on 7 March 1854. At this point, the nation was more divided than ever. The Fugitive Slave Law remained in effect and violence broke out wherever efforts were made to enforce it. Worse yet, Southerners won additional legislative victories like the Kansas-Nebraska Act that, in effect, repealed the Missouri Compromise of 1820 thus allowing the expansion of slavery into the territories. In his address, Emerson reflected on the present state of things and, more importantly, what could be done about it. March 7 was the fourth anniversary of Webster's speech in the U. S. Senate in support of the Fugitive Slave Law. Because Webster's support was key to its passage, Emerson declared that he, "was the life and soul" of the bill (AW 74). In his address, he depicted Webster's moral deficiencies as representative of the moral deficiencies of America. After noting the famous Senator's enormous talents as an intellectual and orator, he turned to Webster's glaring defect, a lack of moral sensibility. "It is a law of our nature," Emerson noted, "that great thoughts come from the heart," but Webster preferred to listen to his head rather than his heart (AW 77). Unfortunately, because of this moral shortcoming, when the crisis of the hour arose, he was found wanting. With no moral core and a strong material inclination, Webster took the wrong side in the debate that was key to America's future. "Here was the question: Are you for man, and for the good of man; or are you for the hurt and harm of man? It was a question: whether man shall be treated as leather? . . . Whether this institution, which is a kind of mill or factory for converting men into monkeys, shall be upheld and enlarged? And Mr. Webster and the country went for the quadruped law" (AW 79). This was a shock to anyone whose moral sensibilities had not been corrupted by gross materialism and the inhumanity involved in the buying and selling of human beings.

Like many other Northerners, Emerson had assumed that decent people would never allow themselves to be tainted by collaboration with such a heinous institution. However, this law that required free citizens to hunt fugitive slaves "found citizens in Massachusetts willing to act as judges and captors." It was now painfully clear that "slavery was no longer mendicant, but was become aggressive and dangerous" even in the Free States (AW 80). Basic principles of morality and common decency were subverted to accommodate the material status quo. Emerson felt this failure most acutely. "It showed that the old religion and the sense of the right had faded and gone out; that, whilst we reckoned ourselves a highly cultivated nation, our bellies had run away with our brains, and the principles of culture and progress did not exist" (AW 80).

The question now was: What can be done? Traditional political means had obviously failed. The system was corrupt throughout. "The events of this month are teaching one thing plain and clear, the worthlessness of good tools to bad workmen, that papers are of no use, resolutions of public meetings, platforms of conventions, no nor laws, nor Constitutions any more" (AW 82). The Federal government had failed to even contain slavery, let alone abolish it. The hope for progress had been dealt a severe blow. The Constitution, which "has not the word slave in it," was ignored when used in arguments against slavery; the Supreme Court had failed to strike down an evil law that insulted the humanity of all; the Missouri Compromise, which limited the expansion of slavery, had been "ridden over," and "state sovereignty in the free states" was ignored as the Fugitive Slave Law became the law of the land (AW 82).

Considering all this, it was now clear that "there is no reliance to be put on any kind of covenant" (AW 83), and that some new means was necessary. Emerson called upon courageous and self-reliant citizens to make a stand against this immoral trend. "To make good the cause of Freedom you must draw off from all these foolish trusts on others. You must be citadels and warriors, yourselves Declarations of Independence, the charter, the battle, and the victory" (AW 83). Regardless of what statute law may say, now was the time to follow a higher law that resided within. Emerson reminded his audience that "Liberty is aggressive, Liberty is the Crusade of all brave and conscientious men. It is the epic poetry, the new religion, the chivalry of all gentlemen." Individuals, empowered by the energy of the Over-Soul, and recognizing the righteousness of their cause, must now act because "there is a Divine Providence in the world, which will not save us but through our own co-operation" (AW 88, 89).

That cooperation grew as opposition to slavery became widespread throughout the North, even as the South grew ever more adamant in their defense of the "peculiar institution." As positions hardened on both sides, violence between pro and antislavery forces became more common in "Bleeding Kansas" and elsewhere. John Brown was the most famous of the antislavery partisans in the Kansas conflict. He visited Concord in the winter of 1857 while on a lecture tour to raise money for his cause. Emerson welcomed him enthusiastically and donated money to buy Sharpe's rifles for Brown's raiders. The growing conflict between pro and antislavery factions in America reached a crisis state in the fall of 1859 when Brown led a raid on the Federal arsenal at Harpers Ferry, Virginia. His goal was to seize weapons to arm Southern slaves whom he intended to liberate by force. The raid failed. Brown was captured, tried, and convicted of treason. He was executed on 2 December 1859 before a crowd of some two thousand spectators. At this point, it was clear to most that the country was headed toward a Civil War and Brown had just shown the way.

When the outbreak of that war finally came in April 1861, Emerson vigorously promoted emancipation to be followed by equal rights for the Freedmen. In the fall of 1862, in a lecture titled "Perpetual Forces," he insisted that after the war, when the nation is re-constructed, it must "Leave slavery out." He encouraged his fellow Americans to "stifle our prejudices against commonsense and humanity and agree that every man shall have what he honestly earns, and, if he is a sane and innocent man, have an equal vote in the state, and a fair chance in society" (LL_2:300). The following year, after Lincoln announced his Preliminary Emancipation Proclamation, Emerson, in "Fortune of the Republic" (1863), celebrated the fact that "slavery is broken, and, if we use our advantage, irretrievably." The war presented an opportunity for the nation to fully embrace, for the first time, the principles of universal freedom and equal rights for all. "For such a gain," he observed, "one generation might well be sacrificed . . . that this continent be purged, and a new era of equal rights dawn on the universe" (AW 153).

Throughout the war, Emerson supported Lincoln and his policies. He was pleased when the Emancipation Proclamation took effect on January 1, 1863, and he publicly applauded the president's courage in taking this bold and controversial step. Not surprisingly, Emerson was attacked by Northern conservatives who believed that the Union could only be restored by accommodating slavery. One of the most prominent of these was Representative Samuel Cox of Ohio, the leader of the conservative Democratic caucus. At a large gathering in New York, just two weeks after the Proclamation went into effect, Cox attacked New England Transcendentalists, Emerson especially, for their part in bringing about this historic development.

Transcendentalism, Cox declared, through its blend of Asian philosophy and Puritan idealism, validated the idea of equality, which made a compromise with slavery impossible.

In his address, which he titled "Puritanism in Politics," Cox asserted that "All the poetic prose and prosaic poetry of Emerson . . . comes from the Dialogues of Kreeshna and Arjoon, called Bhagvat-Geeta . . . This philosophy . . . believes in nothing but the soul. The soul of man is God and nature. No matter, *no color*, nothing but the soul in man; he is all; it is all" (Cox 11). According to Cox, it was this perverse belief in a universal, colorless Over-Soul that led Transcendental reformers like Emerson to embrace the revolutionary notion of equal rights for all regardless of race. Cox was right. This very idea is reflected in Emerson's journal at the time. While speculating on the politics of reconstruction, Emerson insisted, once again, on the need for "absolute Emancipation,—establishing the fact that the United States henceforward knows no color, no race, in its law, but legislates for all alike,—one law for all men" (JMN 15:445).

In his speech, after ridiculing Emerson's belief in the Over-Soul and the divine unity of humankind, Cox asked his audience "Do you wonder, therefore, that since he [Emerson] makes the negro a part of himself, that he holds him to be his equal?" (Cox 11). It was just such Transcendental moonshine as this, Cox believed, that had led directly to the Emancipation Proclamation, followed by a radical push for equal rights. It also, he argued, brought swords into the streets and shattered the peace of a once harmonious and prosperous society. Cox declared that "The painted dream of Universal Emancipation, the offspring of this heathen philosophy, which has been 'pressed' upon the ruling powers in Washington" by Emerson and his "cabal of egotistic zealots" (Cox 12), would render reunion on the basis of the *status ante,* the goal of northern Democrats and "Copperheads," impossible. And that was exactly what it did. After the South was defeated in 1865, slavery was officially abolished with the passage of the Thirteenth Amendment to the Constitution.

Conclusion

In the postwar years, Emerson continued to lend his authority to liberal causes, including racial integration. In an address at Harvard in July of 1867, appropriately titled "Progress of Culture," he celebrated the "fusion of races and religions" in America. He also applauded "the new claim of woman to a political status." He saw the growing crusade for women's rights as "an honorable testimony to the civilization which has given her a civil status new in history" (W 8: 208). For Emerson, equality was not bound by race or gender.

Finally, in 1878, in what would be one of his last public lectures, Emerson spoke again of the need for equality. In a revised version of his "The Fortune of the Republic" address, he summarized his vision for America. "The genius of the country has marked out our true policy," he noted, "opportunity. Opportunity of civil rights, of education, of personal power, and not less of wealth; doors wide open. If I could have it,—free trade with all the world without toll or custom-houses, invitation as we now make every nation, to every race and skin, white men, red men, yellow men, black men; hospitality of fair field and equal laws to all" (W 11:541).

Works Cited

Cox, Samuel S. "*Puritanism in Politics*," *Speech of Hon. S. S. Cox, of Ohio, Democratic Union Association, January 13, 1863*. Van Evrie, Horton, 1863.

Emerson, Ralph Waldo. *The Collected Works of Ralph Waldo Emerson*. 10 Vols. Edited by Alfred R. Ferguson, et al., Harvard UP, 1971–2013. (CW)

__________. *The Complete Works of Ralph Waldo Emerson*. 12 Vols. Edited by Edward Waldo Emerson, Houghton, Mifflin. 1903–1904. (W)

__________. *Emerson's Antislavery Writings*. Edited by Len Gougeon and Joel Myerson, Yale UP, 1995. (AW)

__________. *The Journals and Miscellaneous Notebooks of Ralph Waldo Emerson*. 16 Vols. Edited by William H. Gilman, et al., Harvard UP, 1960–1982. (JMN)

__________. *The Later Lectures of Ralph Waldo Emerson: 1843–1871.* 2 Vols. Edited by Ronald Bosco and Joel Myerson, U of Georgia P, 2001. (LL)

Emerson and the Central Virtue of Reform: A Subjunctive Investigation into the Early Influence on Him of William Lloyd Garrison

Albert von Frank

. . . .so prove it,
That the probation bear no hinge nor loop
To hang a doubt on.

—*Othello*, III.3

A Two-Paragraph Theoretical Introduction

Sometimes an influence important to a writer's inner life arrives covertly or indirectly, disguised by the concurrent preoccupations of the mentality influenced, and so, as sometimes happens, may be overlooked by critics and biographers. Such influence may be further hidden from view if its most important results should differ from what might reasonably be expected. An influence may, for example, set one on a longer or shorter course of development as opposed to provoking an immediate revolution of outlook. It may be that in an environment of active social reform few propositions (if any) are wholly taken up as originally delivered—at least not where the target minds are critical. Such minds, that is, may so construct what "flows in" as to modify or empower some already existent concern. As Emerson said just two weeks after the first of William Lloyd Garrison's epochal lectures of 1830, "It is the nature of the human mind to receive knowledge slowly, not to pass suddenly from ignorance to wisdom, but to intermix the first rays of truth which it receives with its own familiar errors" (*CS* 3: 23, October 31, 1830). Truth, which in this formulation is built on the decay of error, only *promises* to set us free. It is prospective, or, from the present point of view (as experienced), subjunctive. Something in Emerson's thinking at the very outset of the abolitionist crusade made him conceive of liberation as intrinsically gradual. The nature of the "something" that at first held him back from any hearty involvement in the antislavery movement, is worth investigating.

I am not so eager to "prove" the influence of Garrison on Emerson as I am to explore narratives that include such a plausible connection and see if they don't help in our interpretive approach to each or both of these figures. An exploratory nonbinary consideration of the influence question—one not aiming at a mere yes or no conclusion—can lead to a deeper sense of the life of the subject's mind and to more nuanced views of his engagement with topics that, precisely because they *are* emergent and fluxional, do not announce themselves with any great precision. Often the critic who wants to call attention to the genetics of such a transaction will feel a need, for the sake of clarity and emphasis, to isolate its elements from their surroundings or pry them out of an organic embeddedness. Simplification, exaggeration, and/or misrepresentation, however, are typically the result, especially given that influences are always themselves influenced in being taken on. Even calling attention to the likelihood of some particular influence brings publicity to a private mental process, which can falsify the investigator's conclusions by inviting a too emphatic show of discovery or a too great delight in the drama of praise or blame. These are among the complexities explored in the case study that follows.

A Brief Case Study: The Matter of Garrison's Boston Lectures

On Friday evening, October 15, 1830, fresh from a radicalizing sojourn in Baltimore (which included a stint in jail and an education from his friends among the city's Black activists), Garrison delivered at Boston's Julien Hall the first of three uncommonly incisive antislavery lectures.[1] They are among the earliest abolitionist speeches delivered by anyone in Boston and certainly the earliest by Garrison to reject unambiguously the American Colonization Society and its popular though malign plan to transport America's free Blacks to Liberia.

Up to this point Emerson had said substantially nothing about slavery, the Colonization Society, or its project of removal. A slight exception may be found in certain incidental journal jottings made during Emerson's 1826–27 trip to South Carolina and Florida, undertaken for his health, and in an isolated observation, probably from 1826, that newspapers had begun calling the Colonization strategy "A project for extinguishing Volcanoes" (*JMN* 6: 38). The paucity of Emerson's comment and the attention he paid to a mordant witticism testify to his isolation from such antislavery agitation—and influence—as existed by 1830.[2] In the wake of Garrison's Boston lectures, however, Emerson began a new notebook, Blotting Book Psi (*JMN* 3: 205–63), initially devoted to his thoughts on these and related topics, fragments of which he used in sermons delivered to his congregation at Boston's Second Church on consecutive Sundays in November and December and in later exchange deliveries to other Unitarian churches in eastern Massachusetts (*CS* 3: 29–44). If these references to slavery and to the new note in antislavery rhetoric were not inspired by Garrison's disruptive performances, it would be hard indeed to say what prompted them.

A summary of Garrison's lectures may be constructed from the evidence of an unsigned and heretofore overlooked article, "Mr. Garrison's Lectures on Slavery," that appeared in the *Christian Register* shortly after their delivery. The *Register* was a sort of journal of record for Unitarian ministers at this time, including Emerson, as index references in the sixth and tenth volumes of Emerson's *Letters* suggest. Whereas Garrison's subject had been American slavery, the theme throughout was American guilt—the still largely unacknowledged guilt of Northern indifference to Southern slavery and more particularly of New England's economic complicity in its ongoing maintenance. Garrison took as radical a position on these matters as he possibly could have, advocating for the uncompensated and "immediate abolition of slavery . . . as demanded both by justice and expediency."[3] In gauging the broader influence of Garrison's three addresses, it should be noted that this bipolar phrase —"justice and expediency"—was shortly afterwards adopted by the young Quaker poet John Greenleaf Whittier, already, by 1830, an ally of Garrison, as the title of his widely circulated prose exposition of the grounds for slavery's abolition. An exasperated Garrison had found the conservative counterargument from expediency the most frequently advanced as well as the most potent objection to immediate emancipation. "*Expediency!*" he exclaimed, was "the deadliest word in our language."[4] Enlisting the term along with *Justice* as twin concepts properly supportive of abolition, Garrison and Whittier had to reject the popular acceptation of these terms (in legal and prudential contexts) and redefine them so as to show that a moral course of action could offer practical social advantages—White fears and dark imaginings to the contrary notwithstanding.

No evidence exists to show that Emerson analyzed Garrison's rhetorical strategy at this time, and yet it involved an argument that the incipient Transcendentalist delighted in throughout his career: one that did not aim at "saving the appearances," but rather moved beyond the phenomenal world into a correspondent realm of spirit. Quite like Garrison, he grasped the potential for tyranny of a morally misapplied materialism, a potential that must and would, as both felt, give way before the clarity of moral perception that talented reformers and powerful orators would make attractive. Having set his face against such forcible tactics as those simultaneously embraced by Black activists David Walker and Nat Turner, Garrison, in his converting discourse, often targeted linguistic pathologies. By putting language at the persuasive center of his movement and famously demanding that he and his pronouncements be heard, Garrison's approach would have appealed to Emerson, who increasingly saw his own career in such terms.

Further along in this first lecture Garrison endorsed the Quaker policy of boycotting the products of slave labor, whereby individual citizens of the North might withdraw at will from America's slave economy.[5] He pointed as well to the guilt of not abolishing slavery where, as in the District of Columbia, an opportunity to do so manifestly presented itself. He argued that the currently legal interstate traffic in slaves was "scarcely less atrocious in its character" than the old transatlantic trade, outlawed since 1808. One of Garrison's most effective points (among many) amounted to an argument for reparations:

> If a son should inherit property which had been stolen by his father, could he exculpate himself from guilt if he refused to restore it to [its] owner, by the plea that his father stole it, and not he himself? Is it any excuse, then, for a slaveholder who inherits stolen men, to say that it was not he who stole them, but his ancestors?[6]

"*Fiat justitia*," Garrison urged, "*ruat cœlum*." Let justice be done though the heavens fall.

A crucial proslavery argument was disposed of in Garrison's proposition that "the evils which could follow the abolition of slavery [and which it was a point of expediency to avoid], were as nothing compared to those which must result from its continuance." The lecture concluded with Garrison's characteristic denunciation of race prejudice and of the notion "that one color is more incompatible with freedom than another." He instantly collected attention by becoming, through these germinous acts of seeing and saying, a new center of power in Boston.[7]

The second lecture dealt with slavery as it is in theory and as it is in fact. The third occupied itself with an indictment of the Colonization Society along with its racist founding principle "that the blacks must not have their freedom till they can be removed from the country."

What Did Emerson Know and When Did He Know It?

The crucial question in the ordinary genetics of this influence is whether Emerson attended Garrison's lectures. Almost certainly he did not but got at secondhand whatever he may have known about them. As a young minister come only recently (1829) into full charge of his own church, he was heavily burdened with unaccustomed duties—of which, besides the composition of weekly sermons the most pressing involved supervising the construction of a new vestry, tending to the church's charitable efforts, and officiating at weddings and funerals. With none of these activities was Emerson ever comfortable. Moreover, throughout his pastorate Emerson was filled with dread over the precarious health of his wife Ellen, now nineteen years old, who was terminally ill with tuberculosis, intermittently bedridden, and fated to die before winter's end—this despite the devoted care of Emerson's mother Ruth, the abundant though contradictory advice of well-regarded physicians, and the presence of a resident nurse. Adding to Emerson's despair over life on "this sickening planet" (*L* 1: 313), his brothers Charles and Edward were also symptomatic consumptives and, as the event soon proved, equally doomed. Blotting Book Psi, like the sermons of this period, spoke eloquently, often in heterodox terms, of the fear of death and of death's questionably asserted repeal in Christian promises.[8] But, nearly overwhelmed as he was at home and at work, Emerson had no need to go to Garrison's lectures to have registered their radical effect: unlike any previously delivered in Boston, these addresses created a stir for their root-and-branch attack on slavery, for their impossibly bold advocacy of immediate emancipation, and for calling out the cowardice and hypocrisy of most Northern clergy, for whom the Colonization Society had stood for years as the resolving limit to their antislavery concerns. That Emerson's attention was being suddenly called to the issue of slavery is reflected most clearly in Blotting Book Psi, which bore on its front cover verso (*JMN* 3: 204), as a kind of epigraph, a preliminary estimate from the 1830 federal census, cited by Garrison in his first speech, that twelve million free White citizens now occupied the country with, for the first time, more than two million Black slaves. The bare statistics, like Garrison's challenging eloquence, made the issue newly apparent if not yet impossible to ignore—as, indeed, it was, with a few brave exceptions, the long-settled New England custom to do.

Garrison as Model Reformer and Moral Crusader

What stood out for Emerson in the wake of this novel agitation—rather more, it would seem, than any action he might have been led to consider—was the stance and effect of the heroic reformer, above all in his power-conferring isolation. This would have been consistent with Emerson's still unresolved thinking about vocational options, which seemed more and more dependent on the resolution of Ellen's case. The identification of the Reformer as a model moralist addressing a spontaneously gathered secular or unchurched audience—as at Julien Hall or at the Boston Athenaeum (where Garrison's lectures were, in fact, repeated), or at the recently established open-topic lyceums—was likely owing to Emerson's need to understand how the individual might enact self-culture and so progress in a career of moral improvement, even as the churches failed, conspicuously now, in their mission of guidance. Thus, in Blotting Book Psi, Emerson wrote on November 10 about the reformer's own advancing acuity in seeing what few others saw, that an "evil admixture" in something naturally good (as of slavery in society, cruelty in agriculture, or formalism in religion) had to be conceptually distinguished and judged accidental—that is, held exempt from any too-inclusive approval (*JMN* 3: 209). Emerson expressed this kind of analytical discernment metaphorically as a visual process: Inferentially, Garrison simply *sees* better than others, and so sees rightly *for* these others, just as ministers might have done in a traditionally prophetic role. If Emerson brought such an insight into personal focus, as no doubt he did, the conclusion might have been that right seeing was indeed better supported outside the church than inside.

"I, Eye, Ay": Sight as Moral Extension; or How It Is with Every Soul

It is tempting to trace the emergence of a crucial trope—the Emersonian "eye" —to this early working out of the mechanism of free-lance reform:

> This is the merit of every reformer. One man talks of the abolition of Slavery with perfect coolness whilst all around him sneer or roar at his ludicrous benevolence. They with their sinful eyes cannot see society without slaves. He sees distinctly the difference, & knows that the crime is unnecessary. And this is the progress of every soul. What it joined before it now severs & sin & error are perpetually falling away from the eternal soul. (*JMN* 3: 209; Blotting Book Psi, November 10, 1830).[9]

This way of construing the issue—of foregrounding the "one man talk[ing]" in the second sentence and of giving a central place to the recovery of the "eternal soul" in the sixth—arguably marks the emergence of a specifically romantic style of reform, an inward and self-reliant alternative to socially "expedient" options like those offered by the Colonization Society. Emerson's language is influenced as well, of course, by the ancient trope in which Jesus advised the Laodiceans (who were known for compounding and—ironically—exporting eye-salve) to "anoint [their own] eyes with eye-salve, that [they] mayest see" (Revelation 3:18) Emerson's trope broadens the scope of the biblical metaphor, first by breaking its link to the personality of a particular moral teacher and second by locating the effect of right seeing in possibilities for individual moral growth. The Laodiceans and those subsequently who honored the scripture text were being urged to "see" Christ and so follow charismatic authority; modern Americans were being urged (by Garrison and Emerson) to "see" the iniquity of slavery (not to overlook or excuse it) and so to follow the moral promptings of an intuitive revulsion. There are many examples in Emerson's sermons of this sort of modernizing revaluation of the moral life, no small part of which consisted in a revision of the status and purpose of poetic tropes, a point Emerson was to make to famous effect in his Divinity School Address (1838).

Samuel J. May and the Energies of a Hot Conversion

As has just been noted, Emerson regarded the modern (romantic) reformer as a kind of moral visionary, whose right seeing or manner of beholding was in itself curative. But another young Unitarian minister, the Rev. Samuel J. May of Connecticut, visiting Boston, happened to be in the lecture hall that evening. The difference between his enthusiastic response, which would seem to set an upper limit to the function of influence, and what I take to be Emerson's cooler and more searching approval helps us appreciate what is distinctive about the nature and quality of the latter's openness to influence. Like Emerson, May was drawn to the visual metaphor, yet with a more conventional application and a far stronger emphasis on the person of the seer and advocate. The result was to recast influence as an effect of personality, to redirect attention away from the truth and to fasten it, as a form of allegiance, upon the truth-teller himself. Emerson's view was that being influenced by any person, including Jesus (the ordinary requirement of the churches) was a less than adequate substitute for being influenced directly by the truth itself (see *JMN* 4: 45; October 1, 1832).

Indeed, May's response is more recognizable as an instance of influence because it more obviously invokes the model of religious conversion.[10] Remade by the opinions he was hearing, May was the paradigmatic converted attendee that evening at Julien Hall, led then and there to abandon his few remaining doubts and embrace not only the cause of abolitionism but also and at the same time the leadership of Garrison. In Garrison he saw nothing less than the singular, isolated, embattled, and embodied form of the cause. As he later recalled, Garrison had arisen "with an air of calm determination, and delivered such a lecture as he only, I believe, at that time, could have written; for he only had had his eyes so anointed that he could see that outrages perpetrated upon Africans were wrongs done to our common humanity."[11]

Garrison's influence immediately moved the Reverend May to activity, perhaps in part because until that moment he had been a member of the Colonization Society. He and the group he had come with, consisting of his brother-in-law Amos Bronson Alcott and a cousin, the lawyer Samuel E. Sewall, approached Garrison at the lectern when the address was over, expressed their great satisfaction with what had been said, and invited the speaker to Alcott's rooms close by for further talk. As a group they committed that evening to the creation of a regional antislavery society, one of the action-items Garrison had proposed in his lecture.[12] They talked as well about the antislavery newspaper Garrison proposed to edit—the *Liberator*—its aggressive agenda having been fully developed in the three addresses. Whether from enthusiasm, impulsiveness, or the stirring of deep conviction, May was brought by the evening's lecture-language to embrace . . . discipleship:

> Never before was I so affected by the speech of man. When [Garrison] had ceased speaking, I said to those around me: "That is a providential man; he is a prophet; he will shake our nation to its centre, but he will shake slavery out of it. We ought to know him, we ought to help him". . . . Mr. Sewall and Mr. Alcott went up with me, and we introduced each other. I said to him, Mr. Garrison, I am not sure that I can indorse all you have said this evening. Much of it requires careful consideration. But I am prepared to embrace *you*. . . . That night my soul was baptized in his spirit, and ever since I have been a disciple and fellow-laborer of William Lloyd Garrison.[13]

The "Willing Mind" and the New Last Supper

It is clear how far May's response is from Emerson's way—clear, too, what talents would have been extinguished had Emerson exercised the option, as May did, of becoming a sub-Garrison, a valued lieutenant and expeditor of another man's admirable work. Such indeed we certainly know to have been Emerson's view:

> If you take the reform as the reformer brings it to you he transforms you into an instrument. It behoves you to receive into a willing mind, every trait, every bold stroke which is drawn. Let the Age be a showman demonstrating in picture the needs and wishes of the soul: take them into your private mind; eat the book and make it your flesh. Let each of these causes take in you a new form, the form of your character and genius. Then the Age has spoken to you, and you have answered it: you have prevailed over it ("Reforms," *EL* 3: 260).[14]

Being "spoken to" by "the Age" and having responded or "answered" according to one's private "character and genius" rehearses all the core elements of Emerson's extemporized theory of influence. The "new form" that influence most usefully took in Emerson's case was of a novel admiration for "right seeing" and its correlative modes of expression, most notably the dangerous and unsettling talk of the reform hero. The first—the moral potential of vision or of "beholding" or of "bearing witness"—was related to Emerson's theological background; the second—the expression—bore closest relation to Emerson's broadly advancing interest in poetry at this time, partly yet significantly an effect of Ellen's influence. Both the seeing and the saying are best understood as accommodations of revolution-in-general, the ability to say, with accuracy and justification, "I unsettle all things" ("Circles," *CW* 2: 188).[15]

The New Poetry

The eye of the modern poet finds the poetic element in what is scorned, denied, erased, or overlooked in the light of everyday, and so we are led to recognize that which is newly and strikingly seen as important, as a center not of perception merely but of alertness and renewal too. Indeed, such revelation belongs to the reformer and his rhetoric in nearly the same way and nearly to the same degree as it belongs to the poet. As Emerson wrote on May 18, 1831, "The poet casts his eyes on no object soever, not on a tub or shoe but it grows poetical in his eyes. The whole world is a poem to him" (*JMN* 3: 253). Which is to say, things and persons begin to matter; they begin to assert an authentically original status in our attention. Such observation at its sharpest best rescues value, vitality, and truth from the fatigue of stereotypical thought, including, in the issue of slavery, what has been well called the racial imaginary.[16] To separate persons who are enslaved from the total meaning of slavery is to attack the problem as it first exists in the language from which the racial imaginary is constructed. Hence, in some large part, the usefulness of poets, as they may work in verse or lively prose. In Emerson's representation of the function of poetry one seems to have an early, perhaps even a first intimation, of Walt Whitman's democratic-egalitarian aesthetic. An influence that tends in such a direction does not generally culminate in discipleship, with its inherent self-subordination, but rather, or more often, in a "Song of Myself."

In a journal passage of March 4, 1831, Emerson spoke of the "operation of the Holy Spirit" as being "the same in kind in the prophet Isaiah as in the poet Milton" (*JMN* 3: 240). Just as May did not hesitate to call Garrison a "prophet," so Emerson identified the prophet as one who, occupying a more clarified and, therefore, more exalted state of mind than others, "actually *sees* those things to be true which he utters" (*JMN* 3: 240; emphasis added). Again, writing of the public and representative functions of the reformer/prophet/poet, Emerson noted that "What is said by one man, is just trembling on the lips of a thousand more, and is gladly received as connate" (*JMN* 3: 214). By this Emerson likely meant that truth has everywhere and only a human home; he does not mean to imply that Garrison's prophetic message was welcomed at the time—certainly, it was not by more than a few persons predisposed to dissent. Garrison's heroism consisted in his being the first to speak as he did, as a pioneer voice of romantic reform, or as one who utters those things which he sees to be true. In his essay on "Heroism" (1841, based on a lecture of January 1838), Emerson observed that it was of the essence of the definition of heroism that it should work "in contradiction to the voice of mankind, and in contradiction, for a time, to the voice of the great and good" (*CW* 2: 149). Garrison, who would be mobbed in Boston on October 21, 1835, by a crowd of "gentlemen of wealth and standing," had reason to agree. What was generally felt to be most admirable in the 1830 lectures was Garrison's strenuous courage in opposition and the "tart cathartic virtue" of his prescriptions ("Heroism," *CW* 2: 147). Indeed, Emerson's essay on "Heroism" reads at many points like a description of Garrisonian valor.[17]

As a Unitarian minister with concerns appropriate to that role, Emerson was more taken with the process than with its assured result—more attentive, in other words, to the Reformer's effect as heroic change-agent and defender of free speech than to the entailed liberation of actual slaves in actual bondage. He deploys his argument against the conventional objection from expediency, implying that the "discerning eye" of a clear moral vision (see footnote 9 above) will be the effective and, in the new sense that Garrison gave it, the expedient destroyer of slavery. The end of slavery will come when the moral vision modelled by Garrison (his way of seeing the matter) is taught verbally, more or less as Garrison propounded it at Julien Hall. "The genius of the day does not incline to a deed, but to a beholding," said Emerson as late as 1841 ("Introductory Lecture," *CW* 1: 179), but it is the beholding of the universal Reformer that he means, which puts everything in the field of critical vision, as opposed to "acting," which is necessarily partial and local, permanently mortgaged to the limited effect gradually produced. About such beholding there is nothing passive. One sees that Emerson's professional concern with purging "sin & error" from those who, in 1830, stood ignorantly guilty, determined the use he would make of the Reformer's influence—less, once again, to free the slaves directly (were that even remotely possible) than to free the oppressor from his oppressiveness—as Garrison meant to do. That determination has often seemed to critics and historians, at least in Emerson's case, like a limit he voluntarily placed on his imagination, in effect keeping him from the kind of public intervention that Garrison and other influenced reformers mostly urged. In order to release this imaginative constraint (to the extent, say, of being able to write his "West Indian Emancipation" address in 1844), Emerson had to stop thinking so dutifully and desperately as a professional Unitarian. By February 1831 he was a widower; by late 1832, sick himself, he left his pastorate to chart an independent course beyond the church as an institution or body of opinion.

A Non-Lockean "Beginning of Wisdom"

Emerson analogized the separating process not only to a process of right seeing, but also to the cleaving effect of the word of God:

> All our knowledge comes in this way [i.e., by a process of separation and discrimination]. It is when a man perceives the essential distinctness of his mind & his body that he is a metaphysician. It is when the sword of the spirit doth divide his flesh & his spirit that he perceives the immortality of his soul. There is a time when a man distinguishes the idea of felicity from the idea of wealth. It is the beginning of wisdom. There is a time when a man separates God from his Works by a process of his own mind & sees clearly that matter is one thing & the order & forms of matter another. (*JMN* 3: 209) [18]

In this passage and in others nearby in Blotting Book Psi, the Reformer's way of seeing the difference between nature and spirit has, of course, application beyond the cause of antislavery. An awareness of the "essential distinctness" of mind and body, spirit and nature, makes it possible to explore the relation between them, which is arguably the whole business of Emerson's most important early work, the 1836 manifesto, *Nature,* as well as the crux of the problematic misperception at the center of the slavery issue. As a feature of Garrison's antislavery discourse, the distinction locates the slaveholder in a world of bodies, searching for wealth and material comfort at the expense of felicity. "And all external luxuries, the sweetest meats, the softest couch, the rarest music, will be only poison and thorns and strife to our depraved and sick perceptions" (*CS* 3: 26; October 31, 1830). The practical division of "flesh and . . . spirit," the key, Emerson argued, to all the teachings of Jesus (*CS* 3: 23)—which is the deployment of a sanctified seeing—solves the problem of the fear of death, essentially taking over a fundamental task of the Christian religion (*CS* 3: 29; November 20, 1830).

Beginning in late 1830 Emerson consistently related his analysis of right seeing to the effect of the Reformer, as in the following journal entry, written on December 21, 1830, and deployed in his hundredth sermon, delivered five days later. The passage springs to life if we entertain the likelihood that Emerson is here thinking of Garrison—or at very least not excluding him from the company of relevant exemplars. What if attention were transferred from the personal figure of Jesus to the principle by which redeemers work? What if? Might there not then be more redeemers than one? Why the parsimony of Christians? The Universe, as it happens, positively teems with redemption.

> When a truth is presented, it always brings it[s] own authority. . . . I am raised by the reception of a great principle, to its height. And he who communicates, & applies, & embodies, a great principle for me, is my redeemer from the evil to which the want of it would have led me. Bacon showed the inanity of science not founded on observation [i.e., again, right seeing]. So he is the Restorer of science. He has not saved my life; he has not saved my estate; but he has saved me from one error, & to that degree is he honorable in my mind. Newton

> showed the law of gravity & has directed all men to what will be true & will be false touching bodies & so has saved a thousand errors[.]
>
> But here are some more claimants. Harmodius, Aristogeiton, Leonidas, Brutus, Sidney, Washington, Lafayette. All advocates & provers of a principle of far more importance[,] that of [a] right to personal liberty. They are my political saviours. They have made it a matter of conscience to me that I should not submit to arbitrary power. They have made the tyrant feel that he is a tyrant & therefore have weakened wrong & armed right every where. . . .
>
> He that perceives any truth with great clearness cannot contradict it. . . . If he perceives the whole expediency & authority of a moral law[,] he will keep it. (*JMN* 3: 216-217)[19]

The conclusion of this passage makes room for reformers who speak to clarify the moral law. Where all depends on right seeing, language and rhetoric have salvific power.

Emerson and the Cloud of Witnesses

If, again, Emerson did not attend Garrison's lectures, might he have discussed them after the fact with May or Alcott or both? It has long been held that Alcott's acquaintance with Emerson began no earlier than with his visit to Emerson's home in Concord in late November 1835. But he had heard Emerson preach years earlier, for the first time on September 28, 1828, and again on January 24, 1830, not, on either occasion, at the Second Church, but at the Federal Street Church where Emerson happened to be substituting for an ailing William Ellery Channing.[20] If these encounters seem accidental, still Alcott was sufficiently impressed with the young man's sermons to note the fact in his journal. Moreover, Emerson and Alcott had during this period a close mutual friend in George P. Bradford.[21] Later, but before his visit to Emerson's newly purchased home in Concord, Alcott was attending Emerson's Boston lectures, including one on Michelangelo on February 5, 1835.[22] Emerson was reading Pestalozzi in February 1834, probably at the urging of Alcott or Elizabeth Palmer Peabody, Emerson's erstwhile student and Alcott's assistant, beginning this year, at the Temple School.[23] In any event, it seems likely that some contact in Boston would have preceded an invitation to stay overnight out in the country.

If, having heard him preach, Alcott felt he knew Emerson's mind on the subject of Garrison and slavery—or for that matter on free speech and liberal positions generally—he might have suggested to his brother-in-law that even though the Boston churches remained closed to abolitionist speakers, Emerson's might yet be open. May was eager to establish himself as a public advocate of Garrison's principles and getting at least one clerical endorsement would be a crucial furtherance to his effort. He would presumably have had an interview with Emerson to get permission to speak from the Second Church pulpit. That permission was granted, and the discourse duly delivered on May 29, 1831, making Emerson's the first predominantly White church in Boston effectively to endorse Garrison's agenda.[24] The text of May's sermon was published, after some light revisions for a subsequent audience, as *Discourse on Slavery in the United States, Delivered in Brooklyn, [Connecticut,] July 3, 1831* (Boston: Garrison and Knapp, 1832). Even as revised, it closely followed Garrison's treatment, even to the order of topics and such details as the issue of "expediency," the problem of slavery in the District of Columbia, the alarming census figures, and the malignant plans of the Colonization Society. However the ceremony of May's sermon might have come off, clearly Emerson would not shrink from being a personal sponsor of such radicalism.

A Two-Paragraph Theoretical Conclusion

The argument for Garrison's early influence on Emerson rests on a number of suggestive hints in the documentary record but is otherwise conditioned by a dearth of direct evidence. Where does such a fact leave us? Surely it would be helpful if, during the relevant period, Emerson had expressed a judgment of Garrison's agenda, condemning or commending its spokesman by name, in a letter, say, to Alcott. But perhaps it is legitimate, because helpful, to infer a cause—a significant but hypothetical cause—when an array of effects points back to some sufficient origin. Perhaps that is an allowable function of interpretation (construing interpretation as an imputation of meaning) to show how different sequelae might be related, or how, as premised above, Garrison's influence may have ramified over time as it rolled through Emerson's successive purposes.

That last point is worth making because it is an interpretive gesture, after all, and not a mandatory conclusion, to suppose that Garrison's influence must create abolitionists or, in reaction, opponents of abolition. The tendency of much evidence is, of course, to narrow the possibilities, while the essential freedom of ambiguity requires the good offices of interpretation. Where conclusions are not forced by an abundance of evidence, one is not suddenly at a loss for helpful words but is compelled to judge the critical effort by the usefulness of the subject's emergent portrait. Here it is as if Emerson knew that Garrison's best traits, laid out most likely in the essay on "Heroism," served freedom before they served anything more particular. It was a remarkable and instructive decision on Emerson's part to have offered Elijah Lovejoy rather than Garrison as the one named American hero in that defining essay and then nowhere to have identified him as an abolitionist editor, martyred for his opposition to slavery in the proslavery community of Alton, Illinois. Instead, he identified Lovejoy, correctly enough, as one who "gave his breast to the bullets of a mob, for the rights of free speech and opinion, and died when it was better not to live" (*CW* 2: 155).

Notes

1. Garrison wrote these lectures while in jail and delivered them at various cities on his way home after his release, first at the Franklin Institute in Philadelphia, then for "small but respectable audiences" at Broadway Hall in New York, then again at "colored churches" in New Haven and Hartford. (On the composition and delivery of these lectures see Garrison and Garrison, 1: 202–09). Yale student Cassius Marcellus Clay heard Garrison in New Haven and was vividly confirmed in his antislavery views. Scion of a family of Kentucky slave-owners, Clay felt that Garrison's words, having presented him with "a new revelation," were like "water to a thirsty wayfarer" (Clay, 1: 55–56). In September, Garrison offered the series at the Amesbury

and Salisbury [Massachusetts] Lyceum, a performance that prompted the formation of two antislavery societies in the former town, one for men and one for women (Garrison and Garrison, 1: 208–09). J. G. Whittier and family, living in nearby Haverhill and attending the Amesbury Quaker meeting, had a hand in Garrison's speaking arrangements (Woodwell, 85). Clay and Whittier were predisposed toward antislavery positions, but for both Garrison's influence was decisive. The Boston lectures at Julien Hall were given in a space provided by the Universalist freethinker Abner Kneeland when the regular churches, including those of Garrison's native Newburyport, proved inhospitable. See Garrison, *Letters*, 1:111, and Mayer, 644.

2. There was a similar belatedness in the views of Emerson's brother Charles, who was quick to protest the injustice being done by Andrew Jackson's government to the Cherokee Nation in Georgia through a scheme that resembled the Colonization Society's projected expatriation of Blacks. No earlier than April 1835 did Charles declare himself an abolitionist. See Bosco and Myerson, 67, 174; Cole, 234; Charles C. Emerson, 12–30, and *L* 1: 316–17. Lecturing on slavery by Boston's Black abolitionists did not commence until John T. Hilton and Maria W. Stewart first spoke in 1828 and 1831, respectively.
3. "Mr. Garrison's Lectures on Slavery," *Christian Register*, October 23, 1830, 2. Unless otherwise stated, all quotations of Garrison are from this source, though the language may at certain points be that of the reporter's paraphrase. Mayer mentions that the Amesbury lectures were reported in the *Newburyport Herald* on September 28, 1830, from which, he says, "I have extrapolated the outline of the Boston talks" (644).
4. Quoted in Mayer, 129. The position that a just course of thought and action could be declined as inexpedient or rejected for selfish motives was consistently opposed by Emerson as a failure to honor the idea over material advantage, an act he characterized as "Selling so much manhood to buy so much luxury" (*JMN* 12: 158). He further observed that "There is a great deal of unbelief, of distrust in man's nature, of open apology for the wrong on the plea that it is expedient" (*JMN* 12: 154–55). The term seems also an allusion to William Paley's utilitarian doctrine of expediency from his immensely popular *Principles of Moral and Political Philosophy* (1785), which held that whatever is established by God will reflect a divine arrangement for

human happiness in general. Although this doctrine did not weaken Paley's own objection to slavery, it was denounced as pernicious by evangelicals like William Wilberforce. Of Whittier's *Justice and Expediency,* Arthur Tappan ordered 5000 copies to be bound in pamphlet form for distribution to Protestant ministers. In this work Whittier had no purpose beyond reproducing Garrison's arguments from the 1830 lectures, so it may be said to illustrate a type of simple influence, marked by a strict fidelity to its inspiration.

5. For Emerson's approval of the boycott, see his notes for a lost lecture on slavery delivered at Concord in November 1837 (*JMN* 12: 155, 157); this material was used again in the 1841 address "Man the Reformer" (*CW* 1: 147, 155).
6. This reparative argument is close to the position that Emerson finally adopted—belatedly, to be sure, but emphatically—in his "Boston Hymn" (1863): "Pay ransom to the owner, / And fill the bag to the brim. / Who is the owner? The slave is owner, / And ever was. Pay him" (*CW* 9: 383).
7. "Always the seer is the sayer" ("Divinity School Address," *CW* 1: 84). In late 1830 Emerson was on the cusp between careers in the pulpit or behind the lectern. The influence on him of Garrison's example, as might reasonably be inferred, favored the course Emerson finally took in 1833, the date of his first lecture, following his 1832 resignation from the Second Church and an interval of European travel, during which, incidentally, both he and Garrison attended the Westminster Abbey funeral of England's leading abolitionist, William Wilberforce.
8. Emerson's fear led him to exalt further the courage of the hero, which was the role he assigned to the Reformer (and implicitly to Garrison as Reformer) in his lecture on "Heroism," later published in his first collection of *Essays* (*CW* 2: 145–56). His engagement with the subjects of death and slavery during the last months of 1830 and of course beyond Ellen's passing on February 8, 1831, is discussed with sensitivity and historical acumen by Susan Roberson, 50–60, and Robert D. Richardson, 1–27. The relevance of this topical coincidence consists in the thematic interplay among, on the one hand, guilt, the bondage of sin, and death as punishment in traditional religious representations, and, on the other, the new light that antislavery rhetoric cast on the legal and moral significance of the bond/free polarity. The effect of this is, in turn, to construe emancipation and

conversion as mutually interpretive metaphors. An end in freedom is the meaning of each, and yet they differ diametrically as to the implied valuation of will. For the phrase "this sickening planet," see *L* 1: 313. In a lengthy journal passage on overcoming the fear of death, composed on November 3, 1830, Emerson asserts a nexus between this topic and slavery, observing that "the apostles, who never speak of death as dreadful, to whom to die was gain, . . . speak of those who thro' fear of death were all their lifetime subject to bondage" (*JMN* 3: 206).

9. Emerson is still developing this idea seven months later: "Not that man is the Abolisher of Slavery or Intemperance who calls them evils but he whose discerning eye separates between the existence of society & these evils & sees that these may peel off & perish & the institutions remain whole" (*JMN* 3: 272).

10. Were slavery sinful, as Garrison and others maintained, then voluntary emancipation would depend on the sinner's repentance. William E. Gienapp notes (29) that the early Boston abolitionist Amos A. Phelps (1805–47) "argued that immediatism was synonymous with immediate repentance. 'All that follows is the carrying out of the new principle of action, and is to emancipation just what sanctification is to conversion'" (29).

11. Quoted in Mumford, 141. It was a boost to whatever influence was going on that Garrison's speaking revealed a significant division by age between hostile establishment figures and a younger movement party: Garrison was 24 years old at the time of the lectures, May was 33, Alcott and Sewall both 31, and Emerson 27. Henry Ware, Jr., Emerson's erstwhile senior pastor at the Second Church, now on the faculty at the Harvard Divinity School and a persistent critic of Emerson, was 36; Lyman Beecher, a Presbyterian opponent of Unitarianism, was 55. They were prominent among Boston's clerical supporters of the Colonization Society, and both, of course, were appalled by Garrison's aggressiveness. See Garrison and Garrison, 1: 215, for Beecher's patronizing response to the young antislavery speaker, whom he met a few days after attending the first lecture: "'Your zeal,' he said . . . 'is commendable, but you are misguided. If you will give up your fanatical notions and be guided by us [i.e., the clergy], we will make you the Wilberforce of America.'" Indeed, the encounter seems to have been ironically modeled on the Temptation of Christ. See also Garrison and Garrison, 1: 217, for Ware's

censorship of May's first abolitionist sermon, delivered a week after Garrison's lectures. Here one sees that age and position, predictably, offer shelter against influence.

12. This organization, founded November 8 by agreement among Garrison, May, Alcott, and Sewall, was the immediate precursor to the more durable New England Anti-Slavery Society (NEASS), established early in 1832 by an augmented version of this group.
13. Mumford, 142. Italics in the original.
14. The last sentence alludes to John 16: 33, the wording of which would eventually be embodied in the twentieth-century reform slogan, "We shall overcome." Its original context in John undergirds Emerson's gnostic anti-cosmic tendency and offers a view—Emerson's view—of Jesus as a Transcendentalist reform hero.
15. That Emerson did not follow Garrison, May, and Alcott into antislavery activism seems owing in part to his fascination with language as the essential vehicle of communicable truth: Garrison's persuasive power was rhetorical, a fact that would have appealed to Emerson's long-standing interest in classical and modern oratory. But the point to be made is that Garrison's bold reordering of what matters, of what ought to occupy people's attention, is a move away from the temptations of the great world—the world that was to be overcome—and toward a deeper consideration of the status of the humble, the oppressed, and the overlooked. This is not different from the concurrent revolution in Emerson's poetics, provoked, as I have argued elsewhere, by the poetry of Ellen Tucker Emerson. See Carl F. Strauch, 353–77, and "The Ellen Poems, 1828–31," in von Frank, ed., *Ralph Waldo Emerson: The Major Poems,* xiii–xiv and 243–60.
16. The poet Claudia Rankine has pioneered in the study of the racial imaginary, though as yet the concept has not been accorded much historical depth. See Rankine and Loffreda.
17. For discussions of the essay, see Whicher, 65–70, 136–38, and von Frank, "*Essays First Series* (1841)," 114–16.
18. Cf. Ephesians 6: 17 and Hebrews 4: 12. Partly under the contemporaneous influence of Coleridge, Emerson here moves in the direction of the Transcendental persona of *Nature*. The emphasis on the "beginning of wisdom" suggests a quasi-gnostic influence as well, the significance of which is developed in von Frank, "Emerson and Gnosticism," 289–314. Interestingly, Thoreau would make the

same point in similar Pauline imagery: "If you stand right fronting and face to face to a fact, you will see the sun glimmer on both its surfaces, as if it were a cimeter, and feel its sweet edge dividing you through the heart and marrow, and so you will happily conclude your mortal career" (*Walden*, 98). Thoreau's final clause, like Emerson's language in the passage quoted, points up the connection of these concerns to the potent theme of the fear of death.

19. Harmodius and Aristogeiton, heroes of the Athenian democracy, assassinated the tyrant Hipparchus in 514 BCE; they were specifically venerated as "Liberators." Leonidas led the defense of Greece against the Persian king Xerxes. Along with Cassius, Brutus led the conspiracy resulting in the assassination of Julius Caesar in 44 BCE; this pair were likewise popularly known as "Liberators." Algernon Sidney wrote his influential *Discourses Concerning Government*, in part, to oppose the divine right of kings. Garrison may well have felt that such defenders of a "right to personal liberty" were, as "Liberators," a standing endorsement of antislavery work as the vindication of a democratic polity. This list of heroes, of course, is Emerson's, not Garrison's, but the language (especially in the second paragraph) renews what was earlier said about the "clearness" of the reformer's moral vision. The implication is that this was Emerson's plausible context for what thinking he likely did about Garrison and his novel pro-liberty movement.
20. Alcott, 12, 23; von Frank, *An Emerson Chronology*, 1: 46, 70.
21. Mathews, 133–56, esp. 143.
22. Alcott, 56.
23. von Frank, *An Emerson Chronology*, 1: 156.
24. This informal distinction was reenforced on the evening of December 16, 1832, when Arnold Buffum, a Rhode Island Quaker and current president of the New England Anti-Slavery Society, lectured at Emerson's Second Church. Both May's sermon and Buffum's address were announced beforehand in the *Liberator*.

Works Cited

Bosco, Ronald A., and Joel Myerson, *The Emerson Brothers: A Fraternal Biography in Letters*. Oxford UP, 2006.

Clay, Cassius Marcellus. *Memoirs, Writings, and Speeches*, 2 vols. Ohio: J. Fletcher Brennan, 1886.

Cole, Phyllis. *Mary Moody Emerson and the Origins of Transcendentalism*. Oxford UP, 1998.

Emerson, Charles C. "Lecture on Slavery, [1835]." *Emerson Society Quarterly*, vol. 16, 1959, pp. 12–30.

Emerson, Ralph Waldo. [*CS*] *Complete Sermons of Ralph Waldo Emerson*. Albert J. von Frank et al. eds. 4 vols. Columbia, Mo.: University of Missouri Press, 1989-1992.

__________. [*CW*] *Collected Works of Ralph Waldo Emerson*. Alfred R. Ferguson, Ronald A. Bosco, et al. eds. 10 vols. Cambridge, Mass.: Belknap Press of Harvard University Press, 1971-2013.

__________. [*EL*] *Early Lectures of Ralph Waldo Emerson*. Stephen E. Whicher et al., eds. 3 vols. Cambridge, Mass.: Belknap Press of Harvard University Press, 1971-1972.

__________. [*JMN*] *Journals and Miscellaneous Notebooks of Ralph Waldo Emerson*. William H. Gilman et al., eds. 16 vols. Cambridge, Mass., Belknap Press of Harvard University Press, 1960-1982.

__________. [*L*] *Letters of Ralph Waldo Emerson*. Ralph L. Rusk and Eleanor M. Tilton, eds. 10 vols. New York: Columbia University Press, 1939-1999.

Garrison, Wendell Phillips, and Francis Jackson Garrison. *William Lloyd Garrison, 1805–1879*, 4 vols. Boston, MA: Houghton Mifflin, 1894.

Garrison, William Lloyd. *The Letters of William Lloyd Garrison*, 5 vols. Edited by Walter M. Merrill, Harvard UP, 1971.

Gienapp, William E. "Abolitionism and the Nature of Antebellum Reform." *Courage and Conscience: Black and White Abolitionists in Boston*. Edited by Donald M. Jacobs, Indiana UP for the Boston Athenaeum, 1993, pp. 21–46.

The King James Bible Online, (Revelation 3.18), www.kingjamesbibleonline.org/Revelation-3-18/.

Mathews, James W. "George Partridge Bradford: Friend of Transcendentalists." *Studies in the American Renaissance*. Edited by Joel Myerson, Twayne, 1981, pp. 133–56.

Mayer, Henry. *All on Fire: William Lloyd Garrison and the Abolition of Slavery*. St. Martin's Press, 1998.

"Mr. Garrison's Lectures on Slavery." *Christian Register,* 23 Oct. 1830, p. 2.

Mumford, Thomas J. *Memoir of Samuel Joseph May*. Roberts Brothers, 1874.

Rankine, Claudia, and Beth Loffreda, editors. *The Racial Imaginary: Writers on Race in the Life of the Mind.* Fence Books, 2015.

Richardson, Robert D. *Three Roads Back: How Emerson, Thoreau, and William James Responded to the Greatest Losses of Their Lives*. Princeton UP, 2023.

Roberson, Susan. *Emerson in His Sermons: A Man-Made Self.* U of Missouri P, 1995.

Strauch, Carl F. "The Year of Emerson's Poetic Maturity: 1834." *Philological Quarterly*, vol. 34, October 1955, pp. 353–77.

Thoreau, Henry David. *Walden: 150th Anniversary Edition*. Edited by J. Lyndon Shanley, Princeton UP, 2004.

von Frank, Albert J. "*Essays First Series* (1841)." *The Cambridge Companion to Ralph Waldo Emerson*. Edited by Joel Porte and Saundra Morris, Cambridge UP, 1999, pp. 106–20.

__________. "Emerson and Gnosticism." *Emerson: Bicentennial Essays*. Edited by Ronald A. Bosco and Joel Myerson, Massachusetts Historical Society, 2006, pp. 289–314.

__________, ed. *Ralph Waldo Emerson: The Major Poems*. Harvard UP, 2015.

__________. *An Emerson Chronology*, 2 vols. Studio Non Troppo, 2016.

Whicher, Stephen E. *Freedom and Fate: An Inner Life of Ralph Waldo Emerson*. U of Pennsylvania P, 1953.

Whittier, John G. *Justice and Expediency; Or, Slavery Considered with a View to Its Rightful and Effectual Remedy, Abolition*. Haverhill, MA: C. P. Thayer, 1833.

Woodwell, Roland H. *John Greenleaf Whittier: A Biography*. Trustees of the John Greenleaf Whittier Homestead, 1985.

"My thunderbolt has eyes to see": The Civil War, Nationalism, and Manifest Destiny in Emerson and Timrod

Benjamin Crawford

In 1845, an article on the annexation of Texas appeared in *The United States Magazine and Democratic Review* where John O'Sullivan famously discussed "the fulfillment of our manifest destiny to overspread the continent allotted by Providence for the free development of our yearly multiplying millions" (Annexation 5). As Norman Graebner observed: "Manifest destiny conveyed a vision of greatness in all aspects of American life, from the immensity of the nation's territory open for exploration and extension, to its internal development and the quality of its government and civilization" (3). Manifest destiny is an expression of national identity that, coupled with the belief in providential blessing, promotes territorial and cultural expansion. This complicated idea not only motivated much of western expansion in American history, but also had harmful effects on Native Americans. With the advent of the Civil War, the national identity of the United States was torn apart; that the United States were no longer united challenged American nationalism as part of the country established its own separate national identity. Henry Timrod's poem "Ethnogenesis" is one of the most important examples of the Southern desire for a separate national identity during the Civil War, whereas Ralph Waldo Emerson's "Boston Hymn" reflects a dueling Northern sense of nationalism. Both Timrod and Emerson used their poetry to construct opposing perspectives on nationalism and manifest destiny during the Civil War, and each poet offered a unique, yet similar, vision for their respective countries.

Ralph Waldo Emerson's "Boston Hymn"

In the North, national identity was disrupted with the secession of the Southern states, while the abolitionist movement served as a genesis of the move for racial equality. Poets in the North expressed a new sense of nationalism in spite of the challenges of the war, and a great example is Emerson's "Boston Hymn." Composed in 1863 to celebrate the Emancipation Proclamation, "Boston Hymn" praises not only the importance of governmental manumission, but also promotes Northern identity as antithetical to the Southern national identity that Henry Timrod created in "Ethnogenesis." It is very possible that Emerson may have read "Ethnogenesis" in print: after first appearing in a South Carolina newspaper in February 1861, Timrod's poem appeared in the March 30, 1861, issue of the Boston newspaper *Littell's Living Age*. This is significant not only because the paper was published in Boston, near Emerson's home in Concord, but also because two years later, *Littell's Living Age* also republished Emerson's "Boston Hymn" in its February 21, 1863, issue, the poem having originally been published in the February 1863 issue of *The Atlantic Monthly*. At the very least, Timrod's vision of Confederate national identity was present in Northern literary circles, albeit not a popular presence among abolitionists. Although there is no evidence that Emerson read "Ethnogenesis," he was familiar with Timrod's poetry. In an 1873 letter to Paul Hamilton Hayne, John Greenleaf Whittier commented that "[i]n the year '63 I surprised my friends Emerson, Whipple & Holmes by my enthusiastic praise of one or two of [Timrod's] poems which I had seen" (Hubbell 117–18). This implies that during the Civil War, Emerson was familiar with Timrod's poetry enough to dislike the Southern propagandistic sentiments that Timrod expressed, evidenced by Emerson's "surprise."

Interesting parallels between "Ethnogenesis" and "Boston Hymn" suggest that Emerson may be responding to Timrod's depiction of Southern nationalism in the latter poem. "Boston Hymn" can be taken as a rebuttal of "Ethnogenesis" because Emerson offers a perspective on Northern nationalism that counters Timrod's Southern nationalism by suggesting that freedom in America is divinely established, manifest destiny is unavoidable, and that American society should enact justice for enslaved people. The "Boston Hymn" is presented as the voice of God speaking to the

Pilgrims: "The word of the Lord by night / To the watching Pilgrims came" (1–2). By positioning God as the narrator, Emerson implies that the very origin of the United States is divinely directed, and, therefore, divinely blessed. To rebel against the United States is not simply to rebel against the government, but rather to rebel against an institution ordained, according to Emerson's implications, by God. Including divine involvement in the history of America strengthens Northern nationalism by assuring the reader that God is on the North's side. The title "Boston Hymn" imbues a sense of spirituality to the poem. By styling the poem as a hymn, Emerson implies that the freeing of slaves is not simply a positive step toward the complete abolition of slavery, it is also a divinely sanctioned event and, therefore, worthy of a celebratory hymn. Because God is the narrator, the entire poem is filled with religious imagery, from the "word of the Lord" (1) to God's angel whose "name is Freedom" (13). The incorporation of religious imagery strengthens the rhetorical effect of the poem as Emerson begins by imagining God speaking to the Pilgrims, establishing the role of "[m]y angel . . . Freedom" (13) in the New World, a Freedom that will be "your king" (14). Naming the angel "Freedom" harkens not only to the Emancipation Proclamation's legal freeing of millions of African Americans from slavery, but also to the Revolutionary War, a war to which Timrod also referred. Emerson asks the reader if God intended the world to be a place "[w]here tyrants great and tyrants small / Might harry the weak and poor?" (11–12). While Timrod expresses a belief that the South will help the world's poor, Emerson recognizes that it is the power structure of slavery that creates poverty and oppression. While "tyrants great" may refer to political leaders, "tyrants small" could refer to slave owners, for whom the very act of owning slaves constituted tyranny.

In the fourth and fifth stanzas of "Boston Hymn," Emerson expresses a desire for American territorial expansion through the cultural doctrine of manifest destiny. The voice of God narrates the unfolding of the American nation as Emerson signals that it must be God's will for America to expand its territory, ironically criticizing slavery but ignoring the effects of westward expansion on Native

Americans who owned these unincorporated lands. God remarks that the angel Freedom will "cut pathways east and west" (15) and that God will provide America with land " . . . in the West, / As the sculptor uncovers the statue / When he has wrought his best" (18–20). In this context America is the statue and God is the sculptor who makes America into an expression of divine will. God will also provide protection for the country, because the angel will "fend you with his wing" (16), a reassurance about the outcome of the war that was uncertain at the time of the initial reading of the poem in 1863. In these lines Emerson leaves no room for national humility, for that has already been brought on the country by the sin of slavery. By implying the role of God in the formation of America, and in the continued westward expansion of the country, Emerson imagines that there is a divine purpose for the nation despite the temporary loss of the Southern states. These lines sharply contrast with Timrod's assertion that the Confederacy will one day include "lands from sea to sea" ("Ethnogenesis" 93). Emerson's vision of America ignores the formation of the Confederacy and supposes that those states will, one way or another, be reunited to the rest of the country. Both poets include images of an expansive country because they understood manifest destiny as relevant to their respective countries.

"Boston Hymn" imagines a country where those who labor are the ones who prosper economically, which disallows any possibility for the presumed divine legitimacy of slavery that was popular in the South. The Divine narrator instructs readers to "[c]all in the wretch and slave: / None shall rule but the humble, / And none but Toil shall have" (26–28), implying an economy where people are responsible for their own success and not reliant on slavery; those who have profited from enslaving others will now have to work for themselves. More importantly, Emerson directs these lines not just to slaves, but also to socially marginalized non-slaves. That those who rule will be humble implies that they will not be the tyrants, big and small, mentioned earlier in the poem (line 11). Emerson envisions an equitable democracy that is a distinct contrast to the economically imperialistic vision that Timrod provides under the guise of humanitarian motives (see "Ethnogenesis" 97–98).

Emerson goes on to assert that God "will have never a noble, / No lineage counted great" (29–30), a direct contrast to the social structure of the South, where wealth and parochial political power were often concentrated in select slave-owning families. The nation that Emerson envisions will not have nobles in political power as the antebellum South essentially had with its planter class, but rather "[f]ishers and choppers and plowmen / Shall constitute a state" (31–32). Reflecting Emerson's ideal for the United States of America, this vision includes equal economic opportunity alongside racial equality. Emerson's vision was an idealistic but necessary response to the Southern sense of nationalism that promoted a slavery-based society.

The ninth stanza of "Boston Hymn" focuses on the natural environment. God commands his listeners to "[c]ut down trees in the forest, / And build me a wooden house" (35–36). Emerson sees the natural resources of the country as being consumable and intended for use, more specifically to benefit the establishment of a democratic government. Although national identity includes geographical regions, the more important aspect of a nation is stated in the latter line. God commands that a "wooden house" (36) be built for him. This may be a temple or church, places often referred to as a "house of God." The building that is to be God's house is similar to, if not the same, as the building that will serve as a meeting place for people so that "[t]hey shall choose men to rule" (42). Although it is unclear whether these two places, the house of God (36) and the "pine state-house" (41), are the same building, Emerson equates two places that are respectively sacred and secular. By making the buildings similar, or the same, Emerson draws a comparison between them, that the political meeting house is as important as the house of God. That both buildings are mentioned by God strengthens the idea of divine involvement in the political establishment of the United States.

God then calls together, "[t]he young men and the sires, / The digger in the harvest-field, / Hireling, and him that hires" (38–40). In this grouping of people there are no distinctions based on race or social class. They should come together and vote on who should rule different aspects of their society, "[i]n church, and state, and school" (44). For Emerson there should be no difference in the way these social institutions are run. Democracy should apply in both the church house and the "pine state-house" (41). This continues the conflation of nationalism with religion that Emerson weaves throughout "Boston Hymn." The effect of this conflation includes the strengthening of nationalism by including a sense of divine involvement and blessing on the nation, thereby, in a sense, legitimizing the actions of the United States in fighting the rebellious South and ending slavery, while expanding into the West. Emerson imagines God directing the establishment of democracy where all people come together, and where the "[h]ireling, and him that hires" (40) are equal as the Divine narrator expresses interest in the ability of "these poor men" (45) to "make just laws below the sun" (47). This line contrasts with Timrod's assertion that the North would make "laws to stay the laws of Heaven!" ("Ethnogenesis" 74), a line in which Timrod implies that the North will not enact laws that reflect the will of God. Here Emerson counters Timrod's supposition by asserting that the North will indeed "govern the land and sea, / And make just laws below the sun" (46–47). Not only will the laws of the North be just, the laws will "[a]s planets faithful be" (48). Emerson uses this image from nature to imply that the laws of the North will be based on something greater than people's ideas, including Timrod's ideas. The North's laws will come from the heavens, and those laws will be faithful to nature and God's will.

Emerson, speaking through God, continues constructing a sense of Northern nationalism by imbuing the purpose of the country with a sense of moral destiny: "And ye shall succor men; / . . . / Help them who cannot help again" (49–51). When Emerson positions the United States as a country that will help people, he uses this passage to counter Timrod's vision of Southern nationalism. Timrod states that the Confederacy will help "distant peoples" ("Ethnogenesis" 95), and he, too, posits this as the result of divine will ("Ethnogenesis" 101). In "Boston Hymn" there is a connection between "just laws" ("Boston Hymn" 47) and the ability to "[h]elp them who cannot help again" (51). The progression of "Boston Hymn" positions the idea of "just laws" (47) before the ability of the country to help others, a connection that Timrod fails to make in "Ethnogenesis."

Emerson preemptively positions "Boston Hymn" as a poem addressed to the Puritans. By positioning this poem in the historical context of colonial America, Emerson places God's voice prior to the formation of the Confederacy and the claims of Southern nationalism that Timrod makes in "Ethnogenesis." The historical position of "Boston Hymn" also precludes any legitimacy to a secondary government that might incorporate ideas antithetical to those expressed in "Boston Hymn," including slavery. God's warning, "[b] eware from right to swerve" (52), suggests that the country would have the opportunity to stray from the path ordained for it, namely by embracing slavery. God's instructions to the Puritans include manumission as an expression of divine disapproval of slavery (lines 53–68), a marked contrast to Southerners who insisted that slavery was divinely sanctioned. Starting in line 53 God denounces slavery, an issue on which Timrod is silent. God states that, "I break your bonds and masterships, / And I unchain the slave" (53–54). Emerson does two things with these lines. First, he proposes that slavery was never God's will for humanity; and second, Emerson implies that regardless of the laws and proclamations that a government makes, slavery is inherently immoral regardless of its legal status. The description of freed slaves then invokes natural imagery: "[f] ree be his heart and hand henceforth / As wind and wandering wave" (55–56). Although Timrod envisions the wind coming to the South's defense and the ocean's currents being a source of Southern success in international trade ("Ethnogenesis" 52–53 and 104–09, respectively), Emerson appropriates these images as metaphors for freedom. Not only is Freedom a divine institution, but it is also a natural one as Emerson's imagery suggests that freedom is the natural state of existence for human beings.

Emerson then discusses the morally debilitating effects of slavery. Despite Timrod's silence on the issue, Emerson addresses slavery in a straightforward manner. The narrator of "Boston Hymn" contrasts the ideal state of freedom with the reality of slavery, which includes "laying hands on another / To coin his labor and sweat"

(61–62) and follows God's statement that he will "cause from every creature / His proper good to flow" (57–58). By enslaving others, Emerson and God write, the enslaver "goes in pawn to his victim / For eternal years in debt" (63–64). The implication is that those who enslave others owe their victims a debt that can never be paid. However, in the next stanza Emerson suggests financial reparations for slaves, specifically that temporal remuneration is just as important as repenting for the immorality of slavery. Though slaves were viewed as property by their owners, Emerson validated the humanity of enslaved African Americans in some of the most powerful lines of the poem: "Who is the owner? The slave is owner, / And ever was. Pay him" (71–72). By including these instructions for financial reparation to the newly liberated slaves, Emerson suggests a course in public policy for the future.

Suggesting that the South is not exclusively responsible for slavery, Emerson writes, "O North! give him beauty for rags, / And honor, O South! for his shame" (73–74). Though the South should provide "honor" where it has given shame, the North also plays a role in correcting the immorality of slavery, for the slaves it historically allowed within its own borders and for allowing slavery in the South. Emerson looks forward to when the Civil War will end and both parts of the country will, as the United States, enfranchise African Americans as citizens of a country whose economic prosperity they helped create. In lines 77–80, Emerson reiterates the organic nature of freedom, and the natural right that all people have to be under the angel of Freedom. Invoking religious imagery, Emerson states that slavery is a "darkness" (78) in which slaves have been held. Coming out of slavery, then, is a type of salvation that includes coming into the light of Freedom.

Speaking to the land, Emerson and God invoke geographical sections of the country: "Come, East and West and North, / By races, as snow-flakes, / And carry my purpose forth" (81–83). What is most conspicuous in this divine invocation is the absence of the South, which may not have been included because of its rebellion at the time of the composition of "Boston Hymn." Emerson also seems to parody Timrod's reference to "[w]hole leagues of Russian ice and

Artic storm!" ("Ethnogenesis" 29) with the inclusion of "snowflakes" (82) that administer God's will rather than protect the South. Emerson concludes "Boston Hymn" by using imagery from nature, as God goes on to assert that "My will fulfilled shall be" (85) since day or night "My thunderbolt has eyes to see / His way home to the mark" (87–88). Not only is this an assurance that God's will shall be fulfilled, but it also strengthens Emerson's use of natural imagery and the sense of divine involvement in the country.

Henry Timrod's "Ethnogenesis"

When the Southern states seceded from the Union, American national identity underwent a significant shift as the Confederate States formed their own national identity. Meanwhile the Northern states sought to process the loss of the Southern states and to understand what the potential of westward expansion meant for the United States. Discussing antebellum American nationalism, Anders Stephanson comments that "[t]he South . . . began to think of itself as a protonational grouping for which the real meaning of the Union was the liberty for individual states to carry on as they always had, a liberty conceived . . . to include the right to secede" (30). This resulted from "the emergence of sectionalism" (Stephanson 29) in antebellum America, a sectionalism that was centered on a slavery-based economy. As the Confederate States of America became a political entity, an idea of Southern national identity began to take shape that would encompass the Confederacy. One of the elements that helped to consolidate this newly formed national identity was literature, specifically poetry. Timrod utilized his poems to contribute to a Southern national identity that gave a sense of character that was separate from the United States, implied a divine blessing on the Confederacy, and that marginalized the role of slavery in Southern culture. The idea of providential blessing on the Confederacy also helped to grow a Southern sense of manifest destiny that existed prior to the Civil War as a desire to expand Southern influence to the south of the country, primarily to expand the sphere of American slavery (May).

Perhaps no poem better illustrates Southern nationalism than Timrod's "Ethnogenesis." Originally entitled "Ode on Occasion of the Meeting of the Southern Congress," it was first published in the February 23, 1861, issue of the *Charleston Daily Courier*. The poem later appeared with the title "Ethnogenesis" in the January 31, 1862, issue of the *Charleston Daily Courier*, with changes from its original publication in 1861. "Ethnogenesis" also appeared in the postbellum anthology *War Poetry of the South*, published in 1867. According to the epigraph of the poem, it was composed "during the meeting of the first Southern Congress" ("Ethnogenesis") in Alabama in 1861. The positioning of this historical notation under the title strengthens the role of "Ethnogenesis" as an expression of an incipient national identity.

The poem's title is concerned with the political origin of a people. The title of the poem, "Ethnogenesis," implies the formation of a new group identity (the Confederate States of America). By titling the poem this, Timrod also implies the beginning of a new race (*ethno*) of people as well, namely of Southern Whites whose wealth was built on Black slavery. Timrod expresses a sense of national identity throughout "Ethnogenesis" and in lines 1–4, Timrod asks if there will be "another star" (2) in the sky at the formation of the rising Confederate States of America, implying an analogy between the new country and the birth of Christ in an echo of Matthew 2 where the birth of Christ is correlated to a new star appearing. As Abraham Lincoln astutely noted during his second inaugural address, the North and South "[b]oth read the same Bible, and pray to the same God; and each invokes His aid against the other" (734). Speaking of Civil War literary culture and echoing Lincoln, Alice Fahs observes that "Southern poets were equally as confident as their Union counterparts that God was on their side" (79). A primary theme of the first part of "Ethnogenesis" is divine influence and favor for the Confederacy: Timrod writes, "under God, whose thunder need we fear?" (9), echoing Romans 8:31. Insistent that God played a role in establishing the new country, Timrod states that God is the one "who placed us here" (10) as an invocation of manifest destiny. Timrod then remarks that the Confederate flag will appear in “many a distant port” (6), suggesting that the Confederacy will expand its influence over the entire world. The presence of the Confederate flag in “distant port[s]” (6) implies the establishment of embassies that symbolize a strong international presence, and at the very least, an international recognition that the Confederacy sought but never received.

Lines 17–24 of “Ethnogenesis” then suggest a future filled with successful crops of wheat and cotton. To emphasize the importance of cotton, grown with the use of slavery, Timrod capitalizes his description of cotton as the “SNOW OF SOUTHERN SUMMERS!” (24) which will make the South a “happy land” (26). Timrod also suggests that the prosperity brought by cotton will allow the South to rest, the “land shall sleep” (26), as if it were “intrenched behind / Whole leagues of Russian ice and Artic storm!” (28–29). The image of the South being “intrenched” (28) carries military connotations that reveal an expectation of eventual war, but also implies a sense of divinely provided security. The image of the country resting while being surrounded by snow implies a sense of protection by nature, a theme explored elsewhere in “Ethnogenesis” and foreshadowing Emerson’s use of natural imagery in “Boston Hymn.” By imagining that the Confederacy will be divinely blessed, economically affluent, and internationally recognized, Timrod attempts to create a distinct sense of national identity in “Ethnogenesis” that ignores the role of slavery in the antebellum economic success of the South.

Timrod equates the South’s rebellion with the American Revolution when he asks if “the mighty ghosts / Of Moultrie and of Eutaw. . . / Auxiliars such as these?” (41–43) will help the South, to which he answers affirmatively (lines 43–45). Edd and Aileen Parks, in a note on “Ethnogenesis,” remark that the former battle “seems to have symbolized for Timrod the ability of the Confederacy to withstand the Federal navy. The battle of Eutaw Springs . . . symbolized a successful resistance on land” (181). Timrod’s connection of the South with the American Revolution implies that the same self-ascribed legitimacy that the colonies possessed in rebelling against Britain is relevant to the South. This is important to note because it furthers the South’s singular belief in its right to become a separate country from the United States. At the same time, it connects the Confederacy with its antebellum heritage and thereby provides the Confederacy with a sense of its own history. Through motivating a sense of national pride and identity, and by describing the North in denigrating terms, Timrod imagines a historical precedence for the Civil War.

The last lines of section 3 invoke the Biblical story of Israel leaving Egypt (see Exodus 13:17–15:21), with Timrod writing that the South "must pass a redder sea" (83), but only if God "has decreed" (82). Assuming the future will be the result of God's appointment rather than the product of social forces, Timrod also assumes that God "[w]ill surely raise at need / A Moses with his rod!" (85–86) to lead the Confederacy into its self-perceived divinely ordained future. Ironically Timrod implies that the South, the center of slavery in America, would leave the political slavery of the North in its secession. The use of this specific biblical reference serves three purposes in "Ethnogenesis." First, the passage reinforces the poem's implication that the South has divine blessing and guidance, which affirms Timrod's audience's pro-slavery worldview. Second, by implying that the South was a modern type of Israel leaving Egypt, Timrod provides a basis for a common national identity, one that would unite Southerners under the political identity of the Confederate States of America. Third, Timrod implies that the Confederacy is establishing a Promised Land, the destination of Israel after leaving Egypt. In Timrod's poem, the South is no longer a part of the United States, but rather a rising new nation with a separate national identity that is being led by God.

The final section of "Ethnogenesis" envisions the future of the Confederate States of America as Timrod urges his readers to look forward to "the glories which a hundred years / Shall bring us" (92–93). This includes a Southern manifest destiny that will cause the South to range from "sea to sea" (93), presumably still using slavery to drive a cotton-based economy. The country, Timrod writes, will have "wealth, and power, and peace" (94); in addition, Timrod states that the Confederacy will draw satisfaction from "the distant peoples we shall bless, / And the hushed murmurs of a world's distress" (95–96). Despite never directly addressing slavery in "Ethnogenesis," Timrod intimates that the Confederacy will provide "labor to the poor" (97). This will happen, Timrod declares, through divine blessing; according to the poet, "God makes us great and rich!" (101). The final lines of "Ethnogenesis" continue the earlier use of natural imagery, with Timrod admitting that his poetic vision for a Confederate national identity may not be recognized by some people: "The hour perchance is not yet wholly ripe / When all shall own it" (102–03). He then insists that it is through oceanic roads that the Confederacy will gain international recognition, beckoning back to the first section where he wrote of the Southern flag being seen in "many a distant port" (6). By ending "Ethnogenesis" with natural imagery, Timrod implies an organic sense of nationalism because it is through the ocean's currents that Confederate merchants and ambassadors will expand the influence of the South.

Timrod envisions the future nation's economic success, built on the backs of slaves, though never directly addressing slavery. The absence of slavery in "Ethnogenesis" is striking given the importance of the institution to the antebellum Southern economy. As Timrod biographer Walter Cisco observes on Southern beliefs about slavery, "slavery had existed since antiquity . . . and had supported American economic life since colonial times" (48). Cisco's statement applies to the absence of slavery in "Ethnogenesis," where slavery is an unspoken constant in a newly formed nation that, according to Timrod, is and will be divinely blessed and prosperous. By avoiding the topic of slavery, Timrod ignores the immorality of slavery because of his unspoken historical assumption of its morality. Though slavery was a central facet of antebellum Southern culture, by ignoring it and focusing on the assumption of divine blessing for the South, Timrod reinforces the assumptions about slavery that Cisco mentioned. As Mark Twain remarked, Southern attitudes about slavery were that it was "right, righteous, sacred" (49). By ignoring slavery, Timrod strengthened his development of a Southern national identity by satisfying his reader's proslavery beliefs that found political reality in the newly formed Confederate States of America.

Conclusion

In conclusion, both Emerson and Timrod engaged in expressions of nationalism that were reactions to the events of the Civil War. Timrod's "Ethnogenesis" depicts a liminal stage of nationalism in the Confederate States that assumed a national identity distinct from the United States, presumed the presence of divine blessing, and ignored the role of slavery in Southern society. Emerson's "Boston Hymn" expresses a vision of a classless, slave-less society under divine direction that possesses opportunities to expand into the American West. After the war, the sense of national identity in the United States remained divided, with Southerner's referring to the war as "a lost cause," while the North sought to reincorporate Southern states into the country through Reconstruction. Emerson's postbellum inclusion of Timrod's "Ode," a poem addressed to the Confederate dead, in the 1875 anthology *Parnassus*, edited by Emerson, demonstrated that the country was moving slowly towards reconciliation. This reconciliation began by recognizing the loss of life, as well as taking steps to give full rights to African Americans, albeit inadequate steps at the time. Emerson's depiction of the United States in "Boston Hymn" reflects an optimistic vision of the United States going forward.

Works Cited

Cisco, Walter Brian. *Henry Timrod A Biography*. Fairleigh Dickinson UP, 2004.

Emerson, Ralph Waldo. "Boston Hymn." *Poems: A Variorum Edition*. The Belknap Press of Harvard UP, 2011.

__________. "Boston Hymn." *The Atlantic Monthly*, Feb. 1863, pp. 227–28.

__________. "Boston Hymn." *Littell's Living Age*, 21 Feb. 1863, p. 338.

Fahs, Alice. *The Imagined Civil War: Popular Literature of the North & South, 1861–1865*. UNC Press, 2001.

Full Verse Cross Reference Bible. New Living Translation. Tyndale House Publishers, 1996.

Graebner, Norman A., editor. *Manifest Destiny*. Bobbs-Merrill, 1968.

Hubbell, Jay, editor. *The Last Years of Henry Timrod 1865–1867*. Duke UP, 1941.

Lincoln, Abraham. "Second Inaugural Address." *American Speeches Political Oratory from the Revolution to the Civil War*. Edited by Ted Widmer, Library of America, 2006.

May, Robert. *The Southern Dream of a Caribbean Empire, 1854–1861*. LSU P, 1973.

O'Sullivan, John, editor. "Annexation." *The United States Magazine, and Democratic Review (1837–1851)*. J & H. G. Langly, 1 July 1845, *American Periodicals Series Online*, ProQuest.

Parks, Edd Winfield, and Aileen Wells Parks, editors. *The Collected Poems of Henry Timrod: A Variorum Edition*. Athens: U of Georgia P, 1965.

Stephanson, Anders. *Manifest Destiny: American Expansionism and the Empire of Right*. Hill and Wang, 1995.

Timrod, Henry. "Ethnogenesis." *Charleston Daily Courier*, 31 Jan. 1862, p. 4.

__________. "Ethnogenesis." *The Collected Poems of Henry Timrod: A Variorum Edition*. Edited by Edd Winfield Parks and Aileen Parks, U of Georgia P, 2007.

__________. "Ethnogenesis." *War Poetry of the South*. Edited by William Gilmore Simms. New York: Richardson and Company, 1867.

__________. "Ode on Occasion of the Meeting of the Southern Congress." *Charleston Daily Courier*, 23 Feb. 1861 p. 4.

__________. "Ode on Occasion of the Meeting of the Southern Congress." *Littell's Living Age*, 30 Mar. 1861, p. 824.

__________. "Ode." *Parnassus*. Edited by Ralph Waldo Emerson, Boston: James R. Osgood, 1875, p. 258.

Twain, Mark. "Jane Lampton Clemens." *Hannibal, Huck & Tom*. Edited by Walter Blair, U of California P, 1969.

The Multiplicity of Merlin: Emerson's Merlin Poems

Dalicia K. Raymond

Enchanted by Merlin

In the summer of 1848, Ralph Waldo Emerson visited Stonehenge with his friend Thomas Carlyle as part of his English travels. Conversations between Emerson and Carlyle dwelt on English national origins, and as they visited Stonehenge, they allowed themselves to be swept up in the grandiose history and myth this monument holds. Recording his experiences in a journal entry, Emerson recounts gazing upon Stonehenge and pondering theories of its presence, including Merlin's legendary role in magically bringing Stonehenge to England. Emerson questions, "Was this the 'Giants' Dance' which Merlin brought from Killaraus, in Ireland, to be Uther Pendragon's monument to the British nobles whom Hengist slaughtered here, as Geoffrey of Monmouth relates? or was it a Roman work, as Inigo Jones explained to King James; or identical in design and style with the East Indian temples of the sun, as Davies in the Celtic Researches maintains?" ("Stonehenge" 386–87). This consideration reveals Emerson's interest in the monument and his knowledge of Merlin's medieval origins and mythology. Geoffrey of Monmouth, to whom Emerson refers here, is a twelfth century early English author who wrote extensively of Arthurian legends. His work was often the foundation upon which later medieval, and some postmedieval, authors built when writing on Arthur or Merlin. Although Emerson settles on another theory as the most probable for Stonehenge's origins, his consideration of Merlin's contribution to this iconic site of English identity offers a glance into his longer-lived curiosity about Merlin.

In the mid-1840s, Emerson writes the "Merlin (I)" and "Merlin (II)" poems, which allude to Merlin as a bard while Emerson dwells on poetic structures and the power of poetry and language. His visit to Stonehenge mere years after illustrates his continued interest in Merlin and what he represents within Britishness, a connection that is also briefly explored when, in his *English Traits* from 1856, Emerson acknowledges the central role Merlin holds in Arthurian mythology and his connections to British identity's Celtic aspect. It is Celtic ancestors, Merlin included, who Emerson claims, "planted Britain, and gave to the seas and mountains names which are poems, and imitate the pure voices of nature" ("Race" 434). Just a few years later, in his 1860 work *The Conduct of Life*, Emerson writes, "In all ages, souls out of time, extraordinary, prophetic, are born, who are rather related to the system of the world than to their particular age and locality" ("Worship" 582). This declaration echoes themes that permeated his "Merlin" poems over a decade earlier. Emerson is fascinated with prophetic knowledge—knowledge of the inner workings of nature and the universe—and of those whose timelessness allows them to possess it. In 1867, he publishes "Merlin's Song" as part of his collection *May-Day and Other Pieces*. Unlike his earlier "Merlin (I)" and "Merlin (II)" poems, which draw on Merlin as inspiration and reference him through subtle allusions, this poem addresses the mythological character of Merlin explicitly.

In a small passage focused on "Bards and Trouveurs" within his 1872 essay "Poetry and Imagination," Emerson reveals his personal captivation with the medieval Merlin: "There is in every poem a height which attracts more than other parts, and is best remembered. Thus, in Morte d'Arthur, I remember nothing so well as Sir Gawain's parley with Merlin in his wonderful prison" (745). He then quotes a lengthy passage of the conversation between the knight and the magician, centered on Merlin's inability to escape his fate despite having prophetic foreknowledge of it. Although not the only text Emerson draws quotations from in this section on bards, it is by far the longest quoted passage and the one to which Emerson gives the most personally reflective introduction. Finally, in 1876, Emerson publishes "The Harp" as part of his *Selected Poems* and returns to some of the same ideas he originally addressed in "Merlin (I)" and "Merlin (II)" thirty years prior, including the role of the bard, knowledge of nature's secrets, and Merlin's position in Arthurian legend. This long chain of Merlin-related writings demonstrates that throughout his life and career, Emerson is drawn to write about Merlin, whether directly or indirectly. The links between prophetic knowledge, nature, Britishness, and Merlin to which Emerson's prose texts gesture are explored more thoroughly in his four Merlin-related poems.

"Merlin (I)" and "Merlin (II)"

Emerson's paired "Merlin" poems emerge at the intersection of multiple interests he had in the years before and after their composition. Although the poems were finished and published in July 1846, a journal entry five years prior reveals his longing to write poetry with "rhymes as shall not suggest a restrain but contrariwise the wildest freedom" (*Journals* 7:219). Albert von Frank traces the origins of Emerson's interest in the power of rhyme and of his paired "Merlin" poems to a conversation he had with Elizabeth Hoar the week before writing this journal entry (*The Major Poetry* 98). The subject of Merlin and the legend surrounding him offers a prime topic to embody this simultaneously wild and structured form within the content of the poems as well. Merlin as a legendary figure appears in various representations, but the most common two—often intertwined—are those of the wild man and the king's magician and advisor.

The "Merlin" poems, like the medieval figure himself, grapple with prophecy and prophetic knowledge. David Bromwich categorizes Emerson's "successful poems" into three categories: "the Concord Poem," "the Wordsworthian elegy or meditation" and finally "the sort of poem he [Emerson] calls for in 'Merlin,' the shocker or far-fetcher, the prophetic blast," of which Bromwich labels Emerson a "pioneer" (125). Emerson's innovation in these poems' style is a perfect pairing with the uniqueness inherent in the original character Merlin. Although most postmedieval authors tend to draw on Sir Thomas Malory's work for their Arthurian inspiration, Emerson goes further back into the Arthurian corpus to Geoffrey of Monmouth as well. This is rather fitting considering Monmouth's role in developing the character of Merlin from the Celtic wild man into the magical and prophetic advisor of King Arthur. Within Geoffrey of Monmouth's Arthurian works, Emerson perhaps found a kindred soul who shared his interest in prophecy and the tensions of wildness and constraint; Monmouth's works included not only one of the earliest developed accounts of King Arthur, but entire works centered on Merlin. His *Prophetiae Merlini* (*Prophesies of Merlin*) and *Vita Merlini* (*Life of Merlin*) dabble with the multiple facets of Merlin's identity—a multiplicity that seems to echo centuries later in Emerson's "Merlin" poems. The medieval Merlin was predated by the Welsh Myrddin Wyllt, a wild man character who is drawn to the wilderness to learn the secrets of nature and gain prophetic knowledge and/or power. Although Christianization of Merlin's narrative alters the source of his prophetic knowledge in medieval texts, strains of the ancient wild man predecessor remain, and the medieval Merlin continues to be closely connected with the natural world.

Emerson's nineteenth-century "Merlin (I)" and "Merlin (II)" poems are part of the Arthurian Revival, a broader resurgence of interest in Arthurian legends. These two poems are from Emerson's early poems, and their allusions to Merlin are more subtle than his later poems "Merlin's Song" and "Harp." These paired poems focus on the role of the bard, and Emerson uses them as an opportunity to experiment with loosening the constraints of poetic structures by playing with the auditory impact of poetry.

In "Merlin (I)," Emerson draws on the bard figure, tying music and poetry with prophecy. Beginning with lines that critique the "trivial harp" for its lacking, the poem sets formulaic works—the "jingling serenader's art" and the "tinkle of piano strings"—in contrast against the more violent and organic methods of "the kingly bard," who the poem's speaker implies can do what the serenader cannot—"make the wild blood start." This kingly bard's music evokes powerful, unconstrained emotions and more closely exemplifies the wild, unpatterned rhythms of nature. Whereas the "trivial harp" leaves the speaker unfulfilled and longing, the speaker contrasts this against what the "kingly bard" does. In the first four lines, when the speaker criticizes the art of the harp, he focuses not on what the harp sounds like, but on what it fails to do—the speaker tells the harpist that the instrument's ". . . chords should ring as blows the breeze,/ Free, peremptory, clear." Using this conditional grammatical tense both indicates that the harp's art does not do this and implies that the king's bard, introduced five lines later in opposition to the harpist, does. Like the breeze that blows decisively and without restriction of form, so, too, ought music and poetry.

Emerson continues to draw upon nature to render descriptions of what music should sound like as he describes the way the bard plays. A serenade, connected with wooing and love, would generally be filled with soft, gentle notes, and compliments in the lyrics. In contrast, a bard is a role of both musical performer and poet, and in oral cultures, would be entrusted with a community's history. Their storytelling, done in poetic form (likely both for the purpose of performance and remembrance), would also commonly have been accompanied by music. However, while a bard would have memorized poetic accounts, the exact way he told them each time would likely vary as he catered to his audience, expanding upon parts that piqued interest, emphasizing events that would resonate, or altering the pace to accommodate concurrent goings-on. Both his music and his poetry, in a sense being one and the same, would have a sense of innovation and freedom that a serenade would not.

What these hard strikes produce is greater than the soft pleasantness of the harp, serenader, or piano that were dismissed in the speaker's first few lines; the bard instead reveals knowledge and understanding of the universe. The bard's works may not be as delicate or comfortable as gentle musical art, but their authenticity and rawness allow a more visceral response for the speaker. The act of the bard is described with violent terms, he "smite[s]" the chords rather than plays them, and he does so "rudely and hard" in order to accomplish his purpose. The simile Emerson uses here compares the bard's strikes to those made "with hammer or with mace," both of which are exceedingly blunt and destructive weapons. The reward for this unrestrained approach is producing chords that are generative:

That they may render back
Artful thunder, which conveys
Secrets of the solar track,
Sparks of the supersolar blaze.

This result is one of revelation and knowledge, another tie back to the medieval figure of Merlin, who is characterized as being prophetic and possesses knowledge of past, present, and future.

The Merlin that appears in Geoffrey of Monmouth's medieval works often embodies madness and prophetic knowledge concurrently, and this is the same blending of wildness and understanding that Emerson nods to in these lines. For Emerson's speaker, it is only through chaotic, unpatterned action that the universe's secrets can be communicated. The rough and unrefined strikes of the bard may be more aggressive than the serenader's music, but the bard, too, produces a type of "art," one that embodies the freedom and unpredictability inherent in the sounds of nature. Although a serenader would carefully select the notes and chords of his harp or piano, the bard causes "artful thunder," a sound that cannot be predicted or replicated. This type of sound, free from predictable patterns is what the poem's speaker claims communicates the understandings of nature. Just as Merlin's prophetic knowledge was communicated through his madness in Geoffrey of Monmouth's narratives, Emerson seeks to convey something greater through his experimentation with rhymes.

Emerson's own poetic structuring of "Merlin (I)" seeks to put into practice his message about breaking free from the conventions of artistic form. His poem is constructed of five stanzas with a ranging number of lines in each (26, 12, 10, 10, and 19) and playing with his rhyming scheme. The second stanza of his poem addresses this most explicitly as he praises the "art" of the "bard" who "shall not his brain encumber/ With the coil of rhythm and number." Although some editors have glossed the term "coil" in these lines as simply "restraint" (Mikics, "Merlin (I)" 513, n.1), Emerson is playing with contemporary meanings of the term—a "noisy disturbance . . . turmoil, bustle" ("coil, n.2 (1)") as well as a “fuss” (“coil, n.2 (3)”)—and perhaps hinting at another, older meaning of the term a “a selection, a choice” (“coil, n.1”) from the late 1500s. All these meanings align with the basic presumption that the “rhythm and number” in poetry is a burden, but one that the bard does not concern himself with because of the limitations it places upon him. Yet, the abandonment of rhymes in poetry is also not Emerson’s message; he instead wants to use rhymes that generate, rather than limit, meaning within a poem. In essence, rhymes for the sake of rhyming are not productive to Emerson; instead, rhymes should fulfill a more significant purpose in poetry. Albert von Frank suggests that Emerson’s contemplation of the role of rhyme in poetry may have, at least partially, been born from his editing experience with a literary journal in 1839 for which he had to review and select the best sonnets from a large number of submissions (*The Major Poetry* 98).

Emerson mentions Merlin by name only twice in “Merlin (I),” both times intimately connecting Merlin with nature imagery and the previous depiction of a bard. The poem’s first explicit invocation of Merlin tells

> Merlin’s blows are strokes of fate,
> Chiming with the forest tone,
> When boughs buffet boughs in the wood;
> Chiming with the gasp and moan
> Of the ice-imprisoned flood.

Emerson alludes to one of the most common myths about Merlin’s ultimate fate when he discusses “prayers of might from martyrs’ cave,” a reference to Merlin’s cave where some accounts have him being eternally trapped (and which is also a real location, and popular tourist attraction, on the beach below the ruins of Tintagel Castle in Cornwall, England). The second time Emerson explicitly references Merlin is later in the poem:

> Merlin’s mighty line
> Extremes of nature reconciled,—

Bereaved a tyrant of his will,
And made the lion mild.

Here, the speaker presents Merlin's prophecies, his "line," as a moment of unity within the tensions of natural order; one that can drive both man and beast to act against their inherent nature. This same idea of complimentary opposites, the tension between them, and reconciliation of them is one that becomes a topical focus in "Merlin (II)."

Like his subject Merlin, Emerson becomes a bard marrying poetry to unrestricted structure in order to speak on the larger meanings of the universe. In "Merlin I," Emerson accomplishes his aspiration from five years earlier to have rhyme that is free from constraint and instead suggests freedom. Although he begins the poem with alternating rhymes, he breaks from this with a couplet for lines nine and ten followed by an unrhymed line eleven. This initial rhyme scheme of *ABABCDCDEEF* starts like an English sonnet, but then breaks from the expected pattern halfway through the first stanza. From here, Emerson continues to frequently use alternating rhymed lines, but also freely deviates from this rhyme scheme incorporating couplets, eye-rhymes, imperfect rhymes, and unrhymed lines periodically throughout the rest of the poem. In his final stanza, Emerson ties form with content as the poem's speaker tells of the bard:

He shall not seek to weave,
In weak, unhappy times,
Efficacious rhymes;
Wait his returning strength.

The speaker reminds the auditor that rhyming is not a requirement of communicating grand ideas, or of good poetry, but is to be used strategically.

In the paired poem "Merlin (II)," Emerson shifts focus from the compositional theory of poetry to its function within society. Whereas "Merlin (I)" destabilizes the necessity of rigid rhyme schemes, "Merlin (II)" elevates the importance of rhyme. Although the two poems present different perspectives on rhymes in poetry, they are complimentary, rather than oppositional to each other; the first poem of the pair seeks to break free of the limitations of rhyming, but does not discount its value, and the second poem affirms the value rhymes can offer. The opening lines of "Merlin (II)" signal this, stating,

> The rhyme of the poet
> Modulates the king's affairs;
> Balance-loving Nature
> Made all things in pairs.

The message of these lines sets the tone for the rest of the poem. Moreover, the idea of pairs is also carried throughout the rest of the poem's content in addition to being echoed in the overall structure of the two paired "Merlin" poems. The pairings revisited throughout the poem are centered around the balance they create. The poem's speaker draws on sensory-based examples including colors, sounds, and flavors as well as physical body-based examples like pairs of leaves on branches, pairs of hands, and pairs of feet. The poem then considers pairing in the most traditional sense, that of matrimony as it calls the pairing between a groom and bride the "eldest rite" and goes on to explain that

> The animals are sick with love,
> Lovesick with rhyme;
> Each with all propitious time
> Into chorus wove.

This reinforces the understanding that through pairing two things, something new and more powerful emerges. Although rhymes in poetry can fit into a wide range of patterns, Emerson's "Merlin" poems tend to rely on rhymes made between two lines, even when he plays with the placement of those lines (couples, alternating rhymes, etc.). Just as a chorus of voices swells together to generate a new voice that is distinctive from the individuals that make it up, so, too, do the pairings and rhymes on which the poem's speaker dwells. As the poem expounds upon this subject, it references the pairing of thoughts, asserting they are

In equal couples mated,
Or else alternated.

These lines, intentionally or not, allude to the rhyme schemes Emerson has used to weave his Merlin poems—some rhymes are "mated" in couplets, while others are "alternated" in an *ABAB* pattern.

The rest of the stanza contrasts the generative power of paired ideas (like rhymes) that "Adding . . . One to other" combine and support one another against "solitary fancies" characterized as ". . . . bachelors/ or an ungiven maid" and are described as "short-lived wandering to and fro." A thought or line of poetry without a pair is alone and, therefore, limited in its impact, unlike a paired (i.e.,- rhymed) line that remains significant longer as it must be considered in conjunction with its partner. This poem, which keys in on the balance within the universe, was not included by Emerson in his *Selected Poems* in 1876, a fact that surprised his son Edward because it speaks to Emerson's "favorite idea of correspondence, universal rhyme and harmony in Nature, and compensation in life" (Edward Emerson qtd. in *The Major Poetry* 101). This idea is also conveyed in the poem's final stanza as the speaker claims that rhymes exist organically within nature and life, an echo of the concept of nature's balance that was presented at the beginning of the poem:

Subtle rhymes, with ruin rife
Murmur in the house of life.

"Merlin's Song" and "The Harp"

Although interest in Merlin continues to permeate Emerson's thoughts over the next several decades, as shown through the many references to Merlin and prophetic knowledge that appear sporadically in his prose writings, it is in 1867 that he formally revisits the topic of Merlin in his poetry with "Merlin's Song" and again in his 1876 poem "The Harp." His Merlin-related content in "The Harp" actually originates in his poem "May-Day" within the same 1867 collection, *May-Day and Other Pieces*, that "Merlin's Song" appears in; however, the poem was reworked before its inclusion in the 1876 collection with the Merlin section removed and evolved into its own poem under the title "The Harp" (Knight 172). Unlike "Merlin (I)" and "Merlin (II)," in "Merlin's Song," Emerson takes the character of Merlin directly as his subject. Perhaps in a subtle nod to his previous paired poems, "Merlin's Song," is a singular poem divided into two numbered sections, the first is a stanza of thirteen lines and the second a stanza of twenty-seven lines. The first section serves as a prologue to the second, introducing the origins of the "song" that the speaker has learned, yet the wording of the first line of each section leaves some uncertainty: "Of Merlin wise I learned a song" and "Hear what British Merlin sung." The preposition "of" in the first line of the poem could be taken to mean either "from" or "about," but the first line of the second section suggests the speaker is recounting the song that Merlin sang, thereby implying that the speaker has learned this from Merlin. The first section of the poem addresses the force of this song, deeming it "mightier than the strong" and discussing its transformative power over "good men" and "bad men" alike. This song is attributed to Merlin, who in medieval legends gets his prophetic knowledge of the future as a direct gift from God, and the poem's introduction claims "In the heat of the music peals a strain/ Which only angels hear;" potentially alluding to the divine source of Merlin's prophecy.

The second section presents Merlin's song, specifying it is from "British Merlin" (although Arthurian literature largely emerges in the medieval British tradition, there is also a large corpus of French Arthurian literature as well as Arthurian texts in German, Scandinavian, and other literary traditions). Merlin's wisdom, referenced in the first line of section one, is reinforced at the beginning of the song as well; he is described as "of keenest eye and truest tongue." As the most knowledgeable figure in medieval texts due to his prophetic abilities, Merlin was a loyal advisor to

King Arthur and a skilled observer, even outside of his prophetic knowledge. The song the speaker presents speaks to societal conflicts born of human faults, including inequity between those of different social classes. In medieval culture, this would have been between lords, knights, and peasants, but the heart of the idea—the inequity of labor and power—is one that endures throughout the generations into Emerson's own time and beyond.

The speaker alludes to the story of Syndyllan, a medieval lord on the Welsh border who was supposedly killed in battle while bravely defending his land. Syndyllan's bravery and masculine heroics are often praised in texts, such as "Marwnad Cynddylan," an elegy written in the voice of his sister (Brielmaier 210–11). The lines of "Merlin's Song" leading to this allusion criticize those in power who avoid fulfilling their duties to protect their people or who "usurp" what is not theirs. The song carries a warning that focuses on the corruption and weakness bred from prioritizing greed over fulfilling duty. Merlin is the most powerful character in many Arthurian stories, yet rather than using his power to pursue personal gain, he humbly chooses to serve as an advisor for King Arthur.

The poem's end focuses on the role of "cordial speech," which is "The music that can deepest reach." Contrasted with the behavior discussed above, this suggests a preference for diplomacy and alliances over wars and battles. In Arthurian legends, although Arthur, advised by Merlin, engages successfully in brutal battles early in his reign, these are largely to establish himself as rightful ruler; after these initial wars, the court of Arthur, guided through Merlin's prophetic counsel, is known for the *Pax Arthuriana* or "peace of Arthur" that is maintained in Arthur's kingdom. The downfall of Arthur, and his kingdom, is generally ascribed to Mordred, who in most medieval accounts is Arthur's illegitimate child with his half-sister. Mordred's conception generally occurs despite Merlin's prophetic knowledge of it and his attempts to forewarn Arthur of the potential danger Mordred would bring. Like Merlin's own death that Emerson finds so fascinating, here, too, the curse of prophetic knowledge is demonstrated—Merlin may know the future, but this does not inherently mean he can change it. "Merlin's Song" ends with the lines "Of all wit's uses, the main one/ Is to live well with who has none," acknowledging the challenge of being someone with excessive knowledge living in a society or with individuals who lack the same wisdom or willingness to make use of it.

Emerson's poem "The Harp," written almost a decade later in 1876, does not focus exclusively on Merlin, but does directly address Merlin's death. Whereas Emerson's early "Merlin" poems made a reference to the narrative of Merlin's cave, "The Harp" alludes to both this narrative and another variation of Merlin's death that involves Merlin being trapped in a magically created fortress by a woman who learns magic from Merlin as he pursues her romantically. The poem begins with the description of a musician whose "wisdom will not fail" and whose "age cannot cloud his memory" (903). Although these descriptions are already suggestive of Merlin, the allusions in the following lines to the musician's "windy cave," to his prophecy of "the counsel of the gods," and later to his knowledge of ". . . what is writ on Table Round/ Of Arthur and his peers" make it clear that this references Merlin (903). After a lengthy first stanza, the short, two-line second stanza questions the identity, time, and place of the "bard" (903).

The third stanza provides the already known answers to these questions, this time referring to the alternate version of Merlin's fate; the speaker claims that poets should recount the stories told by minstrels:

> Of Merlin locked the harp within,—
> Merlin paying the pain of sin,
> Pent in a dungeon made of air. (903)

In medieval narratives, Merlin's end often comes unhappily through being imprisoned in one of various magical ways by his own apprentice (either from fear of his romantic advances or to jealously guard him); however, the castle of air is one of the happier endings for Merlin as he is kept by his lover there, visited, and is even able to speak with Sir Gawain one final time. Although this set up is similar to the one from *Morte d'Arthur* that Emerson is fond of, the reference to the "dungeon made of air" makes it clear that this is an allusion to a different Arthurian text (*Morte d'Arthur*'s Merlin is trapped in a stone tomb). The figurative comparison of Merlin trapped in a harp allows Emerson to use Merlin's suffering to consider the "griefs of bards" that are reflected in Merlin's supposed agony that suffuses the "melody" (903). Part of this grief is the inadequacy of language to fully express the experience of nature. Emerson goes on to list some of the greatest poets, both ancient and contemporary, asserting that none "can put in verse" the things that a boy sees and hears "on the hills in spring" (903). Although Emerson is a strong believer in the power of poetry, he is also cognizant of the limitations of what it can express.

Breaking Free of Merlin's Spell

Stephen Knight characterizes Emerson's portrayal of Merlin (as poet, musician, bard, and prophet), as "a figure of the poetic muse with wide impact" and "a major wise educator" (Knight 171). This gets to the heart of the many angles from which Emerson's poetry considers Merlin and focuses on the common thread that ties them all together. Through Emerson's works, he returns time and again to ponder Merlin and the power he holds as a bard and prophet, but the magic of writing about Merlin is that his versatility and Emerson's allusions and invocations of him allow Emerson to examine other matters of importance through exploring Merlin's character. As Emerson considers rhyme, language, poetry, nature, balance, and other universal matters, the figure of Merlin provides him an avenue to do so, yet in using Merlin to explore these topics, Emerson, in turn, plays the role of prophetic bard and reveals the depths of Merlin's character.

Works Cited

Brielmaier, Daniel Donovan. *Selves and Subjectivities in Medieval North Atlantic Verse*. 2018. University of Toronto, PhD dissertation.

Bromwich, David. "Emerson and the Ode to W.H. Channing." *Bloom's Modern Critical Views: Ralph Waldo Emerson*, updated edition, Chelsea House Publishers, 2007, pp. 125–36.

"coil, n.1." *OED Online*. Oxford UP, Mar. 2023, www.oed.com/view/Entry/35977.

"coil, n.2." *OED Online*. Oxford UP, Mar. 2023, www.oed.com/view/Entry/35977.

Emerson, Ralph Waldo. *The Annotated Emerson: Ralph Waldo Emerson*. Edited by David Mikics, The Belknap Press of Harvard UP, 2012.

__________. *The Complete Writings of Ralph Waldo Emerson*, Wm. H. Wise, 1929.

__________. "The Harp." *Collected Poems. The Complete Writings of Ralph Waldo Emerson*, pp. 903–04.

__________. *Journals of Ralph Waldo Emerson with Annotations*. Edited by Ralph Waldo Emerson and Waldo Emerson Forbes, vol. 7, The Riverside Press Cambridge, 1912.

__________. *Ralph Waldo Emerson: The Major Poetry*. Edited by Albert J. von Frank, The Belknap Press of Harvard UP, 2015.

__________. "Merlin (I)." *The Annotated Emerson: Ralph Waldo Emerson*. Edited by David Mikics, The Belknap Press of Harvard UP, 2012, pp. 512–14.

__________. "Merlin (I)." *Collected Poems. The Complete Writings of Ralph Waldo Emerson*, pp. 869–70.

__________. "Merlin (II)." *Collected Poems. The Complete Writings of Ralph Waldo Emerson*, p. 870.

__________. "Merlin's Song." *Collected Poems. The Complete Writings of Ralph Waldo Emerson*, p. 898.

__________. "Poetry and Imagination." *Letters and Social Aims. The Complete Writings of Ralph Waldo Emerson*, pp. 727–50.

__________. "Race." *English Traits. The Complete Writings of Ralph Waldo Emerson*, pp. 431–40.

__________. "Stonehenge." *The Annotated Emerson: Ralph Waldo Emerson*. Edited by David Mikics, The Belknap Press of Harvard UP, 2012, pp. 382–93.

__________. "Worship." *The Conduct of Life. The Complete Writings of Ralph Waldo Emerson*, pp. 581–94.

Knight, Stephen. *Merlin: Knowledge and Power through the Ages*, Cornell UP, 2009.

Ralph Waldo Emerson's Nature Poetry

Charles W. Rowe

From an early age, Ralph Waldo Emerson believed he had a poetic temperament. While studying at Harvard Divinity School, he wrote in his journal that he had "a strong imagination & consequently a keen relish for the beauties of poetry" (Gilman 2.238) that made theological and philosophical systems difficult for him to fully grasp. His first wife, Ellen Tucker, wrote poetry, and they both talked of becoming poets. When she died in 1831, Emerson began to develop his intimate, lyric voice by writing hundreds of elegies for her in his notebooks. From then on, Emerson maintained his belief that he saw himself primarily as a poet, telling his second wife, Lydia Jackson, on February 1, 1835 that: "I am a born poet . . . that is my nature & vocation" (Rusk and Tilton 1.435). In his journals and notebooks, he composed thousands of lines of original verse and published what he considered to be the best of these poems in journals, newspapers, and eventually in his two collections of verse, *Poems* (1847) and *May-Day and Other Pieces* (1867).

When Emerson died on 27 April 1882, his poetry was as popular as contemporaries Henry Wadsworth Longfellow and John Greenleaf Whittier. But the popularity of his poetry was short-lived. In 1885, the influential critic Matthew Arnold argued that Emerson's verse is "not the poetry of one of the born poets" (*Discourses* 153). Arnold's critique largely dominated critical views of Emerson's poetry, leading Emerson's verse to remain "among the most underappreciated poetry in American literature" (Morris 189). Yet, Albert von Frank's recent reassessment of Emerson's poetry in his 2011 *Emerson's Poems: A Variorum Edition* has presaged a renewed interest in his verse. If Emerson was not a "born" poet, he was most certainly a poet by vocation. In his introduction to the variorum edition, von Frank rightly asks us to look at Emerson's poetry as a record of Emerson's experimental attempts to represent "the importance of the process and of what was at stake in its conduct" (xxx). In particular, Emerson's nature poems—poems that explicitly explore the affinitive relationship between humans and nature—provide excellent points of entry into Emerson's experimental poetry.

Emerson's first nature poem is "Each and All" from 1834. The poem charts the poet-speaker's gradual acknowledgement that his impulse to dissect nature into parts must be tempered by his poetic imagination's ability to render the dissected parts as composite pieces of what Emerson calls in *Nature* "the perfection of the whole" (28). One day walking in the woods, the speaker is arrested by the song of a sparrow—"I thought the sparrow's note from heaven" (13)—and is so moved that he brings the sparrow and the nest home. The sparrow is not pleased to be removed from her home. Her notes are no longer heavenly to the speaker when heard outside of the environment in which the speaker first heard the sparrow's song. The poet realizes that just because he brought the sparrow home, he "did not bring home the river and the sky" (17). This failure reminds him of his attempt to bring a pile of seashells home:

> I wiped away the weeds and foam,
> I fetched my sea-born treasures home;
> But the poor, unsightly, noisome things
> Had left their beauty on the shore,
> With the sun, and the sand, and the wild uproar. (24–28)

The shells' delicate beauty was covered by "weeds and foam," blushing unseen to the world. The poet liberated them from their dangerous environment so that he could apprehend their hidden beauty from the comfort of his home. Yet at home, they become, "poor, unsightly, noisome things" because the poet has attempted to appropriate the shells for his own pleasure alone. At the end of this sequence, the speaker presents the shells as agents: they "left their beauty on the shore." Their identities are concurrent with the "sun, and the sand, and the wild uproar." He cannot recreate this ecosystem at home; the shells and their environment must be left alone if they are to be appreciated as a part of the "all."

In this poem, the "each" can never be adequately considered without marking its "all" revealing power. Language is the ideal marker of this natural reality, for every new expression of the "each" in the "all" or the "all" in the "each" offers a new space to attempt to chart more adequately an original relationship between the individual consciousness and the natural world in which it is immersed. Stealing a finch's nest or some seashells to bring home will not suffice. Through his lifelong study of natural science, Emerson maintained a material interest in nature. Taxonomic lists, natural specimens, and scientific instruments often lead us towards deeper knowledge of nature. Yet, too narrow a focus on the description and definitions of the "each" can become a distraction. As William Wordsworth renounces the need to dismantle things in order to know them in his poem, "The Tables Turned," "Our meddling intellect / Mis-shapes the beauteous forms of things; / —We murder to dissect" (26–28), Emerson, too, views poetry as a tool aptly suited for countering the scientific impulse to sever and analyze. In Emerson's view, both dissection and poetry can work together to craft a more capacious description of nature. As Emerson claims in reference to Wordsworth in his 1834 lecture "The Naturalist," "I fully believe in both, in the poetry and in the dissection" (Spiller, et al. 1.79). In this sense, "Each and All" dramatizes the speaker's process of accepting the coexistence of the dissection and the poetry.

This is why at the end of "Each and All," when the speaker is so distressed by his meager attempts to understand nature by stealing material objects from it, he suddenly exclaims, "I covet truth" (37). The speaker is self-aware enough to notice that collecting specimens can only bring him so far in his search for truth. He must curb his desire to capture nature and instead strive to let his environment be. When he momentarily does so, he feels a deep sense of awe: "beauty through my senses stole; / I yielded myself to the perfect whole" (47–51). He arrives at a sense of peace and belonging by perceiving himself to be in the middle of things rather than an outsider looking in.

This moment of heightened perception in the poem's final sequence is temporary. Through the poet's repeated attempts to apprehend "the all" through "the each," the speaker has arrived at this brief scene of satisfaction that will not last despite the creation of this poem. The cycle of seeking, failing, and briefly apprehending must continue. Yet even the most sensitive interpreter of this poem, Carl Strauch, reads the poem's conclusion as a celebration: "what gives 'Each and All' its grateful and graceful sense of an accomplished process is the fulfillment of an entirely satisfying sympathy between man and nature" (157). In fact, the poem emphasizes the quicksilver character of "fulfillment." Throughout the poem the speaker seeks "fulfillment" and never obtains it until the end. The speaker has learned to trust that the process of seeking—not any final sought-after product—is the most worthy destination. The poem ends with the speaker's recognition of human finitude. He yields himself to the perfect whole because he is willing to admit that its wholeness is too large for him to grasp for longer than a brief moment. In this sense, the speaker is not fulfilled or satisfied, but resolved to return again to similar scenes in hopes of arriving at similar moments of heightened perception.

Like the poetry of Wordsworth, Samuel Taylor Coleridge, and John Clare, Emerson's nature poetry values the rhythms of rural life over the man-made bustle of the city. His poem "The Snow-Storm" is perhaps his most concentrated meditation on the virtue of rural retreat. The action of the poem is centered around a blizzard that has suddenly made the speaker snow-bound in his home. Emerson unfolds a blank verse lyric conversation between the speaker and the north wind, which he calls the "fierce artificer" (11). Although the first nine lines of the poem encircle the speaker in his home: "Around the radiant fireplace, enclosed / In a tumultuous privacy of storm" (8–9), in the rest of the poem's twenty-eight lines the speaker's perceptions are directed away from the fireplace as if he is traveling the countryside with the north wind. This clever turn on a domestic theme indicates that the poem will seek to unsettle the readers, to enclose them in the tumultuousness of the storm rather than affirming their lucky, pleasant removal from it.

To Emerson, the north wind's ability to shape the snow into organic forms may have seemed to signify other modes of artistic expression, like architecture, music, and poetry. The wind is as solid and ethereal as the air from which great poetry comes. Emerson is certainly playing with the metaphoric suggestions of the figure of a "fierce artificer." The phrase "artificer" comes from John Milton's *Paradise Lost* and refers to Satan's power of deception, and the speaker's tallies of the wind's illusory, and "fanciful" (15) creations in the poem suggest that the poem is about aesthetic deception. The poet, in this sense, is a playful deceiver, too, in that he is attempting to persuade the wind that he can control it through the creation of his poem. The wind teases the speaker with its power, and the poet teases the wind, in turn, with his own imaginative power. We read the poem, in this sense, as spectators of an intriguing dialogue between the wind and the poet.

The "Snow-Storm" is foremost a descriptive poem that details the perceptual experience of a blizzard as it unfolds before the speaker. The poem can be read as a series of ever-deepening identifications between the speaker and the howling wind. Using his physical stasis to his advantage, the speaker imaginatively becomes wind-like, following the wind's fits and starts as assiduously as he can. Through these clipped descriptions, sometimes no more than a few words long, the speaker gives us brief but potent glimpses of the north wind's effects on its landscape: it dabs snow on a "windward stake, or tree, or door" (14); it leaves wreath-like circles on the doors of chicken coops, and then suddenly "fills up the farmer's lane from wall to wall" (20). The wind moves so quickly that, unlike man-made art, it cares not "for number or proportion" (17). It moves through the landscape on its own terms, and the poet perpetually strives to catch up. The speaker's only recourse is to extend the reach of his linguistic resources in these brief glimmers of perception.

After attempting to apprehend the north wind's peregrinations for the majority of the poem, the speaker seems to finally have the deceptive north wind in his grasp. The poet knows he cannot contain the wind, but he is now able to align his active perceptions at least momentarily with the active wind's motions:

And when his hours are numbered, and the world
Is all his own, retiring, as he were not,
Leaves, when the sun appears, astonished Art
To mimic in slow structures, stone by stone,
Built in an age, the mad wind's night-work,
The frolic architecture of the snow. (23–28)

The speedy pace of the north wind's "frolic" slows to a crawl as it takes its seeming exit. In the dawn, it recognizes its momentary dominion over the world, and is now happy to leave. Yet here the speaker acknowledges that he has shaped our view of the north wind. It is "retiring" as if it "were not." Whether the wind is still there or not, the speaker has impelled us to imagine the north-wind's not-ness. We sense that the wind must still be there—the wind never really retires—yet by experiencing the storm with the speaker we are now momentarily capable of imagining its absence.

Through its perceived presences and absences, the wind always leaves traces of itself. In his receptivity to the north wind's "frolic" power, the speaker seems to heed Emerson's claim in his 1834 lecture "The Naturalist," that: "it is fit that man should look upon Nature with the eyes of the Artist, to learn from the greatest Artist whose blood beats in our veins" (Spiller, et al. 1.73). An honest accounting of the relationship between humans and nature should be centered in the belief that the blood beating in the veins of the poet beats also in the veins of the "greatest Artist." The "Snow-Storm" dramatizes a moment of perceptual awareness in which the poet increases his awareness of a convergence between his creative power and the God-like wind's power. The result is an "astonished Art" that encourages readers to cultivate their own ability to be astonished by the experience of a snowstorm.

"Each and All" and "The Snow-Storm" show that the experience of nature can be rendered more vividly when a poet's environment seems to have as much agent power as the poet. But in these poems the human speaker always has the last word. As Emerson further experiments with his poetry, he begins to voice the experience of nonhumans from their imagined perspective. Saundra Morris aptly notes that because for Emerson, "the poet is one who can hear the locutions of nature and translate them into verse" it is important for Emerson "to present the speech of natural objects or forces in direct quotation or paraphrase" (224). This rhetorical maneuver is representative of what Emerson calls his "strange sympathy." After his 1833 visit to the Jardin des Plantes in Paris, Emerson claims in his journal, "I feel the centipede in me—cayman, carp, eagle & fox. I am moved by strange sympathies" (Gilman 4.200). Emersonian sympathy is temperamentally, and happily, "strange" in that it seeks to identify and affirm affinitive experiences of being between previously unidentified or underrepresented natural entities.

An intriguing example of Emerson's "strange sympathy" is his 1841 poem "Woodnotes II." The poem attempts to present a pine tree as a social, living being capable of communicating to humans. In his view, trees should be thought of as communicating beings, whether they speak in the high tones of a prophet or through the silent waving of their boughs. Though he did not have at his disposal the research of twenty-first century dendrologists who have discovered definitive evidence that trees are social beings that indeed communicate with each other using olfactory, visual, and electrical signals (Wohlleben 12–13), Emerson's radically "strange sympathy" with material nature prompted this poetic experiment that enhances the importance of these new scientific findings.

For one of Emerson's earliest readers, the abolitionist and reformer Theodore Parker, Emerson's suggestion that it is possible for a poet to channel the voice of a tree, was too strange to take seriously, "a pine-tree which should talk as Emerson's tree talks would deserve to be plucked up and cast into the sea" (Myerson 238, n.9). Parker may have meant: a tree would never sing about itself for 384 lines in rhymed couplets. Yet Emerson believed that trees have stories to tell, and that poetry may offer one of the best ways to listen to these stories. While in "Woodnotes II" Emerson crafts a pine tree that is undoubtedly an arboreal version of Emerson, the fact that he displaces his own voice into a natural figure is nevertheless a striking poetic act. This rhetorical maneuver forces his readers to experiment with our own human-centered stories of being and provokes us to stretch our moral imaginations in the process.

Perhaps in an attempt to broadcast its song to the widest reach of the American wilderness, Emerson's tree speaks with the vatic intonations of a prophet. A constant feature of its song is its tone of reprobation. Humans have failed to listen to its song so the pine tree has enjoined a single auditor to approach it: "Come, lay thee in my soothing shade / And heal the hurts which sin has made / I will teach the bright parable" (276–78). Its parable is the story of environmental growth and change to which it has borne witness while humans have foolishly focused their energy on making the world in their image. Having been on Earth as long as Jove and Adam, the pine tree has seen nothing but cycles of death and rebirth and will forever watch "o'er the grave of men" (40). The pine tree's vatic tone signals that it is less of a tree than it is a figuration of an exhortative God-like force. It is rooted in our world but not subject to the organic cycle of birth and death.

In repeated variations throughout its song, the pine tree exhorts its auditor to become more receptive to the moralizing influence of the natural world. From its privileged vantage point, the tree claims to have detected that the person listening to its song is alienated from their authentic self. The pine tree wants to intervene in this person's life in hopes of instilling in them a renewed self-trust: "I see thee in the crowd alone; / I will be thy companion." (281–82). Alone in the unthinking crowd, the auditor has learned to mistake "pedant lore" (295) for wisdom. The companionship of this imaginary pine tree is the morally corrective force they need. By identifying with the pine tree, the auditor can learn to look at the natural world not as a "pedant" disinterestedly gathering facts but as one whose primary goal is to affirm their kinship with a living world. Emerson's personification of nature as a primal mind emphasizes this point. Through his friendship with the living, thinking "pine-tree," the auditor can sense that external nature shares his own human nature. Just as humans are thinking beings, nature, too, seems to be a thinking being. From this vantage, the sense of flow one encounters in the forest—the constant rush of the stream, the persistence of the wind, the sense of trees stretching beyond the knowable horizon—mirrors the flow state of poetic creation. In sensing that the "primal mind" that animates nature has an affinitive relationship with the human mind, the auditor can deepen his sense of belonging within his environment.

In his later writing, Emerson admits that this sense of communion between a human and a talking pine tree is impossible to sustain. In an 1850 journal entry, Emerson concluded that his composition of "Woodnotes II" was an attempt to imagine a more direct relationship between humans and nature but "only the reflection or rhyme of some truth" (Gilman 11.271). In part, this statement reflects Emerson's view that moments of divination in his poetry like this one—when God-like nature speaks through natural objects to humans—are rhetorical performances meant to, as Joseph Thomas claims, challenge what Emerson "considered the paltry and paltering ways in which we inhabit the world" (217). The talking tree is a self-consciously extravagant figure meant to waken Emerson's readers. Its performance can only be carried so far, but ideally it leaves a lasting impression. Emerson's claim that his poetry is "only a reflection of some truth" also speaks to his acceptance in his later thinking that the experience of nature is always tempered by the limitation of human perception. If we have no choice but to acknowledge, as Emerson claims in "Experience" that "we do not see directly but mediately, and that we have no means of correcting these colored and distorting lenses which we are, or of computing the amount of their errors" (*Essays and Lectures* 487) then we must accept our imperfect, mediate vision. Of course, humans should always strive to make themselves more receptive to the meaningful correspondences between themselves and the natural world—the process that leads them to their self-formed identities—but they must also assent to the hard fact that their self-formed identities are reflections and rhymes of "some truth."

His acceptance of human finitude is the subject of Emerson's poignant poem "Threnody." Written to honor and grapple with the sudden death of his five-year-old son Waldo in 1842, "Threnody" presents poetic receptivity as both a vulnerability that could dangerously allow a mourning father's grief to subsume him and as the only moral strength that can authorize and support his survival. The poem stages a dialogue between a father mourning his young son's untimely death and the God-like natural force the speaker calls "the deep Heart." The father must attempt to find a path to right action in the face of the disorienting death of his young son. As in the previous poems I have considered, Emerson suggests in "Threnody" that right action can be rooted in poetic practice; the poetic rendering of a speaker's lived experience, in all of its granular joys and sorrows, creates a substantive picture of how a person might live in accordance with their natural world. The conflict at the heart of "Threnody" is whether or not the grieving speaker can continue with their poetic life.

In "Threnody," the "deep Heart" of nature has no cause to mourn a child's death because it sees death as a natural process of life. It is instead troubled by the "blasphemy of grief" (204) that threatens to subsume the father's desire to make poetry. After listening to the father's barren laments, the "deep Heart" tells the father that he should stop weeping; nature is the very power that gives the father the impetus to write this poem. His skillful ability to translate nature's secrets through poetry comes from the same source as his son's death. The father's laments are blasphemous because they have gravely narrowed his poetic vision. Instead of seeing the dynamic flux of nature—in which the poet should always be a participant—the poet sees empty rooms, barren landscapes, and "the world dishonored" by a young boy's death. Yet, at the same time as he listens to the "deep Heart," the father notices on the edges of the view from his window that "my trees repair their boughs" (10). The waving boughs with which he has maintained a friendly affinity are still there despite his son's absence. The line of communication the father has opened through his poetic practice is available even in the face of devastation.

To correct the poet's disorientation in this moment, the "deep Heart" speaks to renew his sense of belonging and identification with his lived environment. The poet and the "deep Heart" have worked in concert with each other for many years. The poet has learned to listen, watch, and feel by conceiving of the natural world as a living being like himself. The "deep Heart" thus reminds him:

> I gave thee sight—where is it now?
> I taught thy heart beyond the reach
> Of ritual, bible, or of speech. . .
> Taught thee each private sign to raise,
> Lit by the supersolar blaze.
>
> (196–98, 201–02)

Perception and affection are the bedrocks of Emerson's environmental poetics. Sight is an activity of illumination by which all "private signs"—seemingly unknowable details of the natural world—can be given meaning. The illumination of sight creates the propitious conditions for the development of a feeling heart "beyond the reach / of ritual, bible, or of speech." Silent, still contemplation of the individual's perceptual process allows the development of a skillful ability to coexist with the environment. Through Emerson's years of careful perceptual awareness, recorded and reflected upon in his journals, letters, essays, lectures, and poems, he has developed his bond with his life-giving environment. The poet has opened himself to this world and, in turn, so has the "deep Heart" of nature opened itself to the poet. The "deep Heart" uses Emerson's own discourse to remind the speaker that their authentic commitment should not be abandoned in this moment of grief.

Grief, as Emerson says in, "Experience," can be severely limiting: "the only thing grief has taught me is to know how shallow it is" (*Essays and Lectures* 472). The "deep Heart" reiterates this view by asking the father if he really wants to "freeze love's tidal flow; / whose streams through nature circling go?" (238–39). The father has lived by a concept of nature as a flow of experience shared by himself and the boughs, the rhodoras, and the wind of his environment. Through his poetic experiments, the father strives to perceive and describe the feeling of being immersed in an enlarging, "tidal flow" of experience. In the negative metaphor of a frozen "tidal flow," the "deep Heart" uses Emerson's own language to remind the poet of the importance of poetic experimentation. In "The Poet," Emerson claims: "the quality of the imagination is to flow, and not to freeze. The poet did not stop at the color, or the form, but read their meaning; neither may he rest in this meaning, but he makes the same objects exponents of his new thought" (*Essays and Lectures* 463). As it is portrayed in this poem, grief destroys the poet's access to the fluxional language of poetry. In grief, everything wears the color of grief. But the poet knows better. The process of making poems keeps the world in flow. It renders the world more vivid and true to his experiences of it. The poet is a maker. He does not "stop" or "rest" in any one "meaning" for long. The "tidal flow" continues, and he continues to adjust to its flow. Poems are momentary resting places through which flux can be closely viewed and reflected upon. But for Emerson, the work always continued.

Works Cited

Arnold, Matthew. "Emerson." *Discourses in America*. Macmillan, 1885, pp. 138–207.

Emerson, Ralph Waldo. *The Collected Works of Ralph Waldo Emerson, Vol. 9, Poems: A Variorum Edition*. Editor by Albert J. von Frank and Thomas Wortham, Harvard UP, 2011.

__________. *The Early Lectures of Ralph Waldo Emerson*, 3 vols., Edited by Robert E. Spiller, et al., Harvard UP, 1959–72.

__________. *The Journals and Miscellaneous Notebooks of Ralph Waldo Emerson*. Edited by William H. Gilman, et al., 16 vols., Harvard UP, 1960–82.

__________. *The Letters of Ralph Waldo Emerson*. Edited by Ralph L. Rusk and Eleanor M. Tilton, 10 vols., Columbia UP, 1939–94.

__________. *Ralph Waldo Emerson's Essays and Lectures*. Library of America, 1983.

Milton, John. *Paradise Lost*. Modern Library, 2008.

Morris, Saundra. "Whim Upon the Lintel: Emerson's Poetry and a Politically Ethical Aesthetic." *Nineteenth-Century Prose*, vol. 40, no. 2, Fall 2013, pp. 189–216.

Myerson, Joel. *The New England Transcendentalists and the* Dial. Fairleigh Dickinson UP, 1980.

Strauch, Carl F. "Emerson and the Doctrine of Sympathy." *Studies in Romanticism*, vol. 6, no. 3, Spring 1967, pp. 152–74.

Thomas, Joseph M. "Poverty and Power: Revisiting Emerson's Poetics." *Emerson: Bicentennial Essays*. Edited by Ronald A. Bosco and Joel Myerson, Massachusetts Historical Society, 2006, pp. 213–46.

Wohlleben, Peter. *The Hidden Life of Trees: What They Feel, How They Communicate—Discoveries from A Secret World.* Greystone, 2016.

Wordsworth, William, and Samuel Taylor Coleridge. *Lyrical Ballads 1798 and 1802*. Edited by Fiona Stafford, Oxford UP, 2013.

Master-Enchanter: Emerson's Extraordinary Influence on John Burroughs

Stephen M. Mercier

John Burroughs (1837–1921) had a lifelong obsession with the figure and writings of Ralph Waldo Emerson. This is demonstrated by admissions from journals and his earliest and final essays. Writing explicitly on Emerson throughout his lifetime, he infused Emersonian perspectives found in the seminal essay "Nature" (1836), including the ability of Nature to heal, its beauty and sublimity, a critique of materialistic society, childlike wonder and curiosity, and spirituality. Thus, Emerson's views on Nature played a particularly influential role in Burroughs's intellectual development, writings, and philosophy.

In her Preface to Burroughs's *The Last Harvest* (1922), published one year after his death, official biographer Clara Barrus attests to his "abiding interest in Emerson" and explains that at the end of his life, Burroughs "hungered for everything that concerned the Concord Sage, who had been one of the most potent influences in his life. . . . he knew well that Emerson would always rest secure on the pedestal where long ago he placed him" (vii).

For readers unfamiliar with the figure of John Burroughs, at the turn of the twentieth century, Burroughs was hailed as the most beloved author of the natural history essay, and his books sold more than one and a half million copies. He wrote twenty-seven books between 1867–1922, comprised of 450 essays. Known mainly for his peaceful woodland rambles and essays about farm life and birdsongs, fans adoringly referred to him as John O' Birds. He was born in Roxbury, New York, and is largely identified as a Hudson River Valley regionalist.

In "An Egotistical Chapter" in *Indoor Studies*, Burroughs blatantly shares with his readers: "as a young man I was an Emersonian" (265) and reflects that when in his early twenties, he started to realize "the power of letters" (266). During this developmental period, he began penning his own essays and first saw them appear in magazines and newspapers. At this especially informative time, Emerson is Burroughs's penultimate influence:

> [T]he master-enchanter of this period of my life and of many following years was Emerson. [I] opened one of his books in a Chicago bookstore, and was so taken with the first taste of it that I then and there purchased the three volumes, —the 'Essays' and the 'Miscellanies.' All that summer I fed upon them and steeped myself in them. (*Indoor Studies* 267–68)

Despite Burroughs forging out on his own as a writer, he acknowledges lifelong gratitude to Emerson: "But to this day I am aware that a suggestion of Emerson's manner often crops out in my writings. . . . my debt to him is great. He helped me to better literary expression, he quickened my perception of the beautiful, he stimulated and fertilized my religious nature" (*Indoor Studies* 268). This last admission conveys three huge claims: Emerson's writings were crucial to Burroughs's development as a literary naturalist, to his ability to perceive beauty, and they also serve as a perpetual incentive to his spirituality. Due to these influences, Burroughs felt a deep affinity with Emerson and continued to view him as a master-enchanter. In addition to explicit considerations, Burroughs's oeuvre contains particularly Emersonian moments that implicitly embed his most meaningful contentions and revelations.

Nature's Ability to Heal and Its Beauty and Sublimity

In "Nature," Emerson explains the healing powers available in Nature, as he contrasts those whose lives have been negatively impacted by their stifling careers and workplaces: "To the body and mind which have been cramped by noxious work or company, nature is medicinal and restores their tone. The tradesman, the attorney comes out of the din and craft of the street, and sees the sky and the woods, and is a man again. In their eternal calm, he finds himself" (27). Quite similarly, Burroughs claims in *Riverby* that Nature heals: "Later in life we go to nature as an escape from the tension and turmoil of business, or for rest and recreation from study, or seeking solace from grief and disappointment, or as a refuge from the frivolity and hypocrisies of society. We lie under trees, we stroll through lanes, or in meadows and pastures, or muse on the shore. Nature 'salves' our worst wounds; she heals and restores us" (220). This essential therapeutic function of spending time in various settings in the natural world has many developmental, physical, and emotional benefits, as many contemporary scholarly studies have shown. Nature may alleviate depression and be essential to a feeling of elation and well-being.

Surely, in many instances, Burroughs promulgates Emersonian recognitions of the healing power of Nature. For example, Burroughs shares his mindset that "Nature we have always with us, an inexhaustible storehouse of that which moves the heart, and fires the imagination, —health to the body, a stimulus to the intellect, and joy to the soul" (*Leaf and Tendril* 3). These elements of health, the rousing of the mind, and the revivification of the spirit are evidence of Burroughs's lifelong adoption of Emersonian themes. Nature often helped heal Burroughs's sorrow when he was down spirited. In addition to the healing qualities available in Nature, Burroughs's awareness of beauty was enhanced by Emerson.

In his section "Beauty" in "Nature," Emerson focuses on aesthetic qualities and their according emotional responses: "Nature satisfies the soul purely by its loveliness, and without any mixture of corporeal benefit. I have seen the spectacle of morning from the hill-top over against my house, from day-break to sun-rise, with emotions which an angel might share" (27). The emphasis on beauty in "Nature" propelled Burroughs to recognize and pronounce aspects of the beautiful in many of his own accounts. A passage reminiscent of Emerson's "spectacle of morning from the hill-top" shows Burroughs's sensory immersion as he revels in the scents and sounds of his native fields: "The moist, hot, fragrant breath of the fields—mingled odor of blossoming grasses, clover, daisies, rye—the locust blossoms, dropping. What a humming about the hives; what freshness in the shade of every tree; what contentment in the flocks and herds!" (*Leaf and Tendril* 29). Then, he pronounces the beauty of the atmosphere: "Go to the top of a hill on such a morning, say by nine o'clock, and see how unspeakably fresh and full the world looks. The morning shadows yet linger everywhere, even in the sunshine; a kind of blue coolness and freshness, the vapor of dew tinting the air" (*Leaf and Tendril* 29). Envisioning the entire planet as beautiful, Burroughs maintains an Emersonian vision capped off with biblical allusion as he finds, "an endless series of beautiful and wonderful forms forever flowing out of itself. From the highest heavens of the telescope to the minutest organisms of the microscope, all is beautiful and wonderful, and passeth understanding" (*The Summit of the Years* 15). Certainly, there are many attestations to the beautiful in Burroughs's writings that extended from his descriptions of pretty local wildflowers to the astral splendor of the outer cosmos.

In "Nature," Emerson provides readers with the example of the stars to illustrate sublime aspects of the natural world. Emerson's depiction is epiphanic and demonstrates the extreme appreciation that would blanket many of Burroughs's most powerful descriptions. Emerson's strong opening concrete example is also spiritual in its guise: "But if a man would be alone, let him look at the stars. The rays that come from those heavenly worlds, will separate between him and vulgar things. One might think the atmosphere was made transparent with this design, to give man, in the heavenly bodies, the perpetual presence of the sublime" (23). The stars afford awe in contemplating their grand significance as Emerson elaborates on his vision: "Seen in the streets of cities, how great they are! If the stars should appear one night in a thousand years, how would men believe and adore and preserve for many generations the remembrance of the city of God which had been shown! But every night come out these preachers of beauty and light the universe with their admonishing smile" (23). Here Emerson develops a contrast between civilized society and inspirited Nature, as he bestows the cosmos with soul. At the same time, he adds religious connotations, framing them as "preachers" who remind us to remain reverent. Due to his extreme appreciation, Emerson's awareness of a sublime universe becomes implicitly imbued in Burroughs's own writings, and Emerson's emotive exclamations serve as a model for how he responds to natural phenomena.

In fact, Burroughs interprets many aspects of Nature and scientific knowledge in a similar fashion, invoking an epiphanic reverence that is omnipresent in many of his accounts. Like Emerson's grand visions, his reflections are charged with notions of soul and spirit and pervaded with the sublime. In *Riverby*, Burroughs encourages his readers to garner more invigorated impressions of Nature to elicit "a vivid and original sense of the beauty and significance that surrounds us" and wants us to feel a profound sense of awe: "How often do we really see the stars? Probably a great many persons never see them at all,—that is, never look upon them with any thrill of emotion" (232). Prompted by Emerson, he stresses the stars' "ineffable splendor and significance" (232). Burroughs's paean continues with a revitalized vision:

> How overwhelming and awe-inspiring! His thought goes out like a lightning flash into that serene abyss, and then the veil is drawn again. One's science, one's understanding, tells him he is a voyager on the celestial deep, that the earth beneath his feet is a star among stars, that we can never be any more in the heavens than we are now, or any more within reach of the celestial laws and forces; but how rare the mood in which we can realize this astounding fact, in which we can get a fresh and vivid impression of it! To have it ever present with one in all its naked grandeur would perhaps be more than we could bear. (233)

In this exclamatory passage, one can also glean Emersonian emphasis on "the now" that occurs at the beginning of "Nature," as well as similarly bold Whitmanesque poetic proclamations. Here, Emerson's sublime visions are a catalyst for Burroughs's own particular account of the stars. The inclusion of the "lightning" flash is a nod to what he saw as Emerson's quality of thought as electric. Burroughs repeatedly framed Emerson's thinking and style as electric, claiming his "daring affirmations" are "the very electricity of thought" (*Under the Apple Trees* 223). This quality is stimulating and suggestive: "His page is full of moral electricity, so to speak, which begets a state of electric excitement in the reader's mind" (*Literary Values* 229). As Burroughs aligned his views with science, he also embraced Emerson's more grandiose visions. Thus, Emerson allowed him to break free from many critics figuring him as solely a regionalist writer who offered small-scale glimpses of Nature. Urged by Emerson's text, he extended his considerations to the largest possible scale and wished for his readers to do the same. However, he saw society's increased preoccupation with greed as an obstacle toward appreciating Nature's vital life-sustaining forces.

Critique of Materialistic Society

In "Nature," Emerson argues for the central importance of simple living, noting the damaging consequences of straying away from high moral fortitude. Such immoral desires are corruptive and engender false views: "When simplicity of character and sovereignty of ideas is broken up by the prevalence of secondary desires, the desire of riches, the desire of pleasure, the desire of power, the desire of praise,—and duplicity and falsehood take the place of simplicity and truth, the power over nature as an interpreter of the will, is in a degree lost; new imagery ceases to be created, and old worlds are perverted to stand for things which are not" (33). Although mainly known for his more peaceful depictions of wildflowers, birds, and wildlife about his cabin, emboldened by Emerson, Burroughs also crafted harsh social critique against these aforementioned desires.

Burroughs implanted Emersonian views to fortify his own contention that a simple life tied to the earth is more conducive to high ethical standards than those distractions and frivolities offered by civilization. Throughout his career, Burroughs emphasizes the necessity of direct contact with real natural elements, such as the atmosphere and soil. For him, immersion in Nature leads to a strong moral character that is incompatible with desires for material possessions and what he termed mammon worship. Burroughs is in complete agreement with Emerson's contention that there is an "advantage which the country-life possesses for a powerful mind, over the artificial and curtailed life of cities" (34). To ameliorate these corrupting influences of greed and economic materialism,

Burroughs offers himself as an example of one who lives more of a simple life in accord with the family farm.

Country living is idealized as Burroughs's paean for the farmer reaches its climax at the end of "Phases of Farm Life" in *Signs and Seasons* (1886). The farmer becomes the archetypal figure in contact with Nature, who demonstrates "direct contact with the soil and with the elements; the watching of the clouds and of the weather; the privacies with nature, with bird, beast, and plant; and the close acquaintance with the heart and virtue of the world. The farmer should be the true naturalist; the book in which it is all written is open before him night and day, and how sweet and wholesome all his knowledge is" (*Signs and Seasons* 247–48). Hailing the pastoral ideal, Burroughs cannot sing enough praises about growing up on a farm: "Where the cow is, there is Arcadia; so far as her influence prevails, there is contentment, humility, and sweet, homey life" (*Signs and Seasons* 254). In fact, during his childhood in Roxbury, New York, his family raised cows and sold milk and butter to New York City, and during his later years at his estate Riverby in West Park, New York, Burroughs would tend berry bushes and fruit trees.

The benefits of farming are multifold, including bonds formed with barnyard animals as well as "intimacy with nature, with bird and beast, and with the quickening and elemental forces; his cooperation with the clouds, the sun, the seasons, the heat, wind, rain, frost!" (*Signs and Seasons* 260–61). The Emersonian theme of a restorative nature once again comes to the fore: "Nothing will take the various social distempers which the city and artificial life breed out of a man like farming, like direct and loving contact with the soil. It draws out the poison. It humbles him, teaches him patience and reverence, and restores the proper tone to his system" (*Signs and Seasons* 260). By invoking the healing and restorative powers of Nature over materialistic consumer desires, Burroughs carried Emerson's dictums in "Nature" with him into the very principled manner in which he lived out his life to make proud Emerson his spiritual father-figure. Surely, he preferred the simple life over materialistic desires and vanities and related advice procured through Emerson to his vast readership into the twentieth century.

Childlike Wonder and Curiosity

As a remedy for becoming hardened against Nature through economic materialistic endeavors, Burroughs recommends cultivating childlike wonder and curiosity. This he also garnered from "Nature," where Emerson makes a critical distinction between perceptions of Nature during adulthood versus childhood: "To speak truly, few adult persons can see nature. Most persons do not see the sun. At least they have a very superficial seeing. The sun illuminates only the eye of man, but shines into the eye and heart of the child. The lover of nature is he whose inward and outward senses are still truly adjusted to each other; who has retained the spirit of infancy even into the era of manhood" (23). Furthermore, placing yourself within the forest is a catalyst for obtaining the fountain of youth: "In the woods, too, a man casts off his years, as the snake his slough, and at what period soever of life, is always a child. In the woods, is perpetual youth" (Emerson 24).

Many of Burroughs's accounts are laden with the sense of discovery, expectancy, and the spirit of youthful inquiry that sees wondrous occurrences in a wide range of phenomena. In fact, throughout his career, he emphasizes to readers that they also should always maintain a childlike curiosity and find the miraculous in the near-at-hand, thereby embracing Emerson's proclamations as dictums. These fabulous sensibilities escort him as he encounters immediate surroundings, such as the forest, meadow, or mountain, as heightened experiences through sensory immersion:

> Indeed, when I go to the woods or the fields, or ascend to the hilltop, I do not seem to be gazing upon beauty at all, but to be breathing it like the air. . . . What I enjoy is commensurate with the earth and sky itself. It clings to the rocks and trees; it is kindred to the roughness and savagery; it rises from every tangle and chasm; it perches on the dry oak-stubs with the hawks and buzzards; the crows shed it from their wings and weave it into their nests of coarse sticks; the fox barks it, the cattle low it, and every mountain path leads to its haunts. I am not a spectator of, but a participator in it. It is not an adornment; its roots strike to the centre of the earth. (*Birds and Poets* 170)

Thus, an Emersonian notion of beauty permeates Burroughs's passage, saturating his literary naturalism. In "Nature," Emerson writes famously: "Standing on the bare ground,—my head bathed by the blithe air, and uplifted to infinite space,—all mean egotism vanishes. I become a transparent eye-ball. I am nothing. I see all. The currents of the Universal Being circulate through me; I am part or particle of God. . . . I am the lover of uncontained and immortal beauty" (24). Just as Emerson allows Nature to "circulate through" him, Burroughs allows himself to "be breathing it in like the air." Burroughs's notion of beauty extends to well beyond the "pretty," to subsume more rugged components of the natural world, along with the "chasm," and "hawks and buzzards." Furthermore, he fuses himself to the environment as a "participator," mirroring Emerson's "part or particle of God."

Becoming a Literary Naturalist

In "Nature," Emerson finds correlations between the natural world with moral and spiritual values: "Every natural fact is a symbol of some spiritual fact" (32). He locates "analogical import" between phenomena and human traits, putting forth that "man is an analogist, and studies relations in all objects" (32). Accordingly, "He is placed in the centre of beings, and a ray of relation passes from every other being to him" (32). He keenly realizes the merit in joining the facts of natural history with human experience: "All the facts of natural history taken by themselves have no value, but are barren like a single sex. But marry it to human history, and it is full of life. . . . Whole Floras, and Linnaeus's and Buffon's volume, are but dry catalogues of facts; but the most trivial of these facts, the habit of a plant, the organs, or work, or noise of an insect, applied to the illustration of a fact in intellectual philosophy, or, in any way associated to human nature, affects us in the most lively and agreeable manner" (Emerson 32–33). Burroughs took Emerson's notion of correspondence and inserted it into his own brand of what he labelled literary naturalism. In fact, he uses Emerson's directions here as a cue. His overarching methodology of getting readers interested in natural history is to wed natural history to personal human experience.

In *Indoor Studies* (1889) Burroughs explicitly spells out his developmental criteria for the literary naturalist, who must join the human with nonhuman Nature to create interest for readers. Personal associations are the key to developing relatable and emotional attachments and sentiment. This comes across as an anthropocentric approach to literary art:

> Unless knowledge in some way issues in life, in character, in impulse, in motive, in love, in virtue, in some live human quality or attribute, it does not belong to literature. Man, and man alone, is of perennial interest to man. In nature we glean only human traits,—only those things that in some way appeal to, or are interpretive of, the meaning or ideal within us. Unless the account of your experience to field or forest, or to the bowels of the earth, or to the bottom of the sea, has some human interest, and in some measure falls in with the festival of life, literature will none of it. (Burroughs 70)

Thereby, Burroughs adopts Emersonian correlation tactics as rhetorical strategies to garner emotional connections for his readers and pull their heartstrings, asserting that we all find fascination in living species "because we dimly read themselves there, or see their own lives rendered in new characters on another plane," and that even features of the landscape effectively "serve as vehicles for the expression of our natural emotions" (*Indoor Studies* 70).

In "Nature," Emerson presents a challenge to his readers to become the best read naturalists as he criticizes their separation from Nature and consequent ignorance: "We are as much strangers in nature, as we are aliens from God. We do not understand the notes of the birds" (50). Implicit here is the call for a deeper connection to the natural world and a realization of the soul's omnipresence. He also compels readers to learn more about the flora and fauna in their nearby surroundings with "devout attention to truth" (51). Furthermore, in endeavoring to discover Nature, one must enter the task with an "entire humility" (51). Burroughs took Emerson's words as a personal summons to become the "best read naturalist." In particular, he set out to decipher the "notes of the birds," famously known as John O' Birds, writing dozens of essays upon ornithological ethology. Indeed, Burroughs spent much of his life trying to understand birds' behaviors and songs.

Burroughs gives full credit to Emerson's enormous influence for sparking his "love of nature" and on his literary naturalism:

> I suppose Emerson influenced me most, beginning when I was about nineteen . . . [He] is spirit seemed to blend with Nature, and to reveal the ideal and spiritual values in her works. I think it was this, or something like it, that stimulated me and made bird and tree and sky and flower full of a new interest. It is not nature for its own sake that has mainly drawn me; had it been so, I should have turned out a strict man of science; but nature for the soul's sake—the inward world of ideals and emotions. (qtd. in Barrus *Our Friend John Burroughs*)

In *Indoor Studies*, Burroughs harps on the notion of human interest as an essential quality for literary naturalism. Significantly, in Emersonian fashion he includes the soul: "I should think more meanly of my own books than I do, if I did not believe that my account of bird, or flower, or forest, or stream, contained some stimulus or quality, or suggestion, which the reality itself does not hold, and which is purely the gift of the spirit. Your fact or observation is not literature until it is put in some sort of relation to the soul" (253). Literary naturalism consists of accurate first-hand observations even as they are often transmuted through the writer's emotions and personal associations. Even as Burroughs argues for the intrinsic value of species and habitats and believes that the vast forces of the universe held human beings in special favor, he nonetheless realizes the value in linking aspects of Nature to human experiences in generating literary naturalism as a form of art.

In fitting with his sentimental and nostalgic constitution Burroughs paints his own "soul," if you will, out upon the world in many of his woodland rambles, yet he never falsifies the facts he observes. At the same time, he posits that to become the best read naturalist, one must combine emotion and science, for "Love is the measure of life: only so far as we love do we really live" (*Leaf and Tendril* 3).

Emersonian Spirituality

In the opening paragraph of "Nature" Emerson infuses spirituality. Yet he departs from traditional dogma, heralding his readers to forge their own immediate connections with their world and forego their ancestors' preconceptions, thereby breaking free of a constraining preordained conformity and a "retrospective" age: "Why should not we also enjoy an original relation to the universe? Why should not we have a poetry and philosophy of insight and not of tradition, and a religion by revelation to us, and not the history of theirs?" He sets forth an ambitious agenda and initiation of discovery, nonconformity, and emphasis on the present. Similarly, as if cued by Emerson's radicalism, Burroughs casts off previous generations as he frames Nature as a blessing one can find presently in one's midst: "The beauty of the natural religion is that you have it all the time; you do not have to seek it afar off in myths and legends. . . . It is of to-day; it is now and here; it is everywhere" (*Accepting the Universe* 117).

Burroughs expounds upon what he calls "religious value," as he draws on Emersonian themes to frame his reflections of Nature as a church:

> Amid the decay of creeds, love of nature has high religious value. This has saved many persons in this world—saved them from mammon-worship, and from the frivolity and insincerity of the crowd. It has made their lives placid and sweet. It has given them an inexhaustible field for inquiry, for enjoyment, for the exercise of all their powers, and in the end has not left them soured and dissatisfied. It has made them contented and at home wherever they are in nature—in the house not made with hands. This house is their church, and the rocks and the hills are their altars, and the creed is written in the leaves of the trees and in the flowers of the field and in the sands of the shore. A new creed every day and new preachers, and holy days all the week through. Every walk to the woods is a religious rite, every bath in the stream is a saving ordinance. (*Accepting the Universe* 116)

In the above passage, Burroughs first harkens Emerson's call to dispense of religious dogma, even while he insists on the saving graces of Nature. Like Emerson, Burroughs recognizes the dangers of placing "value" on material possessions and soul-damaging corruption of greed. In direct contrast, in Nature people may gain a sense of wholesome peace. Moreover, citizens can learn about natural history, even as they engage in outdoor recreation and creative play. With many religious signifiers, such as "church," "altars," and "creed," "holy days," and "religious rite," Burroughs figures a natural world suffused with spirit. Situating his discussion in biblical terms, Burroughs's most revelatory passages are cued by his reaping of Emersonian spirituality. His grander visions are laden with figurations of religious imagery due to the license he received from Emerson, whose texts helped him imagine Nature as a church.

Emerson's Enduring Legacy

Until his death in 1921, Burroughs continually reflected back on Emersonian dictums by which he lived: "Emerson says, 'The day does not seem wholly profane in which we have given heed to some natural object.' It is such little incidents as I have been relating that redeem many of my own days, and give to my pastimes a touch of something I would not willingly miss from them" (*The Summit of the Years* 256). Certainly, Emerson's immense influence has traversed well beyond his lifetime into the twentieth century and beyond. Clara Barrus explains that while Burroughs was in his final days suffering from illness, he made efforts to revise his essay on Emerson titled "Flies in Amber." Barrus asked Burroughs to compose a conclusion and then, she relates, "he sat up in bed, and wrote the closing sentences, which proved to be the last he ever penned" (*The Last Harvest* 96). Burroughs caps his literary career with these final enchanting words in tribute to Emerson:

> Let us keep alive the Emersonian memories: that such a man has lived and wrought among us. Let us teach our children his brave and heroic words, and plant our lives upon as secure and ethical a foundation as he did. Let us make pilgrimages to Concord, and stand with uncovered heads beneath the pine tree where his ashes rest. He left us an estate in the fair land of the Ideal. He bequeathed

us treasures that thieves cannot break through and steal, nor time corrupt, nor rust nor moth destroy. (102)

Works Cited

Barrus, Clara. *Our Friend John Burroughs*. Houghton Mifflin, 1914.

Burroughs, John. *Accepting the Universe*. Russel and Russel, 1920.

__________. *Birds and Poets*. 1877, Houghton Mifflin, 1904.

__________. *Indoor Studies*. 1889, Houghton Mifflin, 1904.

__________. *The Last Harvest*. 1922, Russel and Russel, 1968.

__________. *Leaf and Tendril*. 1908, Houghton Mifflin, 1908.

__________. *Literary Values*. 1902, Houghton Mifflin, 1904.

__________. *Riverby*. 1894, Houghton Mifflin, 1904.

__________. *Signs and Seasons*. 1886, Houghton Mifflin, 1904.

__________. *The Summit of the Years*. 1913, Houghton Mifflin, 1908.

__________. *Under the Apple Trees*. 1916, Houghton Mifflin, 1916.

Emerson, Ralph Waldo. "Nature." *Selections from Ralph Waldo Emerson*. Edited by Stephen E. Whicher, Houghton Mifflin, 1960.

Writing Dawn and Day in the Work of Mary Oliver and Ralph Waldo Emerson

Jeff Westover

Mary Oliver shows her devotion to Ralph Waldo Emerson's ideas throughout her work. She even wrote an introduction to a collection of his writing. The first of two epigraphs to Oliver's 2002 volume *What Do We Know* ("the invisible and imponderable is the sole fact") is from Emerson's "Poetry and the Imagination." The epigraph to *The Blue Iris* (2004) is from "Gifts," and the second epigraph to *Swan* (2010) is "'tis curious we only believe as deep as we live," from "Beauty." She addresses him directly in "From Percy (Nine)," writing,

> Emerson, I am trying to live,
>
> as you said we must, the examined life.
> But there are days I wish
>
> there was less in my head to examine,
> not to speak of my busy heart. (*Red Bird* 39)

Oliver refers to him again a few pages later in "Not This, Not That" (*Red Bird* 47). Similarly, after naming him in "More Evidence," she exclaims, "how the elegance of his can make me weep over my own inadequacy" (*Swan* 52). In "Rhapsody," the seventh section of *The Leaf and the Cloud* (2000), Oliver writes,

> I am so busy among
> Shelley's long poems, Plato, Godwin's
> Enquiry, Carlyle concerning
> the failed revolution that bloody sorrow, and,
> as always, Emerson. (*Leaf and the Cloud* 34)

These examples are not likely to be comprehensive, and they are all explicit references to Emerson or quotations from his work. Beyond such references, Emerson's ideas about nature, language, the soul, beauty, God, and undoubtedly other subjects leave their mark on Oliver's writing.

Paying Tribute by Paying Attention

Like Emerson, Oliver pursues "an original relation to the universe" (Emerson, *Essays and Lectures* 7). One way she achieves this is through her emphasis on morning scenes, which are moments of promise and awakening to the world and the inner self. With the dawn comes light, the enabling of vision, and a sense of opportunity. Oliver also represents episodes of heightened attention to the natural world, allowing insights to emerge organically, as Emerson says they should in "The Poet" (*Essays* 450). Although Emerson valued the importance of common daily experience, his rhetoric is often more high-flown than Oliver's. Moreover, for Emerson, "Every touch should thrill" (*Essays* 448), whereas Oliver's epiphanies are often more ordinary. Nevertheless, both writers highlight the beauty and wonder of nature in relation to themselves as well as their readers. As Mark Johnson observes, "Emersonian rapture is at the core of her work, and informs her sense of what poetry does" (82).

Indeed, throughout her writing Oliver pays homage to Emerson by paying attention to nature. She invites her readers to join her in the adventure of exploring the self by exploring the world. As she writes in her introduction to the volume of Emerson, "The one thing he is adamant about is that we should look—we *must* look—for that is the liquor of life, that brooding upon issues, that attention to thought even as we weed the garden or milk the cow" (*Upstream* 69). Oliver emphasizes the centrality of such looking in poem after poem throughout her career. In "To Begin with, the Sweet Grass," for example, she insists, "Look, and look again. / This world is not just a little thrill for the eyes" (*Evidence* 37).

Both Emerson and Oliver describe their reverence for nature and its centrality to their inner life in key passages from their writing. In *Nature* Emerson famously writes about his experience in transcendent terms: "Standing on the bare ground,—my head bathed by the blithe air, and uplifted into infinite space,—all mean egotism vanishes. I become a transparent eye-ball; I am nothing; I see all; the currents of the Universal Being circulate through me; I am part or particle of God" (*Essays* 10). Oliver closely echoes Emerson's idea of being nothing and seeing everything in her poem "Entering the Kingdom" (from *Twelve Moons*, 1979), but she avoids his oracular rhetoric. Writing in a more muted vein, she explains that

> The dream of my life
> Is
> . . . .
> To learn something by being nothing
> A little while but the rich
> Lens of attention. (*Devotions* 406)

The enjambment and understatement of these lines emphasize the poet's desire, focus, patience, and poise rather than Emerson's ecstasy. Oliver articulates an aspiration, whereas Emerson makes a revelation. Her phrasing allows a reader to imagine that the lens of her attention may belong to a microscope or a camera as much as to an eye, while the lulling l- and z-sounds of "lens" reinforce her dreamy atmosphere. The accent on *lens* calls attention to the word as an image and as an instrument of vision, so that we become aware not only of what is seen but of our relationship to it and to the means of seeing it. As Kirsten Hotelling Zona points out regarding Oliver's work, "the more acutely we look beyond ourselves, the more palpable becomes the lens through which we look" (125).

At the same time, through the ongoing action signified by the participle in her title ("Entering"), Oliver conveys something of Emerson's transcendental moment. By alluding in her title to Jesus' statement that "The Kingdom of God is within you" (Luke 17: 21), Oliver allies her poem with a tradition of spiritual interiority that also parallels Emerson. However, she adapts the biblical statement in a surprising way, because she portrays an animal kingdom instead of a paradisal one. As Diane S. Bonds puts it, in Oliver's poetry

"The Kingdom of God is replaced by all the 'small kingdoms' of nature, kingdoms possessing their own kind of infinitude" (8). This is borne out in a companion poem: in "The Other Kingdoms" Oliver refers to trees, snow, and "creatures, with their / thick fur, their shy and wordless gaze" (*Devotions* 93).

Artist of the Ordinary

Oliver is profoundly Emersonian in forging a first-hand relation to the world, but she is less heady when it comes to her figurations of cosmic oneness. In the essay "The Perfect Days," for instance, she offers a low-key account of an important epiphany:

> Once, years ago, I emerged from the woods in the early morning at the end of a walk and—it was the most casual of moments—as I stepped from under the trees into the mild, pouring-down sunlight I experienced a sudden impact, a *seizure* of happiness. . . . I made no struggle toward it; it was given. Time seemed to vanish. Urgency vanished. Any important difference between myself and all other things vanished. I knew that I belonged to the world, and felt comfortably my own containment in that totality. (*Long Life* 33–34)

Oliver shares with Emerson a profound reverence for nature, a respect for the intensely lived moment, and a harmonious union with all things. Her experience of unity parallels Emerson's, but her calm tone differs from his ecstatic utterance. Oliver goes on to emphasize this difference, explaining, "I did not feel that I understood any mystery, not at all; rather that I could be happy and feel blessed within the perplexity" (*Long Life* 34).

Oliver's eschewal of mysticism marks a difference in her work from nineteenth-century Transcendentalism. She characteristically describes her raptures in down-to-earth terms. At the same time, the continuities between herself and her forebear outweigh such differences in rhetoric and temperament. Her communion with nature does have a lot in common with Emerson's enthusiastic surrender to the Oversoul. After all, although she disclaims the visionary, she does portray the experience as a *seizure* by some power beyond herself. (Perhaps Oliver's word alludes to *carpe diem*, the Latin motto meaning "seize the day." If so, the day has seized her, not the other way around.) Moreover, both writers emphasize the emphatic goodness and wonder of being alive, and the role nature plays in making them aware of that. Emerson and Oliver consistently portray existence as a privilege and adventure.

Readers of the preceding excerpts may notice a further similarity: both writers use the verb *vanish*. For Emerson, it is "egotism" that vanishes, whereas for Oliver it is an oppressive sense of time and difference. Although the specific objects of the verb differ for each writer, the overall meaning of their statements is similar. They both express the alleviation of a burden or the removal of a barrier. Moreover, both writers represent their particular interaction with nature as a spiritual zenith. Oliver makes this explicit when she points out later that her "sudden awareness" had a lasting impact, shaping important decisions she made later in life. Both writers strive to show that their experience of nature defines them.

Morning Consciousness in Emerson and Oliver

Emerson and Oliver revisit the moment of their union with the world by focusing on the individual day and daily life. For both, the day represents the opportunity to live a full life. They explore ways of interacting with the landscape and fellow living creatures in order to make their lives meaningful. Dawn and sunrise become metaphors for possibility and newness, whereas day serves as a trope for what the individual makes of that possibility. (As Emerson insists in such texts as *Nature* and "Poetry and Imagination," the natural world readily supplies symbols for human thought.) Emerson and Oliver offer positive and negative visions of the day, but they both emphasize the value of attentive daily living.

As she makes plain in her poems, Oliver was in the habit of rising early in order to witness the dawn. She even named one book *Why I Wake Early* (2004), and another, *A Thousand Mornings* (2012). A consciousness of the dawn is prevalent throughout her work, to such an extent that morning scenes can help readers understand her poetic goals over all. As she puts it in "Morning Poem" (from *Dream Work*, 1986), "Every morning / the world / is created" (*Devotions* 345). Emerson shows his own commitment to daily mindfulness in the following passage from *Nature*: "I see the spectacle of nature from the hill-top over against my house, from day-break to sun-rise, with emotions an angel might share. The long slender bars of cloud float like fishes in the sea of crimson light. From the earth, as a shore, I look out into that silent sea. I seem to partake its rapid transformation: the active enchantment reaches my dust, and I dilate and conspire with the morning wind" (*Essays* 15).

Emerson's topsy-turvy likening of the sky to a sea provokes a thrilling dizziness, imparting to his readers a sense of the morning's splendor. The comparison of the sky to a sea turns his vista upside down, figuring the sunrise as a disorienting but enlivening perception. Emerson's reference to dust intensifies the drama of the sky's "rapid transformation" and further connects his personal perception to the natural world. Dust may designate the earth beneath his feet, but it is also a metaphor for his body, a metaphor he elaborates on in the final clause of the passage. The metaphor derives from the Bible: "all are of the dust, and all turn to dust again" (King James Version, Ecclesiastes 3:20b). By drawing a parallel between the motion of the morning wind and himself, Emerson plays on the etymology of *conspire*. This verb shares the same Latin root as *inspire* and *spirit*. By writing, "I dilate and conspire," Emerson means that he is both partnering with the natural force of the wind and (etymologically speaking) "breathing together" along with it, sharing in its expansive morning rhythms as one's lungs dilate, or expand, with air when taking in a breath. Together with the analogy comparing the body to dust, Emerson's wordplay encourages his readers to experience his description of the dawn as an act of creation, as when God made Adam, breathing life into his nostrils (Genesis 2:7). In Hebrew, the words for human being (*'adam*) and ground (*'adhama*) are similar (*Oxford Annotated Bible* 4). This interpretation of the passage from *Nature* shows that it is a clear parallel to Oliver's poetic claim that the world is born anew each day.

In his 1844 essay "Nature" (not his book of the same name), Emerson writes that "It seems as if the day was not wholly profane, in which we have given heed to some natural object" (*Essays* 542). This idea is central to Oliver's writing. As Emerson's friend and protégé Henry David Thoreau writes in *Walden*, "Morning is when I am awake and there is a dawn in me" (394). (When Thoreau built the cabin on Walden Pond that he wrote about in his book, he did so on territory owned by Emerson.) Like Emerson, Oliver uses the resources of poetry to dramatize the wonders of the natural world and the potential significance of morning time. She aims to be vitally aware of the world's beauty and of the mystery and excitement of life. She shares with Thoreau a keen sense of wakefulness as meaningful *awareness*, as living vividly. Like Thoreau, she subscribes to the view that "To affect the quality of the day, that is the highest of arts" (394). As she puts it in "October" (from *New and Selected Poems*, 1991–92): "I want to love this world / as though it's the last chance I'm ever going to get / to be alive / and know it" (*Devotions* 309). She drives home the point just as forcefully in the form of the question that ends "The Summer Day" (from *House of Light*, 1990): "Tell me, what is it you plan to do / with your one wild and precious life?" (*Devotions* 316).

Oliver follows Emerson and Thoreau in seeking to live a spiritually abundant life every day, even in demanding circumstances. As Emerson puts it in "Works and Days," "He only is rich who owns the day" (*Collected Works*, VII: 85). The benefit of this ideal is that it can motivate one to fulfill the aspiration. The drawback is that there are inevitable moments of difficulty, ennui, and languor in any life. The potential for disillusionment presents a major challenge for writers espousing such an ideal. In fact, both Emerson and Oliver demonstrate their concern about such disillusionment and spiritual failure. Oliver often leavens her portraits of these phenomena with calm good humor. For his part, Emerson provides a somber portrait of spiritual inadequacy in "Days," one of his best poems.

Before discussing "Days," however, let us consider a prose passage by Emerson. The passage will provide an aid to understanding his poem. In "Works and Days," an essay from *Society and Solitude*

(1870), Emerson writes, "The days are ever divine. . . . They are of the least pretension and of the greatest capacity of anything that exists. They come and go like muffled and veiled figures, sent from a distant friendly party; but they say nothing, and if we do not use the gifts they bring, they carry them as silently away" (*Collected Works*, Vol. VII: 85). This scenario is played out in "Days":

> Daughters of Time, the hypocritic Days,
> Muffled and dumb like barefoot dervishes,
> And marching single in an endless file,
> Bring diadems and fagots in their hands.
> To each they offer gifts after his will,
> Bread, kingdoms, stars, and sky that holds them all.
> I, in my pleached garden, watched the pomp,
> Forgot my morning wishes, hastily
> Took a few herbs and apples, and the Day
> Turned and departed silent. I, too late,
> Under the solemn fillet saw the scorn. (*Collected Poems* 178)

Emerson depicts the day as bearing gifts of "diadems and fagots," meaning crowns and bundles, terms that he further defines in the expanding catalog of "Bread, kingdoms, stars, and sky." By contrasting the "few herbs and apples" that he hastily takes with the increasing magnitudes of "kingdoms, stars, and sky," the poem takes the measure of the speaker's mistake, which accounts for the scorn he sees on the face of the departing Day. The poem memorializes the speaker's failure to seize the day and make the most of it.

As I have mentioned, Oliver offers a host of poems about the morning, possibility, and the hopeful outlook associated with the beginning of a day. Most of these poems are quite celebratory, but some of her work expresses the kind of regret Emerson displays in "Days." In "The Kookaburras" (from *House of Light*, 1990), for example, the poet remembers an opportunity to respond to fellow living beings, an opportunity she squandered: "The kookaburras, kingfishers, pressed against the edge of / their cage, they asked me to open the door." Years later, she suffers remorse in visceral terms: "The sun shines on the latch of their cage. / I lie in the dark, my heart pounding." Having seen the birds and deciphered their plight from the look in their eyes, the poet said "*no*, and walked away." The poem begins with an epigram, or something like the moral of the story: "In every heart there is a coward and a procrastinator" (*Devotions* 321). The poet's refusal to release the birds exemplifies the cowardice of this opening assertion. The last word of the line, *procrastinator*, means a person who defers a task. The English word includes *cras*, which is the Latin word for tomorrow. Instead of living for the day, fully in the moment, the poet shows how she made the mistake of living for a vaguer later.

Another piece by Oliver shares the tone of regret in "The Kookaburras." In the first of "Three Prose Poems" included in *Winter Hours* (1999), Oliver writes, "*Oh, yesterday, that one*, we all cry out. *Oh, that one!* How rich and possible everything was! How ripe, ready, lavish, and filled with excitement—how hopeful we were on those summer days, under the clean, white racing clouds. *Oh, yesterday!*" (*New and Selected* 2: 113). The refrain of this piece expresses a lament for something unrecoverable except through memory. The recollection may seem Wordsworthian in its apparent spontaneity, but it is haunted rather than tranquil. The piece expresses the misguided but common state of consciousness that reaches toward the past with frustrated longing. Dwelling on the plenitude of a cherished moment is understandable, but such dwelling blinds one to the new potential of the present, benighting the mind and foreclosing the possibility of a new opportunity.

Making Your Own Days

In contrast to the prose poem and "The Kookaburras" are many morning poems with a more optimistic outlook. Take "First Happenings," for instance. Launching this prose poem with her wonderful title, Oliver rushes headlong into the following rhapsody: "A morning-glory morning with its usual glory, dawn particularly startling with citrons and mauves, petunias in the garden flashing their tender signals of gratitude. The sunflowers creak in their grass-colored dresses" (*New and Selected* 2: 8). The poet conveys the exuberance of daybreak by repeating "morning" and "glory," offering an array of exotic colors, using forceful verbs (*flashing*, *creak*), and combining brisk rhythm with compact consonance in the final five words of the first sentence. Oliver's sunflower metaphor positively dances with imaginative abandon. The effect is to dazzle the reader with her paean to the morning, to wake one up with the sun's rising splendor.

In "Sunrise" (from *Dream Work*, 1986), Oliver compares the ideas of living and dying for "an idea, / or the world." This comparison leads to a meditation on martyrs who die

> brilliantly,
> letting
> their small bodies be bound
>
> to the stake,
> creating
> an unforgettable
> fury of light. (*New and Selected* 1: 125)

Shifting abruptly from this grisly image, Oliver goes on to explore the idea of oneness among all living beings. In the burgeoning light of "this morning,"

> I thought
> how the sun
> blazes for everyone
> just
> so joyfully
> as it rises
> under the lashes
> of my own eyes, and I thought
> I am so many!
> What is my name? (*New and Selected* 1: 125–26)

Oliver's insight echoes Jesus' remark in the Sermon on the Mount that God "maketh his sun to rise on the evil and the good" (Matthew 5:25). Moreover, by putting the contrast between dying violently and living joyfully at the center of her poem, she makes the case for a universal consciousness. Her "I am so many!" echoes Walt Whitman's "I contain multitudes" (246). This jubilation leads the speaker to a lively sense of union with all others in the penultimate stanza of "Sunrise." Her form of witness (the etymological meaning of *martyr*) demonstrates that a continuing commitment to the unity of all living beings is as honorable as dying for an idea. Living mindfully in compassionate union with others constitutes "another one / of the ways / to enter fire" (*New and Selected* 1: 126). "Sunrise" exemplifies the claim Oliver makes in "For the Man Cutting the Grass" that "every poem must . . . reach the regions of shared experience, and therefore is not one man's poem more than another's" (732).

Oliver assiduously cultivates a morning consciousness throughout her poetry. As she writes in poem 6 of "In Blackwater Woods," she aspires to "bring to each blue and cloudy morning a / suitable exuberance" (*White Pine* 31). In "This Morning" (*Devotions* 4) from *Felicity* (2015), she invites her readers to recognize the wondrous in the midst of the ordinary. The poem describes the hatching of birds and the blind cries of the chicks "chirping for food." It focuses on their instinct and provides a catalog of things they do not yet know, including "the sky that's waiting" for them and the fact that they have wings. The implication is that the chicks will, with good luck, someday use those wings to fly, and the sky is anticipating or looking forward to their action. The poem ends with the plain but joyful statement that "just like that . . . / a miracle is / taking place" (*Devotions* 4). Oliver uses the present progressive tense to bring the reader directly into the moment, so that we experience the miracle happening now. The poem also gets its expressive power from the contrast between what the chicks do not know and what the human witness does. The promise of the moment, its beauty and pathos, unfold in each line of this short poem.

Oliver repeats this kind of performance, and with similar brio, again and again in her morning poems. Echoing "Softest of Mornings" (*Devotions* 193), in "Why I Wake Early" (from the book of the same name, 2004), she greets the sun with glee, telling the story of how the sun makes a fresh day:

> Hello, sun in my face,
> Hello, you who make the morning
> and spread it over the fields
> and into the faces of the tulips
> and the nodding morning glories. (*Devotions* 171)

Later in the poem, it turns out that what the sun does is reciprocated by the poet when she says, "Watch, now, how I start the day / in happiness, in kindness" (*Devotions* 171). The gusto of this response is quite charming, increasing the pleasurable impact of the poem on readers, and reminding them of the importance of making the most of their own days.

As she does in "This Morning," Oliver makes great use of the present tense in "Why I Wake Early," drawing her readers into the intimate moment between the sun and herself. She intensifies this effect by making the present time of the poem as immediate as possible through the sustaining action of the sun ("make . . . / and spread"). When you read the poem, you experience an intense, unfolding event just as it happens. The reader is in the middle of the action, watching the sun's mighty rise in the sky, and then joining the sun itself to watch the poet *now* as she begins her day. The change of perspective is exhilarating because Oliver forces the reader to slow down by presenting a series of staccato monosyllables in the penultimate line, spotlighting *now* by surrounding it with commas that function as caesurae, and immediately rhyming *now* with *how*. There is a satisfying, ceremonial quality to this slowing rhythm, for the poet returns thanks to the sun by offering it her own hours. It is as though she has clapped her hands to make us pause and watch her, so that we notice how well she will engage the coming day.

In "Morning at Blackwater" (from *Blue Iris*, 2004), Oliver offers a beautiful hymn to the morning:

It's almost dawn
and the usual half-miracles begin
within my own personal body as the light
enters the gates of the east and climbs
into the fields of the sky, and the birds lift
their very unimportant heads from the branches
and begin to sing; and the insects too,
and the rustling leaves, and even
the most common of earthly things, the grass,
can't let it begin—another morning—without
making some comment of gladness, respiring softly
with the honey of their green bodies, and the white
blossoms of the swamp honeysuckle, hovering just where
the path and the pond almost meet,
shake from the folds of their bodies
such happiness it enters the air as fragrance,
the day's first pale and elegant affirmation.
And the old gods liked so well, they say,
the sweet odor of prayer. (*Devotions* 166)

The sun rises in the form of "light" that "climbs / into the fields of the sky." Oliver's trope is like Emerson's flip-flopping of sky and sea in the passage above from *Nature*. Oliver's sky is turned into a field, which similarly inverts Earth and heaven, jostling readers' mental habits and exhilarating them by sharing the thrill of daybreak. The poem is also a tribute to "half-miracles," or to the ordinary course of the dawn. Sunrise brings light to rouse ordinary creatures who wake with song and excitement—an enthusiastic "gladness" that arises from the mere fact of being.

Exuberance Is Beauty

Oliver's exuberance is embedded in her syntax: most of the poem is one extended sequence. The sentence structure emphasizes the action of rising by moving from "light," which "climbs," to "birds" that "lift / their very unimportant heads" in a common ascent. But this rising motion leads to a further paratactic progression of events set off by dawn. The emergence of day unleashes a great joy among "that most common of earthly things, the grass." Oliver's reference to grass pays homage to Whitman, who chose the image as the emblem of his lifework by naming it *Leaves of Grass*. In the sixth section of "Song of Myself," moreover, he calls the grass a "uniform hieroglyphic," noticing that it grows everywhere and can be enjoyed by everyone (193). Oliver's word choice ("unimportant" and "most common") emphasizes the ordinariness of the event, but by mixing mundane features with the great gladness of all creatures, the poem paradoxically enacts the splendor it seeks to communicate. This paradox is wonderfully summed up in the opening phrase "the usual half-miracles."

By paratactic, I mean that the parts of the sentence are joined by coordinating conjunctions (*and*, in this case). The feature is important to notice because each event is rendered equally important and equally part of greeting the new day with "gladness." The equal weight given to all creatures' praise of the day is expressed in the poem's very syntax. Those *ands* unify the creatures and highlight their importance. This unity recalls Whitman's descriptions of the grass in "Song of Myself" and Emerson's visionary oneness with the world in the transparent eyeball passage from *Nature*.

A New Day Dawns

It is notable that Oliver opens and closes *Devotions*, a selection of poems spanning her career, with poems about morning time. The last poem in *Devotions* is called "Morning in a New Land" (from *No Voyage and Other Poems* 1963):

> In trees still dripping night some nameless birds
> Woke, shook out their arrowy wings, and sang,
> Slowly, like finches sifting through a dream.
> The pink sun fell, like glass, into the fields.
> Two chestnuts, and a dapple gray,
> Their shoulders wet with light, their dark hair streaming,
> Climbed the hill. The last mist fell away,

And under the trees, beyond time's brittle drift,
I stood like Adam in his lonely garden
On that first morning, shaken out of sleep,
Rubbing his eyes, listening, parting the leaves,
Like tissue on some vast, incredible gift. (*Devotions* 442)

The Adamic poet looking at a new world, waking from the sleep that preceded creation, sums up the morning consciousness I have explored in this essay: dawn is a promise to realize before the day is out, the natural world appeals to our shared sense of beauty and refreshes the soul, and one should strive to live life fully and meaningfully. Oliver's use of the word *shake* vividly unites the opening of the bird's wings (lines 1–2) with the speaker's waking consciousness (line 10). There is a rapturous quality to this motion that corresponds to other moments in Oliver's writing, such as the seizure she describes in "The Perfect Day." Similarly, the honeysuckle blossoms in "Morning at Blackwater" "shake" sheer happiness from "the folds of their bodies" in the form of "fragrance." Building on this exuberance at the end of "Morning in a New Land," Oliver likens the world to a gift, as Emerson often did. For both writers, the point is to accept the gift with thanks, humility, and love.

Thank you to Jericho Williams for his advice about improving an earlier draft.

In this essay I have tried to honor the memory of two friends: Cheryl Hindrichs, who knew how to live, and Scott Kost, who gave me a set of Emerson's writings and a rotating calendar inscribed with Psalm 90:12 when I was in high school.

Works Cited

Bonds, Diane S. "The Language of Nature in the Poetry of Mary Oliver." *Women's Studies*, vol. 21, 1992, pp. 1–15.

Emerson, Ralph Waldo. *Collected Poems and Translations*. Library of America, 1994.

__________. *The Collected Works of Ralph Waldo Emerson*. Volume VII. Harvard UP, 2007.

__________. *Essays and Lectures*. Library of America, 1983.

The Holy Bible. King James Version. (Ecclesiastes 3.20), Oxford University Press, n.d.

__________. (Genesis 2.7), *The King James Bible.* Oxford UP, n.d.

__________. (Luke 17.21), *The King James Bible.* Oxford UP, n.d.

__________. (Matthew 5.25), *The King James Bible.* Oxford UP, n.d.

Johnson, Mark. "'Keep Looking': Mary Oliver's Emersonian Project." *Massachusetts Review*, vol. 46, no. 1, 2005, pp. 78–98.

The New Oxford Annotated Bible. New Revised Standard Version. Oxford UP, 1994.

Oliver, Mary. *The Blue Iris: Poems and Essays.* Beacon, 2004.

__________. *Devotions: The Selected Poems of Mary Oliver*. Penguin, 2017.

__________. *Evidence*. Beacon, 2009.

__________. "For the Man Cutting the Grass." *Georgia Review*, vol. 35, no. 4, 1981, pp. 730–33.

__________. *The Leaf and the Cloud.* Da Capo-Perseus, 2000.

__________. *Long Life: Essays and Other Writings*. Da Capo-Perseus, 2004.

__________. *New and Selected Poems*. Volume 1. Beacon, 1992.

__________. *New and Selected Poems*. Volume 2. Beacon, 2005.

__________. *Red Bird*. Beacon, 2008.

__________. *Swan*. Beacon, 2010.

__________. *A Thousand Mornings*. Penguin, 2012.

__________. *Upstream: Selected Essays*. Penguin, 2016.

__________. *What Do We Know*. Da Capo-Perseus, 2002.

__________. *White Pine: Poems and Prose Poems*. Houghton Mifflin, 1994.

__________. *Why I Wake Early*. Beacon, 2004.

Thoreau, Henry David. *A Week on the Cord and Merrimack Rivers. Walden. The Maine Woods. Cape Cod*. Library of America, 1985.

Whitman, Walt. *Poetry and Prose*. Library of America, 1982.

Zona, Kirstin Hotelling. "'An Attitude of Noticing': Mary Oliver's Ecological Ethic." *ISLE*, vol. 18, no. 1, 2011, pp. 123–42.

RESOURCES

Chronology of Ralph Waldo Emerson's Life

1803	Emerson is born on May 25 in Boston.
1807	In April, his brother John dies from tuberculosis.
1811	Emerson's father dies on May 12, less than two weeks before Emerson turns eight.
1812	Emerson begins study at Boston Latin School. He studies math and writing as well as Latin and Greek and begins writing poetry.
1814	Emerson's sister Mary Caroline passes. In November, his family moves to Concord to live in a house built by Emerson's grandfather.
1815	Emerson's family moves back to Boston.
1817	He begins attending Harvard College.
1820	In January, Emerson begins writing in a journal, which he will continue to do for more than fifty years.
1821	He is elected "Class Poet"; in August, he graduates from Harvard.
1822	Emerson publishes an essay entitled: "The Religion of the Middle Ages" in *The Christian Disciple*.
1823	His brother William leaves for Germany, and Emerson steps in to lead the school.
1824	Emerson closes the school in December.

1825	In February, he begins studying at Harvard's Divinity School.
1826	Emerson becomes licensed to preach as a Unitarian in October and begins a stint as a minister. He visits Charleston, South Carolina, as part of an effort to help remedy a sickness related to his lungs.
1827	He meets Ellen Louisa Tucker in December.
1828	Emerson becomes engaged to Tucker.
1829	He begins work as a junior pastor at Second Church in Boston in January and is later promoted to pastor in July. Emerson and Ellen Tucker are married in September.
1831	At 19, Ellen Tucker dies as a result of tuberculosis.
1832	Emerson resigns from Second Church in December and then embarks on his first trip to Europe three days later. While there, he meets Thomas Carlyle, William Wordsworth, and Samuel Taylor Coleridge, among others, and the places he visits over the course of the next eleven months include: England, Scotland, Switzerland, France, Italy, Sicily, and Malta.
1833	Emerson returns to the United States in October.
1834	He meets Lydia Jackson in Plymouth in March; his brother Edward dies due to tuberculosis in October; Emerson moves to the Old Manse in Concord eight days later.

1835	He becomes engaged to Jackson in January and begins a lecture series during the same month. In September, he marries Lydia "Lidian" Jackson and in November starts another lecture series.
1836	Another brother, Charles Emerson, dies due to tuberculosis in May. *Nature*, Emerson's first book, is published in September and his first son, Waldo, is born on October 30.
1837	Emerson delivers "The American Scholar" address at Harvard's Phi Beta Kappa graduation ceremony in late August and his first antislavery address in Concord in November.
1838	In late April, Emerson speaks against the removal of members of the Cherokee nation and other tribes. He writes a letter to President Van Buren that is later printed in newspapers. In July, he delivers his famous "Divinity School Address" at Harvard.
1839	His second child Ellen is born in February.
1841	In March, his *Essays: First Series* is published, and his third child (Edith) is born in November.
1842	Son Waldo dies of scarlet fever in January, and Emerson struggles immensely during the course of the next two years. He travels to New York in February and begins a stint as editor of *The Dial* in March.
1844	The final issue of the *Dial* is published in April; in July, his fourth child Edward is born. He delivers another antislavery speech ("Emancipation of the Negroes in the British West Indies") in August; in September, he buys fourteen acres at Walden Pond. In October, *Essays: Second Series* is published.

1845	Henry David Thoreau moves to a cabin on Walden Pond in July. Emerson begins a winter lecture series in Concord in December.
1846	His First collection of poetry (*Poems*) is published in December.
1847	By Emerson's invitation, Thoreau leaves Walden Pond and moves in with Lidian and the children in September. In October, Emerson travels for a second time to Europe, where he meets Charles Dickens, Alexis de Tocqueville, and Alfred, Lord Tennyson.
1848	Emerson begins a lecture series in London in June and returns from Europe in late July.
1849	Another lecturer series begins in February in Massachusetts. *Nature, Addresses, and Lectures* are published in September.
1850	*Representative Men* is published in January, and Emerson begins a midwestern lecture tour in May.
1851	Emerson begins another lecture series in Pittsburgh and delivers "Fugitive Slave Law Address" in Concord in May.
1852	In November, Emerson starts another midwestern lecture tour, which lasts through February 1853.
1853	His mother, Ruth Emerson, passes away in November.
1854	In March, Emerson gives his second "Fugitive Slave Address" in New York; in August, he offers the commencement address at Williams College. Emerson meets Walt Whitman in December and Henry David Thoreau's *Walden; or Life in the Woods* is published.

1855	In August, he offers the commencement address at Amherst College, and in September, addresses the women's rights convention in Boston.
1856	*English Traits* is published in August.
1857	Emerson embarks on another midwestern lecture tour in January and February.
1858	He begins a lecture series in Boston in March.
1859	His brother, Robert Emerson, dies in May. Emerson delivers a speech at John Brown's memorial service in Boston in December, following Brown's execution after his failed raid at Harper's Ferry, West Virginia in October.
1860	He offers another lecture tour in the Midwest in January and February and publishes *The Conduct of Life* in December.
1861	Emerson begins a lecture series in Boston in April. The American Civil War begins on April 12.
1862	Fellow naturalist and friend Henry David Thoreau passes due to tuberculosis in April, and Emerson offers his eulogy "Thoreau," which is published in *The Atlantic Monthly* in August.
1863	Aunt Mary Moody Emerson dies at 88 in May; Emerson lectures throughout the year.
1864	Emerson attends Nathaniel Hawthorne's funeral in May.

1865	The American Civil War concludes on April 9, and President Abraham Lincoln is assassinated five days later. On April 19, Emerson presents an address at the Lincoln Memorial Service in Concord.
1866	Emerson goes on a midwestern lecture tour early in the year and starts a lecture series in Boston in April. He earns an honorary law doctorate from Harvard University in July.
1867	His second collection of poems (*May-Day and Other Pieces*) is published in April. He offers commencement address at Harvard entitled "The Progress of Culture" in July.
1868	Brother William Emerson dies in September.
1870	*Society and Solitude*, a collection of essays, is published in March; Emerson begins a lecture series at Harvard in April.
1871	Emerson visits California, where he meets John Muir and Brigham Young; he embarks on a midwestern lecture tour in November.
1872	Emerson delivers an address entitled "What Books to Read" at Howard University in January. Emerson's health begins to decline; he travels to Europe and later Egypt beginning in October.
1873	He returns from overseas in May.
1874	*Parnassus*, an anthology of Emerson's favorite poems, is published in December.
1875	*Letters and Social Aims* is published in December.

1876	*Selected Poems* is published in November.
1880	Emerson gives his 100th lecture at the Concord Lyceum in February.
1882	Emerson dies as a result of pneumonia at the age of 78 in Concord.

Works Consulted

Atkinson, Brooks, editor. *The Essential Writings of Ralph Waldo Emerson*. Modern Library, 2000.

Bosco, Ronald. "Ralph Waldo Emerson, 1803–1882: A Brief Biography." *A Historical Guide to Ralph Waldo Emerson*. Oxford UP, 2000, pp. 9–58.

Porte, Joel, and Saundra Morris. "Chronology of Emerson's Life." *The Cambridge Companion to Ralph Waldo Emerson*. Cambridge, 1999, pp. xvi–xviii.

von Fronk, Albert J. *An Emerson Chronology*, 2 vols. Studio Non Troppo, 2016.

Wayne, Tiffany. *Critical Companion to Ralph Waldo Emerson*. Facts On File, 2010.

Works by Ralph Waldo Emerson

Nonfiction

Nature. 1836

Essays: First Series. 1841

Essays: Second Series. 1844

Nature; Addresses and Lectures. 1849

Representative Men. 1850

English Traits. 1856

The Conduct of Life. 1860

Society and Solitude. 1870

Letters and Social Aims. 1875

Natural History of the Intellect. 1893

Poetry

Poems. 1846

May-Day and Other Pieces. 1867

Selected Poems. 1876

Bibliography

Anderson, John Q. *The Liberating Gods: Emerson on Poets and Poetry.* U of Miami P, 1971.

Arsić, Branka, and Cary Wolfe, editors. *The Other Emerson.* U of Minnesota P, 2010.

Atkinson, Brooks, editor. *The Essential Writings of Ralph Waldo Emerson.* Modern Library, 2000.

Baker, Carlos. *Emerson Among the Eccentrics.* Viking, 1996.

Bercovitch, Sacvan. *The Rites of Assent: Transformations in the Symbolic Construction of America.* Routledge, 1993.

Bishop, Jonathan. *Emerson on the Soul.* Harvard UP, 1964.

Boller, Paul. F. *American Transcendentalism, 1830–1860: An Intellectual Inquiry.* G.P. Putnam's Sons, 1974.

Bosco, Ronald A., and Joel Myerson. *The Emerson Brothers: A Fraternal Biography in Letters.* Oxford UP, 2004.

__________, editors. *Emerson in His Own Time: A Biographical Chronicle of His Life, Drawn from Recollections, Interviews, and Memoirs by Family, Friends, and Associates.* U of Iowa P, 2003.

Branch, Michael P., and Clinton Mohs, editors. *"'The Best Read Naturalist': Nature Writings of Ralph Waldo Emerson."* U of Virginia P, 2017.

Brooks, Van Wyck. *The Life of Emerson.* The Literary Guild, 1932.

Brown, Lee Rust. *The Emerson Museum: Practical Romanticism and the Pursuit of the Whole.* Harvard UP, 1997.

Buell, Lawrence. *Emerson.* The Belknap Press of Harvard UP, 2003.

__________. *Literary Transcendentalism: Style and Vision in the American Renaissance.* Cornell UP, 1973.

Burton-Christie, Douglas. "Nature, Spirit, and Imagination in the Poetry of Mary Oliver." *Cross Currents,* vol. 46, no. 1, 1996, pp. 77–87.

Cavell, Stanley. *Emerson's Transcendental Etudes.* Stanford UP, 2003.

__________. *In Quest of the Ordinary.* U of Chicago P, 1988.

Chiasson, Dan. "Ecstasy of Influence: Ralph Waldo Emerson's American Poetry." *The New Yorker*, 31 Aug. 2015, www.newyorker.com/magazine/2015/09/07/ecstasy-of-influence.

Christensen, Laird. "The Pragmatic Mysticism of Mary Oliver." *Ecopoetry: A Critical Introduction*. Edited by J. Scott Bryson, Utah State UP, 2002, pp. 135–52.

Clark, Prentiss. "'Pulse for Pulse in Harmony with the Universal Whole': Hearing 'Self-Reliance' Anew." *Nineteenth-Century Literature*, vol. 69, no. 3, 2014, pp. 319–41.

__________. *Ralph Waldo Emerson: A Companion*. McFarland, 2022.

Cole, Phyllis. *Mary Moody and the Origins of Transcendentalism*. Oxford UP, 1998.

Conner, Frederick William. *Cosmic Optimism: A Study of the Interpretation of Evolution by American Poets from Emerson to Robinson*. U of Florida P, 1949.

Corrigan, John Michael. *American Metempsychosis: Emerson, Whitman, and the New Poetry*. Fordham UP, 2012.

Delbanco, Andrew. *The War Before the War: Fugitive Slaves and the Struggle for America's Soul from the Revolution to the Civil War*. Penguin, 2018.

Ellison, Julie. *Emerson's Romantic Style*. Princeton UP, 1984.

Emerson, Ralph Waldo. *The Major Poetry*. Edited by Albert J. von Frank, The Belknap Press of Harvard UP, 2011.

__________. *The Major Prose*. Edited by Ronald A. Bosco and Joel Myerson, The Belknap Press of Harvard UP, 2015.

Fahs, Alice. *The Imagined Civil War Popular Literature of the North and South, 1861–1865*. U of North Carolina P, 2001.

Fast, Robin Riley. "Moore, Bishop, and Oliver: Thinking Back, Re-Seeing the Sea." *Twentieth Century Literature*, vol. 39, no. 3, 1993, pp. 364–79.

Field, Peter S. *Ralph Waldo Emerson: The Making of a Democratic Intellectual*. Rowman and Littlefield, 2002.

Fletcher, Angus. *A New Theory for American Poetry: Democracy, The Environment, and the Future of Imagination*. Harvard UP, 2004.

Fuller, Randall. *Emerson's Ghosts: Literature, Politics, and the Making of Americanists*. Oxford UP, 2011.

Garvey, T. Gregory, editor. *The Emerson Dilemma; Essays on Emerson and Social Reform*. U of Georgia P, 2001.

Gilmore, Michael. *American Romanticism and the Marketplace*. U of Chicago P, 1985.

Gougeon, Len. *Emerson and Eros: The Making of a Cultural Hero*. Albany State U of New York P, 2007.

__________. "Emerson and Race." *Ralph Waldo Emerson in Context*. Edited by Wesley Mott, Cambridge UP, 2013, pp. 196–213.

__________. Emerson, Self-Reliance, and the Politics of Democracy," *A Political Companion to Ralph Waldo Emerson*. Edited by Daniel Malachuk and Allan Levine, UP of Kentucky, 2011, pp. 185–220.

__________. "'Fortune of the Republic:' Emerson, Lincoln, and Transcendental Warfare," *ESQ: A Journal of the American Renaissance*, vol. 45, nos. 3 & 4, 2001, pp. 258–324.

__________. "Militant Abolitionism: Douglass, Emerson, and the Rise of the Anti-Slave," *The New England Quarterly*, vol. 85, no. 4, Dec. 2012, pp. 622–57.

__________. "Transcendental Politics and Economics," *The Oxford Handbook of Transcendentalism*. Edited by Joel Myerson, Sandra Petrulionis, and Laura Dassow-Walls, Oxford UP, 2010.

__________. *Virtue's Hero: Emerson, Antislavery, and Reform*. U of Georgia P, 1990, 2010.

Gougeon, Len, and Joel Myerson, editors. *Emerson's Antislavery Writings*. Yale UP, 1995.

Graebner, Norman A., editor. *Manifest Destiny*. The Bobbs-Merrill Company, 1968.

Graham, Vicki. "'Intro the Body of Another': Mary Oliver and the Poetics of Becoming Other." *Papers on Language and Literature*, vol. 30, no. 4, 1999, pp. 352–72.

Greenham, David. *Emerson's Transatlantic Romanticism*. Palgrave, 2012.

Gregg, Edith W., editor. *One First Love: The Letters of Ellen Louisa Tucker to Ralph Waldo Emerson*. The Belknap Press of Harvard UP, 1962.

Gross, Robert A. *The Transcendentalists and Their World.* Farrar, Straus and Giroux, 2021.

Gura, Philip F. *American Transcendentalism: A History.* Hill and Wang, 2007.

Habich, Robert D. *Building Their Own Waldos: Emerson's First Biographers and the Politics of Life-Writing in the Gilded Age*. U of Iowa P, 2011.

Hanegraaff, Wouter J. *Western Esotericism: A Guide for the Perplexed.* Bloomsbury, 2013.

Hanlon, Christopher. *Emerson's Memory Loss: Originality, Communality, and Late Style*. Oxford UP, 2018.

Harding, Brian. "'Frolic Architecture': Music and Metamorphosis in Emerson's Poetry." *Nineteenth Century American Poetry*. Edited by Robert A. Lee, Barnes and Noble, 1985, pp. 100–17.

Hatch, Nathan O. T*he Democratization of American Christianity*. Yale UP, 1989.

Hodder, Alan D. "Asian Influences," *The Oxford Handbook of Transcendentalism*." Edited by Joel Myerson, Sandra Petrulionis, and Laura Dassow-Walls, Oxford UP, 2010.

__________. *Emerson's Rhetoric of Revelation*. Pennsylvania State UP, 1989.

Hubbell, Jay, editor *The Last Years of Henry Timrod 1864–1867*. Duke UP, 1941.

Hurth, Elisabeth. "William and Ralph Waldo Emerson and the Problem of the Lord's Supper: The Influence of German 'Historical Speculators.'" *Church History*, vol. 62, no. 2, 1993, pp. 190–206.

Irmscher, Christoph. "Linen Shreds and Melons in a Field: Emerson and His Contemporaries." *The Cambridge History of American Poetry*. Edited by Alfred Bendixen and Stephen Burt, Cambridge UP, 2014, pp. 192–216.

Katopodis, Christina. "The Music of the Spheres in Emerson, Fuller, and Thoreau: Lyell's *Principles* and Transcendental Listening." *ISLE*, vol. 28, no. 3, 2021, pp. 839–67.

Kidd, Thomas S., editor. *The Great Awakening: A Brief History with Documents*. Bedford/St. Martin's, 2008.

Knutson, Andrea. *American Spaces of Conversion: The Conductive Imaginaries of Edwards, Emerson, and James*. Oxford UP, 2011.

LaRocca, David. *Emerson's English Traits and the Natural History of Metaphor*. Bloomsbury, 2013.

Lothstein, Arthur S., and Michael Brodrick, editors. *New Morning: Emerson in the Twenty-First Century*. SUNY P, 2008.

Lucas, Rose. "Drifting in the Weeds of Heaven: Mary Oliver and the Poetics of the Immeasurable." *Rhizomes*, vol. 13, 2006, www.rhizomes.net/issue13/lucas.html.

Lundblad, Michael. "Emersonian Science Studies and the Fate of Ecocriticism." *ISLE*, vol. 10, no. 2, 2003, pp. 111–34.

Lysaker, John T. *After Emerson*. Indiana UP, 2017.

__________. *Emerson and Self Culture*. Indiana UP, 2008.

Mann, Thomas. *God of Dirt: Mary Oliver and the Other Book of God*. Cowley Publications, 2004.

Matthiessen, F.O. *American Renaissance: Art and Expression in the Age of Emerson and Whitman*. Oxford UP, 1941.

May, Robert. *The Southern Dream of a Caribbean Empire, 1854–1861*. Louisiana State UP, 1973.

McMurry, Andrew. "Framing Emerson's 'Farming': Climate Change, Peak Oil, and the Rhetoric of Food Security in the Twenty-First Century." *ISLE*, vol. 19, no. 3, 2012, pp. 548–66.

McNew, Janet. "Mary Oliver and the Tradition of Romantic Nature Poetry." *Contemporary Literature*, vol. 30, no. 1, 1989, pp. 59–77.

Meehan, Sean Ross. "Ecology and Imagination: Emerson, Thoreau, and the Nature of Metonymy." *Criticism*, vol. 55, no. 2, 2013, pp. 299–329.

__________. *Mediating American Autobiography Photography: Emerson, Thoreau, Douglass, and Whitman*. U of Missouri P, 2008.

__________. "Metonymies of the Mind: Ralph Waldo Emerson, William James, and the Rhetoric of Liberal Education." *Philosophy and Rhetoric*, vol. 49, no. 3, 2016, pp. 277–99.

__________. "'Nature's Stomach': Emerson, Whitman, and the Poetics of Digestion." *Walt Whitman Quarterly Review*, vol. 28, no. 3, 2011, pp. 97–121.

__________. "The Environment of Liberal Education: Emerson, Berry, and the Rhetoric of the Commonplaces." *ISLE*, vol. 26, no. 2, 2019, pp. 358–78.

Mellard, Joan. "Mary Oliver, Poetic Iconographer." *Language and Literature*, vol. 16, 1991, pp. 65–73.

Morris, Saundra. "'Meter-Making' Arguments: Emerson's Poems." T*he Cambridge Companion to Ralph Waldo Emerson*. Edited by Joel Porte and Saundra Morris, Cambridge UP, 1999, pp. 218–42.

__________. "The Threshold Poem, Emerson, and 'The Sphinx.'" *American Literature*, vol. 69, no. 3, 1997, pp. 547–70.

Mott, Wesley T., editor. *Ralph Waldo Emerson in Context*. Cambridge UP, 2013.

__________. *'The Strains of Eloquence': Emerson and His Sermons*. Penn State P, 1990.

Myerson, Joel. *A Historical Guide to Ralph Waldo Emerson*. Oxford UP, 2000.

__________, editor. *Transcendentalism: A Reader*. Oxford UP, 2000.

Newfield, Christopher. *The Emerson Effect: Individualism and Submission in America*. U of Chicago P, 1996.

Olander, Renée. "An Interview with Mary Oliver." *The Writer's Chronicle*, vol. 27, 1994, pp. 1–8.

Plekon, Michael. *Uncommon Prayer: Prayer in Everyday Experience*. U of Notre Dame P, 2016.

Poirier, Richard. *Poetry and Pragmatism*. Harvard UP, 1992.

Porter, David. *Emerson and Literary Change*. Harvard UP, 1978.

Reynolds, David S. *Beneath the American Renaissance: The Subversive Imagination in the Age of Emerson and Melville*. Alfred A. Knopf, 1988.

Richardson, Robert D. *Emerson: The Mind on Fire: A Biography*. U of California P, 1995.

__________. *Emerson on the Creative Process*. U of Iowa P, 2009.

__________. *Three Roads Back: How Emerson, Thoreau, and William James Responded to the Greatest Losses of Their Lives*. Princeton UP, 2023.

Robinson, David M. *Apostle of Culture: Emerson as Preacher and Lecturer*. U of Philadelphia P, 1982.

__________. *Emerson and the Conduct of Life: Pragmatism and Ethical Purpose in the Later Work*. Cambridge UP, 1993.

Rose, Anne C. *Transcendentalism as a Social Movement, 1830–1850*. Yale UP, 1981.

Schirmeister, Pamela. *Less Legible Meanings: Between Poetry and Philosophy in the Work of Emerson*. Stanford UP, 1999.

Schmidt, Leigh Eric. *Restless Souls: The Making of American Spirituality from Emerson to Oprah*. HarperCollins, 2005.

Sealts, Merton M., Jr. *Emerson on the Scholar*. U of Missouri P, 1992.

Sederat, Roger. *Emerson in Iran: The American Appropriation of Persian Poetry*. SUNY P, 2019.

Smith, Gayle L. "The Language of Identity in Emerson's 'The Sphinx.'" *ESQ: A Journal of the American Renaissance,* vol. 29, 1983, pp. 136–43.

Stephanson, Anders. *Manifest Destiny: American Expansionism and the Empire of Right*. Hill and Wang, 1995.

Stowe, William. "Linnaean Poetics: Emerson, Cooper, Thoreau, and the Names of Plants." *ISLE*, vol. 17, no. 3, 2010, pp. 567–83.

Strauch, Carl F. "The Year of Emerson's Poetic Maturity: 1834." *Philological Quarterly*, vol. 34, Oct. 1955, pp. 353–77.

Tharaud, Barry, editor. *Emerson for the Twenty-First Century: Global Perspectives of an American Icon*. U of Delaware P, 2010.

Thompson, Roger. *Emerson and the History of Rhetoric*. Southern Illinois UP, 2017.

Timrod, Henry. *Collected Poems of Henry Timrod: A Variorum Edition*. Edited by Edd and Aileen Parks, U of Georgia P, 2007.

Uechi, Naomi. "Emersonian Transcendentalism in Frank Lloyd Wright's Unity Temple." *ISLE*, vol. 7, no. 2, 2000, pp. 95–113.

Von Frank, Albert J. *An Emerson Chronology*. 2nd edition, 2 volumes, Studio Non Troppo, 2016.

Walls, Laura Dassow. *Emerson's Life in Science: The Culture of Truth*. Cornell UP, 2003.

Wirzbicki, Peter. *Fighting for the Higher Law: Black and White Transcendentalism Against Slavery*. U of Pennsylvania P, 2021.

Worley, Sam McGuire. *Emerson, Thoreau, and the Role of the Cultural Critic*. SUNY P, 2000.

Yoder, R.A. *Emerson and the Orphic Poet in America*. U of California P, 1978.

About the Editor

Jericho Williams is assistant professor of English at University of Alaska Fairbanks. His prior publications include two edited volumes, *Critical Insights: Frederick Douglass* and *Critical Insights: The Color Purple,* as well as articles in *The Thoreau Society Bulletin*, *Studies in American Culture*, *South Atlantic Review*, *The James Fenimore Cooper Society Journal*, *Supernatural Studies*, *The New Centennial Review*, *Studies in American Naturalism*, and *Journal of the Georgia Philological Association*. His forthcoming research will appear in *Nathaniel Hawthorne Review* and *The Oxford Handbook of African American Women's Writing.*

Contributors

Christopher Allan Black received his PhD in English and American literature from Oklahoma State University (Stillwater, Oklahoma). He is currently an assistant professor of teaching and member of the American literature faculty at the University of Memphis, where he teaches courses in eighteenth- and nineteenth-century American literature and composition. He is associate editor of *The James Fenimore Cooper Society Journal*. His first book *The Anti-Gallows Movement and Republican Social Justice Reform in Antebellum Literature 1772–1862* is currently forthcoming with Lexington Books an imprint of Rowman and Littlefield. He is the recipient of three National Endowment for the Humanities summer research fellowships. In the summer of 2022, Dr. Black was an NEH Summer Research Fellow for the Institute: "Transcendentalism and Social Reform: Activism and Community Engagement in the Age of Thoreau," in Concord, Massachusetts.

Joshua Boyd is chair of the general education division and associate professor of English at Faith Baptist Bible College, Ankeny, Iowa, where he teaches American, British, and world literature as well as writing and public speaking. His dissertation examined hospitality through the works of several American travel writers in the nineteenth century. He has published articles on American authors such as Margaret Fuller, Henry David Thoreau, and Mark Twain.

Benjamin Crawford currently teaches at the University of Alabama. His primary academic interests include ecocriticism and religion, along with their intersections throughout early American literature. In addition to teaching early American literature, he has also published research on Philip Freneau, David Humphreys, and Washington Irving.

LuElla D'Amico is an associate professor of English and coordinator of women's and gender studies at the University of the Incarnate Word. Her primary research interests lie in girlhood studies and women's religious writing in early and nineteenth-century American literature, and she has published on authors such as Margaret Fuller, Louisa May Alcott, and Elizabeth Stuart Phelps. She has edited a volume about the history of girls' series books in the United States titled *Girls' Series Fiction and American Popular Culture* and is co-editor (with Robin Cadwallader) of *Reading Transatlantic Girlhood in the Long Nineteenth Century*. Dr. D'Amico currently serves as president of the Harriet Beecher Stowe Society.

Susan L. Dunston is professor emerita at New Mexico Tech University where she taught philosophy, American literature, and writing to science and engineering students. She is a past president of the Emerson Society and received the Society's Distinguished Achievement Award in 2020. She is the author of *Emerson and Environmental Ethics* (Lexington, 2018) and *The Romance of Desire: Emerson's Commitment to Incompletion* (Fairleigh Dickinson University Press, 1997) as well as essays on Emerson's writings and philosophy in the *Journal of Speculative Philosophy*, *ESQ*, *The Journal of American Culture*, *ATQ*, and chapters in *Approaches to Teaching the Works of Ralph Waldo Emerson*, *Emerson for the Twenty-First Century*, *Ralph Waldo Emerson in Context*, and *Romanticism and Philosophy*.

Robert C. Evans was I. B. Young Professor of English at Auburn University at Montgomery until he was awarded emeritus status upon his retirement in 2021. He earned his PhD from Princeton University in 1984. In 1982, he began teaching at AUM, where he has been named Distinguished Research Professor, Distinguished Teaching Professor, and University Alumni Professor. External awards include fellowships from the American Council of Learned Societies, the American Philosophical Society, the National Endowment for the Humanities, the UCLA Center for Medieval and Renaissance Studies, and the Folger, Huntington, and Newberry Libraries. He is the author or editor of over seventy books and of more than five hundred essays, including recent work on various American writers.

Len Gougeon, distinguished professor of American literature, emeritus at the University of Scranton, is the author of *Virtue's Hero: Emerson, Antislavery, and Reform*, and *Emerson & Eros: The Making of a Cultural Hero*. He is co-editor (with Joel Myerson) of *Emerson's Antislavery*

Writings. He has published numerous scholarly articles on nineteenth-century America in such journals as *The New England Quarterly*, *American Literature*, *Walt Whitman Quarterly Review*, *Studies in the American Renaissance*, *Modern Language Studies*, and others. His essays appear in several collections including *The Oxford Handbook to Transcendentalism*, *The Cambridge Companion to Henry David Thoreau*, *Thoreau at 200: Essays and Reassessments*, *A Political Companion to Ralph Waldo Emerson*, *Teaching Emerson*, and others. He is currently at work on a study titled *Culture and Conflict: Old England, New England, and the Civil War: How a Clash of Cultures Ignited an International Campaign for Racial Equality and Human Rights*.

Amy Leshinsky received her EdD from Northeastern University, where she wrote her dissertation on the experiences of secondary English distance educators using Intelligent Agents to target student engagement in asynchronous classrooms. During the height of the pandemic in 2020, Leshinsky provided professional development to school districts on best practices in educational technology. She received an MA in English from Boston College and a MAT from Tufts University. She has been a guest lecturer on human rights violations in literature at many universities including Notre Dame and the University of Connecticut, Storrs. Her work has been published in various books, newspapers, and journals. Leshinsky spent nearly 20 years teaching English, and currently teaches at Roger Williams University, where she was the 2022 recipient of the Faculty Excellence in Teaching Award.

Stephen M. Mercier is recognized as a leading John Burroughs expert in the fields of American literature and ecocriticism. He has edited two academic journal special issues on John Burroughs for *ATQ: Nineteenth C. American Literature and Culture* (2007) and *The Hudson River Valley Review* (2008). In 2010, he published an article titled "John Burroughs and the Sentimental: Revaluing the Literary Naturalist" in *ISLE: Interdisciplinary Studies in Literature and Environment,* the premiere journal in the study of environmental literature. In 2012, he published a book chapter titled: "Epic Narratives of Evolution: John Burroughs and Loren Eiseley." Furthermore, he has also served as a keynote speaker at the biennial "Sharp Eyes" John Burroughs Conference and at Slabsides

Day celebrating the legacy of this famous literary naturalist of the Hudson River Valley. Dr. Mercier is a lecturer of American and environmental literature at Marist College in Poughkeepsie, New York.

Dalicia K. Raymond is a professor of English at Spartanburg Methodist College. Her research centers on magic in medieval literature, with interest in the dynamics of gender, power, and difference and on the characters Merlin and Morgan le Fay. She also holds interest in how medieval culture, characters, and narratives are used and represented in post-medieval texts and culture, an interest inclusive of nineteenth-century literature, modern-day popular culture, and everything in between. She has previously published essays on magic in the medieval poem *Sir Gawain and the Green Knight* and on Morgan le Fay as magical practitioner in *Le Morte D'Arthur*.

Charles W. Rowe received his PhD in English literature from the CUNY Graduate Center. He is an adjunct assistant professor of English at Hunter College. He teaches nineteenth-century British and American poetry, Shakespeare, and contemporary fiction. His scholarly focus is transatlantic Romantic poetry. He has written, spoken, and published on the philosophical and poetic affinities shared between British and American romantic authors Percy Bysshe Shelley and Walt Whitman and is currently working on an essay about the late-eighteenth century British poet William Cowper's influence on Romantic poetry.

Jeff Westover is professor of English at Boise State University, where he teaches literature. He is currently co-editing *Marianne Moore and the Archive*, forthcoming from Clemson University Press. He is the author of *The Colonial Moment: Discoveries and Settlements in Modern American Poetry*, which was selected as an outstanding academic title by *Choice* magazine in 2005. *The Colonial Moment* addresses depictions of imperialism by Marianne Moore, Robert Frost, William Carlos Williams, Langston Hughes, and Hart Crane. He has published articles about Elizabeth Bishop (*Elizabeth Bishop and the Literary Archive*), W.S. Merwin (*Genre*), H.D. (*Classics in Modernist Translation*), Thylias Moss (*CLA Journal*), and sonnets by Black poets (*A Companion to Poetic Genre*). He contributed articles about Amy Tan and Maxine Hong Kingston for *Critical Insights* volumes edited by Linda Trinh Moser and Kathryn West. Other publications include essays about Lorine Niedecker, Wallace Stevens, James Merrill, Herman Melville, and Henry James.

Albert von Frank, professor of English, Washington State University, Emeritus. His publications with a focus on Emerson include *The Trials of Anthony Burns: Freedom and Slavery in Emerson's Boston* (1998); *An Emerson Chronology*, 2nd ed, 2 vols. (1994, 2016); editor, with R. H. Orth, David Hill, and Linda Allardt, of *The Poetry Notebooks of Ralph Waldo Emerson* (1986); with Teresa Toulouse, Andrew Delbanco, Ronald A. Bosco, and Wesley T. Mott, *The Complete Sermons of Ralph Waldo Emerson*, 4 vols. (1989–1992); *Ralph Waldo Emerson: The Major Poems* (2015), and, with Thomas Wortham, of vol. 9 of *The Collected Works of Ralph Waldo Emerson: The Poems, A Variorum Edition* (2014). Among his essays are "The Composition of Nature: Writing and the Self in the Launching of a Career" in *Biographies of Books: The Compositional Histories of Notable American Writings* (1996); "Mrs. Brackett's Verdict: Magic and Means in Transcendental Antislavery Work" in *Transient and Permanent: The Transcendental Movement and Its Contexts* (1999); "Essays: First Series (1841)" in *The Cambridge Companion to Ralph Waldo Emerson* (1999); "Emerson and Gnosticism" in *Emerson: Bicentennial Essays* (2006); and (with Larry J. Reynolds), "Emerson, John Brown, and Transcendental Idealism: A Colloquy" in *South Central Review* (2011). He served for 12 years as editor of *ESQ: A Journal of the American Renaissance*.

Trevor B. Williams, a PhD candidate at Villanova University, is writing his dissertation on the French philosopher Emmanuel Falque, applying his concept of animality to questions in sacramental theology. He was recently awarded the Founders' Circle Prize by the Society for the Study of Christian Spirituality. His recent publications appear in *New Blackfriars*, *The Heythrop Journal*, *Spiritus*, *Logos*, and the *Journal of the American Oriental Society*.

Index